My
Samsung Galaxy S® 4

Steve Schwartz

800 East 96th Street,
Indianapolis, Indiana 46240 USA

My Samsung Galaxy S® 4

Copyright © 2014 by Pearson Education

ISBN-13: 978-0-7897-5157-7
ISBN-10: 0-7897-5157-7

Library of Congress Control Number: 2013940863

Printed in the United States of America

First Printing: August 2013

Trademarks

All terms mentioned in this book that are known to be trademarks or service marks have been appropriately capitalized. Que Publishing cannot attest to the accuracy of this information. Use of a term in this book should not be regarded as affecting the validity of any trademark or service mark.

Galaxy S 4 images are provided by Samsung Electronics Co., Ltd.

Warning and Disclaimer

Every effort has been made to make this book as complete and as accurate as possible, but no warranty or fitness is implied. The information provided is on an "as is" basis. The author and the publisher shall have neither liability nor responsibility to any person or entity with respect to any loss or damages arising from the information contained in this book.

Bulk Sales

Que Publishing offers excellent discounts on this book when ordered in quantity for bulk purchases or special sales. For more information, please contact

U.S. Corporate and Government Sales
1-800-382-3419
corpsales@pearsontechgroup.com

For sales outside of the U.S., please contact

International Sales
international@pearsoned.com

Editor-in-Chief
Greg Wiegand

Acquisitions Editor
Michelle Newcomb

Development Editor
Charlotte Kughen

Managing Editor
Kristy Hart

Senior Project Editor
Betsy Gratner

Copy Editor
Apostrophe Editing Services

Senior Indexer
Cheryl Lenser

Proofreader
Williams Woods Publishing Services

Technical Editor
Christian Kenyeres

Editorial Assistant
Cindy Teeters

Cover Designer
Mark Shirar

Compositor
Nonie Ratcliff

Contributor
Guy Hart-Davis

Contents at a Glance

Table of Contents

4   Placing and Receiving Calls   99

9   Messaging, Chatting, and Socializing   253

10   Installing and Using Applications   283

About the Author

Steve Schwartz got an early start as a computer industry writer and author. Immediately after buying an Apple II+ in 1978, he began writing regularly for the computer magazines of the day. Since then, he has written hundreds of articles for major publications, including *Macworld*, *PC World*, *InfoWorld*, and *Computerworld*. He is also the author of more than 60 books on technology, game and computer topics, including guides to business/productivity software (Microsoft Office, Access, and FileMaker Pro), Internet software (Internet Explorer, Outlook Express, Entourage, and Gmail), and graphics/image-editing software (Picasa, Picture It!, Digital Image Suite, and CorelDRAW). Following his best-selling *My Samsung Galaxy S III*, this is Steve's second book in the *My* series.

Before becoming a full-time writer in 1990, Steve served as editor-in-chief for *Software Digest* and technical services director for Funk Software. He also authored the first trade paperback on the then-new Nintendo phenomenon: *Compute!'s Guide to Nintendo Games*.

Steve has a Ph.D. in psychology, consults on game design, database design, and technology issues, and lives in the fictional town of Lizard Spit, Arizona. You can see the complete list of his published books at http://www.siliconwasteland.com/misc.htm.

Dedication

To Sydney and Spooky

Acknowledgments

I'd like to extend my special thanks to the following individuals:

- The talented Que editorial and production team: Michelle Newcomb, Todd Brakke, Betsy Gratner, Charlotte Kughen, Cheryl Lenser, Nonie Ratcliff, and San Dee Phillips.

- Carole Jelen of Waterside Productions

- Mieshel and Dane Thompson

We Want to Hear from You!

As the reader of this book, *you* are our most important critic and commentator. We value your opinion and want to know what we're doing right, what we could do better, what areas you'd like to see us publish in, and any other words of wisdom you're willing to pass our way.

We welcome your comments. You can email or write to let us know what you did or didn't like about this book—as well as what we can do to make our books better.

Please note that we cannot help you with technical problems related to the topic of this book.

When you write, please be sure to include this book's title and author, as well as your name and email address. We will carefully review your comments and share them with the author and editors who worked on the book.

Email: feedback@quepublishing.com

Mail: Que Publishing
           ATTN: Reader Feedback
           800 East 96th Street
           Indianapolis, IN 46240 USA

Reader Services

Visit our website and register this book at quepublishing.com/register for convenient access to any updates, downloads, or errata that might be available for this book.

Introduction

About This Book

My Samsung Galaxy S 4 is specifically about configuring, using, maintaining, and troubleshooting a Samsung Galaxy S 4. Although much of its information is applicable to other Android phones, it will be most helpful to those of you who either own or intend to get a Samsung Galaxy S 4.

The Need for a Book

If this is your first smartphone, you'll quickly discover that learning to use it entails a considerably steeper learning curve than mastering an ordinary phone. Actually, it will probably help you to think of your S 4 as a handheld computer that also has the capability to place and receive phone calls. For many users, the calling capabilities of the S 4 are secondary to all the other wonderful things you can do with it.

Although each carrier offers a free, downloadable manual with *general* explanations of how the phone works and how to use the standard applications (or *apps*), the manuals seldom provide sufficient detail to enable you to comfortably use the various phones' features or to understand the impact of setting particular options. That's where this book comes in. Rather than waste hours of your time figuring these things out, I've spent that time on your behalf—in many cases, through hours of experimentation. And no, not every answer can be found online—easily or, in some cases, at all. For instance, I spent 6–8 hours figuring out why Group Play worked only with the demo song and not with the 40+ songs I downloaded to the phone. (See "Sharing Songs with Group Play" in Chapter 12 for the answer to that question.)

How to Read This Book

Although the chapters are presented in what is intended to be a logical order (based on *what* I think you need to know and *when* you'll need to know it), it may sometimes feel like you have to understand *everything* about the phone before you can do *anything* with it. Placing a call, for example, requires you to know how to interact with the touchscreen and, optionally, how to select a phone number or person's name in Contacts.

Although you'll do well to at least skim through the entire book (to avoid being overwhelmed by that "need to know everything" feeling), I recommend that you start by working your way through the basics provided in Chapters 1 through 3 and only then jump to whatever chapter you want to tackle next.

Smartphone "Facts of Life"

When reading this book, there are some important facts you should know:

- At its launch, five major U.S. carriers announced they'd carry the Galaxy S 4: AT&T, Sprint, T-Mobile, Verizon, and U.S. Cellular. From a hardware perspective, each of these phones is identical.

- On a software basis, however, there are some differences between carriers. First, many add their own applications (*apps*) to the standard ones that come with every S 4, and they sometimes make minor modifications to the standard apps, too. For example, when you first launch Contacts on an AT&T S 4, you're notified that your address records will be backed up to your AT&T Address Book.

Second, each carrier has its own method of updating the phone's operating system and apps. To be applicable to every carrier's S 4, this book explains how to use the software that *all* S 4's have in common; little mention is made about carrier-specific apps and updating procedures. For such information, you should refer to the carrier's online manual and support.

• App and operating system (OS) updates can be delivered or downloaded whenever the app developers and your carrier, respectively, see fit. Thus, like all Android cell phones, the S 4 is a *moving target* and subject to change. This book, on the other hand, is static text—correct at the time it was written. When a new version of the OS is applied to your phone, the steps to perform some procedures, what you see onscreen, and the options available in certain Settings categories may change slightly. However, based on past OS updates, even if this happens to an app here or a procedure there, the material in this book should still be sufficiently relevant for you to determine how to work with and use the new features and options. In other words, you're still far better off with this book in your hands than without it!

Status or
Notification
Bar

Widget

Google Quick
Search bar

Apps

Home screen
page indicator

Primary
shortcuts

In this chapter, you become familiar with the basics of setting up and operating your new phone. Topics include the following:

→ Familiarizing yourself with the phone hardware, operating system, interface, and customization options

→ Charging the battery

→ Turning the phone on and off

→ Restoring a dark display

→ Adjusting the volume

→ Using a headset or headphones

→ Setting up voicemail

→ Placing and receiving calls

→ Creating and registering a Gmail account

→ Creating a Samsung account

→ Connecting to a Wi-Fi network

→ Changing the phone's default language

Galaxy S 4 Essentials

Welcome to *My Samsung Galaxy S 4*. In this chapter and Chapter 2, you become familiar with the fundamentals of operating and interacting with your new Android-based phone.

About the Galaxy S 4

As the latest entrant in Samsung's all-star lineup of Galaxy S-series phones, the Galaxy S 4 is a fast, feature-laden smartphone. This section discusses the phone hardware, the Android operating system that powers the S4, the interface you use to interact with it, and available customization options.

The Hardware

To create a powerful, flexible smartphone, Samsung equipped the Galaxy S 4 with the following features:

- 1.9GHz quad-core processor, running the Android 4.2.x (Jelly Bean) operating system
- HD Super AMOLED, 1920 × 1080-pixel, 441 ppi, 5" touchscreen display
- 2.0-megapixel front-facing camera; 13-megapixel rear-facing camera with 4x digital zoom and HD video recording
- 16, 32, or 64GB internal memory; 2GB RAM; and support for up to 64GB of additional memory with a microSDHC card
- 2.5G, 3G, and 4G/LTE network support
- Wi-Fi (802.11 a/b/g/n/ac), Bluetooth 4.0, and NFC connectivity
- GPS (global positioning system)
- IR (infrared) LED; MHL (Mobile High-definition Link) 2.0

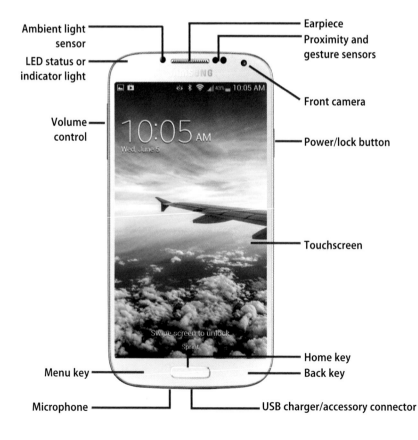

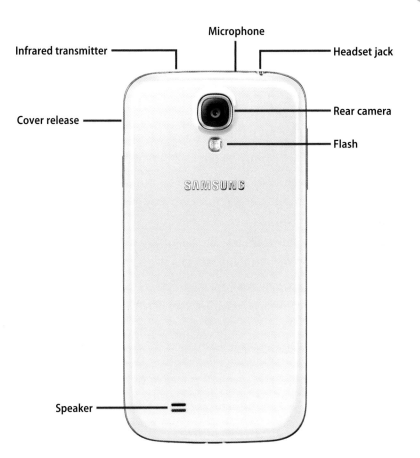

The following are the key hardware components of the Galaxy S 4:

Power/Lock button. Press the Power button to turn the phone on or off and to manually darken (lock) or restore the screen.

Volume control. Press this context-sensitive hardware control to raise (top part) or lower (bottom part) the volume of the current activity, such as conducting a call or playing music.

Microphones. Speak into the bottom microphone when participating in a call, giving voice commands, or using the phone's speech-to-text feature. The top microphone is used for noise cancellation and stereo recording.

Earpiece. When you're not using a headset, call audio is transmitted through this front speaker. The external speaker on the back of the phone is used to play music, ringtones, and other audio.

Headset jack. Port for connecting a compatible 3.5mm wired headset or headphones; enables 5.1 channel sound when playing media.

Front camera. Low-resolution (2-megapixel), front-facing camera for taking self-portraits and participating in video chats.

Rear camera. High-resolution (13-megapixel), rear-facing camera for taking pictures and high-definition movies.

Flash. Illuminates photos shot with the rear-facing camera (unless you've disabled it for the shot).

Touchscreen. Touch-sensitive screen; displays information and enables you to interact with the phone.

Menu, Home, and Back keys. Press these hardware keys to interact with the operating system and installed applications.

USB charger/accessory connector. Enables the phone to be connected with the supplied USB cable to a computer (for file transfers) or to the charger head and a wall outlet (to charge the phone's battery).

LED Status or indicator light. Displays a flashing or steady light to indicate that the phone is performing its startup sequence, denoting notifications (such as newly received email or text messages), or showing the charging status.

Ambient light, proximity, and gesture sensors. The ambient light sensor enables the screen's brightness to adjust to current lighting conditions. The proximity and gesture sensors detect how close an object is to the phone and whether particular gestures are occurring. During calls, the proximity sensor determines when your face is pressed to the screen and locks the keypad to prevent accidental key presses.

Adding a Memory Card

In addition to using the S 4's built-in memory for storing email, photos, music, apps, and other material, you can purchase a memory card (up to 64 GB) to increase the phone's available storage—much like adding a second hard disk to your computer. For information on installing, formatting, or removing a memory card, see "Viewing and Expanding Storage" in Chapter 19.

The Android Operating System and TouchWiz

Just like a computer, every smartphone has an *operating system* that controls virtually every important activity that the phone can perform, as well as the ways in which you interact with it. On the Galaxy S 4, the operating system is Android 4.2.x (Jelly Bean).

Like many of the other major cell phone manufacturers, Samsung has customized the Android operating system to differentiate its phones from those of competitors. Samsung's TouchWiz touch interface is that operating system customization. Even though phones from other manufacturers run Android 4.2.x, TouchWiz ensures that Galaxy S 4 phones operate in a similar—but never identical—fashion to such phones.

Note that operating system updates are periodically made available to phones through the carriers.

The Interface

Much of what you do with the phone involves using its touchscreen. The Home screen consists of five customizable pages that you can optionally expand to seven. On it, you can place shortcuts to the applications (*apps*) that you use most often, as well as small applications called *widgets* that run directly on the Home screen. To interact with the touchscreen, you tap app icons to launch programs, flick up or down to scroll through lists, pinch and spread your fingers to change the current magnification, and so on. Chapter 2 explains in detail how to work with the touchscreen interface.

Easy or Standard Mode

If you're new to cell phones (or just to *Android* phones), you can elect to use a Home screen variant called Easy Mode. Although the material in this book is based on Standard Mode, you may want to use Easy Mode until you're comfortable with the phone. See "Setting the Home Screen Mode" in Chapter 2 for instructions and information about switching modes.

Widget

Apps

Home screen
navigation dots

Customization

One of the main reasons for buying a smartphone such as the Galaxy S 4 is
that you can do considerably more with it than you can with an ordinary
telephone or cell phone. Much as you can do with a computer, you can
customize your phone by populating the Home screen with custom
arrangements of widgets and application icons, change the Home and lock
screens' background *(wallpaper),* install additional useful applications, and
set preferences (*settings*) for the system software and installed applications.
When you're comfortable with the phone's basic operations and are ready to
start customizing it, read Chapter 3.

CHANGING SYSTEM SETTINGS

To change certain operating system features (such as choosing a new Wi-Fi network or adjusting the screen timeout interval), you need to access the Settings screen. There are several ways you can do this:

- From any Home screen page, press the Menu key, and tap Settings in the pop-up menu that appears at the bottom of the screen.

Settings ————

- On any Home screen page, tap the Apps icon, ensure that the Apps tab is selected, and then tap the Settings icon.

Apps tab ————

Settings icon ————

- If you've created one, tap a Settings shortcut icon on a Home screen page.

Settings shortcut ——

- Open the Notification panel by dragging the status bar downward, and then tap the Settings icon.

Charging the Battery

The Galaxy S 4 includes a two-piece wall charger that consists of a special USB cable and a charger head. You charge the phone's battery by connecting the assembled wall charger to the phone and a standard wall outlet. It's recommended that you fully charge the phone before its first use.

It isn't necessary to wait until the battery is almost fully discharged before charging. In fact, the phone's manual recommends that you *not* wait because repeatedly letting the battery completely drain can reduce its capability to store a charge.

Connecting to a Computer

The battery also charges while the phone is connected to a computer by the USB cable. See "Transferring Files over USB" in Chapter 15 for instructions on making the connection.

1. Plug the large end of the USB cable into the charger head.

2. Plug the small end of the USB cable into the bottom of the phone.

3. Plug the charger head into a wall outlet. The LED indicator light glows while the phone charges.

4. When the LED changes color and the indicator shows 100%, the phone is fully charged. Disconnect the USB cable from the wall outlet and phone.

Charging While the Phone Is On
If you need to complete a call or use apps when the battery is almost drained, you can continue to use the phone while it charges.

Powering On/Off

Although many people prefer to simply leave their phones on, you can turn yours off whenever you like—to conserve the battery, for example.

- To turn on the phone, press and hold the Power button until the phone vibrates and begins its normal startup sequence (approximately 4 seconds).

Power button

- To turn off the phone, press and hold the Power button for 1–2 seconds. In the Device Options menu that appears, tap Power Off. Tap OK in the Power Off dialog box to confirm that you want to shut down your phone.

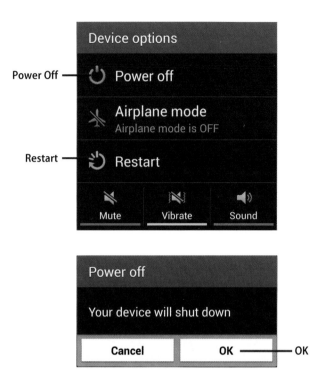

Restarting the Phone

You can also restart the phone from the Device Options dialog box. If you've been running the phone continuously for several days, periodically restarting clears memory fragmentation—enabling you to start again with a clean slate.

THE SETUP WIZARD AND SAMSUNG SMART SWITCH

The first time the phone is turned on (and after any Factory Data Reset), a setup wizard automatically launches and displays its Welcome screen. You can respond to its prompts to set up some essential services, such as creating or signing in to a Google account and Samsung account, configuring your Wi-Fi settings, and adding an email account. The sections in this chapter show you how to establish these basic settings manually—without the wizard's assistance.

If the S 4 isn't your first cell phone, you may ease the transition from your old phone by visiting www.samsungsmartswitch.com and downloading the free content-transfer computer program. Currently supported phones include the iPhone, BlackBerry, LG, Nokia/Symbian, Galaxy S II, Galaxy S III, Galaxy Note, and Galaxy Note II. When you run Smart Switch, selected content is backed up from the old phone to your computer and then transferred to the S 4. If you're an iPhone user, Smart Switch can even transfer your iTunes music, videos, and podcasts, as well as recommend matching or similar Android apps to the iOS apps installed on your iPhone.

AT&T Setup Wizard

Samsung
GALAXY

Welcome to AT&T Ready2Go!

Select language

English

If you are visually impaired or hard of hearing, tap Accessibility below to change the accessibility settings

Accessibility

Next >

Darkening and Restoring the Display

Depending on your *screen timeout* setting, the display automatically turns off during periods of inactivity. In addition to waiting for this timeout to occur, you can manually darken the display to conserve the battery or maintain privacy by pressing the Power button on the right side of the phone.

Restoring a Dark Display

1. Press the Power button on the right side of the phone to make the *lock screen* appear. (The lock screen also appears when you turn on the phone.)

Dimmed, Not Dark

The display automatically dims for a brief period before it turns black. To restore a dimmed display, tap any blank spot on the touchscreen.

2. Swipe in any direction to dismiss the lock screen.

Working with a Locked Phone

You can secure the phone by assigning a password, PIN, or pattern, for example, to require more than a simple finger swipe to dismiss the lock screen. See "Securing the Lock Screen" in Chapter 17 for instructions.

Setting the Screen Timeout Interval

1. On the Home screen, tap Apps, followed by Settings.

2. Select the My Device tab.

3. Tap Display.

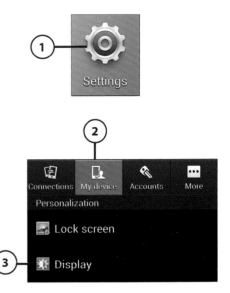

4. Tap Screen Timeout.

5. In the Screen Timeout dialog box, select a new timeout interval or tap the Cancel button to retain the current setting.

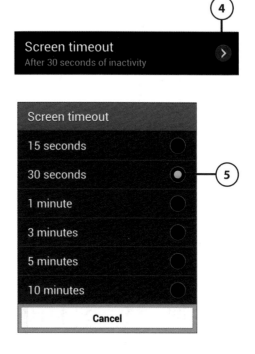

It's All About Trade-Offs

Substantial juice is needed to power the phone's gorgeous display, so the sooner it dims during idle periods, the longer the current charge will last. The key is to select a screen timeout that enables the phone to sit idle as long as possible before dimming and still have sufficient charge to meet your daily calling and app requirements.

To avoid timeouts when you're reading or viewing material onscreen, enable the Smart Stay setting. (In Settings, select the My Device tab, scroll down and tap Smart Screen, and ensure that Smart Stay is checked.) If the front-facing camera detects that you're looking at the screen, it prevents the normal timeout from occurring.

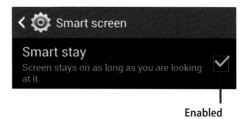

Enabled

>>>Go Further

LOCK SCREEN OPTIONS

If your screen locking method is Swipe (the unprotected default) and you've enabled certain options in Settings, you can perform actions on the screen in addition to simply clearing it. For instance, you can flick the icon of a favorite app to clear the lock screen and launch the app. If the screen displays a new message indicator, you can tap it to launch Messaging and view the conversation. Finally, if you've enabled Wake Up In Lock Screen, you can simultaneously clear the screen and perform an action by saying a key phrase, such as "Play music." For information about setting lock screen options, see Chapter 17.

Launch Messaging

Launch Phone

Adjusting the Volume

You can press the volume control on the left side of the phone to adjust voice volume during a call, media playback volume, or ringer volume (when you're neither playing media nor participating in a call). The volume control is context-sensitive instead of being a general volume control; what is affected when you press the control depends on what you're doing.

1. To change the volume, press the volume control on the left side of the phone. A context-sensitive control appears.

2. To raise or lower the volume, drag the slider. You can also press the top part of the hardware volume control to raise the volume or press the bottom part to lower the volume.

3. *Optional:* To adjust other common volume settings, tap the Settings icon and drag the sliders that appear.

Adjust Everything at Once

You can also open Settings to adjust the various volumes. On the Home screen, press the Menu key, and—in order—tap Settings, My Device tab, Sound, and Volume. Adjust the volume sliders by dragging and tap OK.

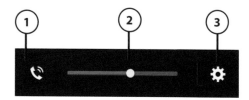

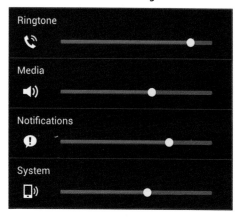

Volume settings

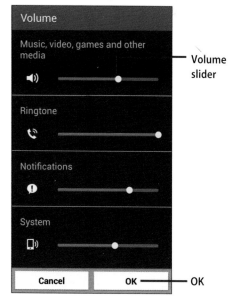

Volume dialog box

Using a Headset or Headphones

By connecting the headset that's included with the Galaxy S 4 (or any other compatible 3.5mm wired headset or headphones), you can improve the phone's audio quality. For example, the Music app supports 5.1 channel sound when a headset is connected. And a wired or a wireless (Bluetooth) headset is handy for making hands-free calls.

Using a Wired Headset or Headphones

1. Plug any compatible headset or headphones into the jack at the top of the phone.

2. Adjust the volume for whatever you're currently doing (taking a call, playing media, and so on) using the phone's or the headset's volume control. For instructions on the former, see "Adjusting the Volume," earlier in this chapter.

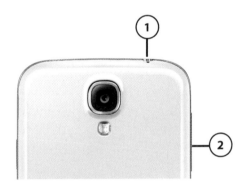

Using a Bluetooth Headset

Although a few Bluetooth headsets support stereo (making them suitable for listening to music), most are mono devices intended primarily for hands-free phone calls. With a maximum range of 30 feet, using a Bluetooth headset enables you to place the phone nearby and conduct a conversation. Unlike using a speakerphone, the audio is routed directly to your ear and the headset's microphone won't pick up as much ambient noise.

Working with a Bluetooth headset involves two steps: pairing the headset and phone (a one-time procedure) and using the headset for calls. The procedures for pairing and answering calls are specific to your headset and are explained in the headset's instructions. As an example, the following tasks illustrate how to use a Jabra EasyGo Bluetooth headset with the Galaxy S 4.

Pairing the Headset with the Phone

1. On the Home screen, tap Apps, followed by Settings.

2. Select the Connections tab at the top of the screen.

3. In the Network Connections section, enable Bluetooth by dragging the slider to the On position, turn the Bluetooth headset on, and then tap Bluetooth.

Check Your Headset's Manual

Your Bluetooth headset may require more than simply turning it on to enter pairing mode. The Jabra EasyGo, for example, can be paired with two devices. You must hold down the Answer button for 5 seconds to initiate the second pairing.

4. *Optional:* If the headset doesn't appear in the Available Devices list, tap the Scan button.

5. Tap the headset's name to pair it with the phone.

6. A confirmation appears when pairing is successful.

Using the Headset for Calls

1. Turn on the headset and place it in your ear. If Bluetooth isn't currently enabled, open the Notification panel by dragging the status bar downward. Tap the Bluetooth icon to enable it.

When the Headset Won't Connect

If a previously paired Bluetooth headset refuses to connect to the phone, open the Notification panel, and then disable and re-enable Bluetooth.

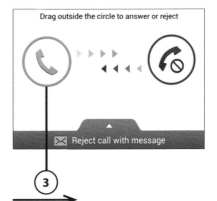

2. To place a call, dial using any of the methods supported by the phone (see "Placing Calls" in Chapter 4).

3. To receive an incoming call, tap the headset's Answer/End button or drag the green Accept Call icon to the right.

Adjusting the Volume

While on a call, you can adjust the volume by pressing the volume control on the left side of the phone or on the headset.

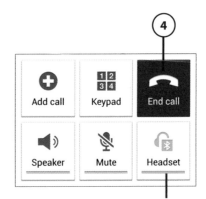

4. To end the call, tap the headset's Answer/End button or tap the End Call icon on the phone. When you finish using the headset, you can remove it from your ear and turn it off.

Headset enabled

>>>Go Further

IN-CALL OPTIONS

During a call, you can freely disable or enable the headset by tapping the Headset icon. In addition, your headset may support a variety of in-call options. For example, you can also use the Jabra EasyGo to reject incoming calls, redial the last number, mute the microphone, and place the current call on hold to switch between two conversations (if you have call waiting). Refer to your headset manual for instructions.

Setting Up Voicemail

After your phone is activated, one of the first things you should do is set up voicemail. Doing so identifies the phone number as yours and ensures that callers have an opportunity to leave a message when you're unavailable.

Note that the exact process of setting up and using voicemail is specific to each provider. Providers may even include their own app that you can use to review and manage your voicemail. (See "Using Voicemail" in Chapter 4 for instructions on accessing voicemail and changing your settings.)

1. On any Home screen page, tap the Phone icon.

2. On the Phone keypad, press and hold 1 (the speed dial number reserved for voicemail) or tap the Voicemail icon.

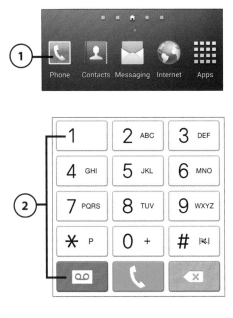

3. When prompted, record your name, enter a password, and select or record a greeting. When you finish reviewing voicemail options, tap the End Call icon.

Gmail and Your Phone

Your phone runs on Android, the Google operating system. To use and connect to any Google service (such as Google Play, the source for Android apps that run on your phone), you must have a Gmail account—Google's free email service. If you don't have an account, you should create one now. The final step is letting your phone know your Gmail account username and password, enabling it to access Google services.

Do It the Easy Way

Although you can create a Gmail account using your phone, a lot of typing is required. It's easier to use your computer's web browser (as described next). On the other hand, if you don't have access to a computer or would *prefer* to create the account using your phone, go to Settings; select the Accounts tab; and tap Add Account, Google, and New.

Creating a Gmail Account

1. On your PC or Mac, launch your web browser: Internet Explorer, Safari, Firefox, or Chrome, for example. Type **www.gmail.com** in the address box and press Enter/Return.

2. Click the Create an Account button in the page's upper-right corner.

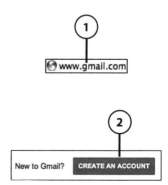

3. Enter the requested registration information on the Create a New Google Account page.

Name
First   Last

Choose your username
                              @gmail.com

Create a password

Confirm your password

Birthday
Month   ⇕   Day   Year

Gender
I am...   ⇕

Mobile phone
🏳 ▾

Your current email address

Prove you're not a robot

prosperous
                    istumdin

Type the two pieces of text:
                              C ⏴) ▣

Location
United States   ⇕

I agree to the Google Terms of Service and Privacy Policy

✓ Google may use my account information to personalize +1's on content and ads on non-Google websites. About personalization.

[Next step]

ACCOUNT-CREATION TIPS

>>>Go Further

The most common, desirable Gmail usernames are taken. To get one based on your name or your company's name, try adding numbers at the end (sschwartz972), separate words with periods (steve.schwartz), or combine two or more unusual words (hamstringwarrior). Your username can be any combination of letters, numbers, and periods.

Your password must contain at least eight characters and can be any combination of uppercase letters, lowercase letters, and numbers. The Password Strength rating indicates how secure your proposed password is.

If possible, resist the temptation to use your Internet service provider (ISP) account password for Gmail, too. If you use one password everywhere on the Internet and someone learns it, all your accounts could be compromised. The most secure passwords combine uppercase letters, lowercase letters, and numbers (such as hA73rTv91).

Registering Your Gmail Account

If you just created a Gmail account using your computer's browser, you need to add the account to your phone. (To see if the account is already registered, open Settings and select the Accounts tab. If Google is listed in the My Accounts section, the account is registered, and you can skip the following task.)

1. On the phone's Home screen, tap the Apps icon.

2. Tap the Gmail icon.

Accounts tab

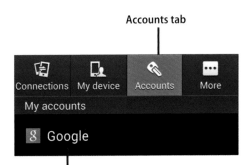

Registered Gmail account

3. On the Add a Google Account screen, tap Existing. (If you don't have a Google/Gmail account, tap New and follow the onscreen prompts, or perform the steps in "Creating a Gmail Account.")

4. Enter your Gmail username and password. Tap the right-arrow icon to continue.

5. Click OK to agree to the Terms of Service.

6. On the Backup and Restore screen, the check box determines whether important phone data will be routinely backed up to your Gmail account. Ensure that the box is checked or unchecked according to your preference, and then tap the right-arrow icon.

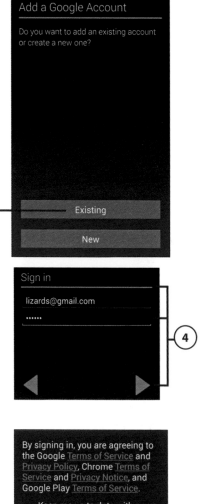

Add a Google Account

Do you want to add an existing account or create a new one?

Existing

New

Sign in

lizards@gmail.com

By signing in, you are agreeing to the Google Terms of Service and Privacy Policy, Chrome Terms of Service and Privacy Notice, and Google Play Terms of Service.

☑ Keep me up to date with news and offers from Google Play.

Cancel   OK

Backup and restore

Use your Google account to back up your apps, settings (such as bookmarks and Wi-Fi passwords), and other data.

You can change your backup settings anytime in Settings.

☑ Keep this phone backed up with my Google Account

7. Tap Sync Now.

8. A sync is performed and your Gmail account's Inbox displays. Press the Home key when you want to exit from Gmail.

lizards@gmail.com

Account not synced

This account isn't set up to sync automatically.
Touch **Sync Now** to sync mail once, or **Change Sync Settings** to set up this account to sync mail automatically.

⑦ ──────── Sync now

Change sync settings

⑧

Inbox
lizards@gmail.com

》 **Google Play**   May 8
☐ New Angry Birds + More Top Games and   ★
Great Gatsby Soundtrack — [image: Google

》 **Google Play**   May 1
☐ Dr. Oz's Fave Apps + New Android Games   ★
and Music Hits from $3.99 — [image: Google

Creating a Samsung Account

Certain Samsung applications that are supported on the Galaxy S 4, such as ChatON, Music Hub, and SamsungDive, require you to sign up for a free Samsung account. If you didn't create the account or log into an existing one when you ran the setup wizard, you can create the account now—or the first time you use an application that requires it.

1. On the Home screen, tap Apps, followed by Settings.

2. Select the Accounts tab and tap Add Account.

3. Tap Samsung Account. (If the account's dot is green, you've already added a Samsung account to this phone and can skip the remaining steps.)

4. Tap Create New Account.

Status

5. Create the account by entering an email address and password to use for the account, as well as the other requested information. Scroll to see the additional fields. Tap the Sign Up button.

6. Review the Terms and Conditions, tap I Accept All the Terms Above, and then tap the Agree button.

7. Open the account verification email message on your phone or computer and follow the account activation instructions. When you finish, the Samsung account is marked with a green dot on the Add Account screen, indicating that it's recorded on your phone.

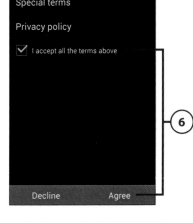

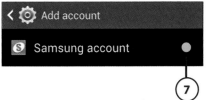

Placing and Receiving Calls

Although Chapter 4 covers placing and receiving phone calls in detail, here's a quick summary of the process. For other outgoing call options, such as calling someone with a Contacts record, see Chapter 4.

Placing a Call

1. Tap the Phone icon at the bottom of any Home screen page.

2. Using the onscreen keypad, enter the number to dial.

Country Code and Area Code Prefixes

When calling a number outside of your cell phone's area code, be sure to enter the recipient's area code. It's only necessary to enter a country code, such as 1 for the United States and Canada, when you're dialing a country that uses a different code than yours.

3. Tap the green phone icon to dial the call.

Receiving a Call

1. When a call is received, the caller is identified by name and number (if he has a Contacts record), by number (if there's no matching Contacts record), or by Private Caller (if the caller has blocked caller ID).

2. Do one of the following:

   • To accept the call, drag the green phone icon in any direction.

   • To reject the call and send it to voicemail, drag the red phone icon in any direction.

   • To reject the call by sending a text message of explanation, drag the Reject Call with Message tab upward and select a message to transmit.

3. When the call is completed, tap End Call.

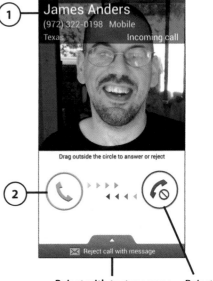

Reject with text message   Reject

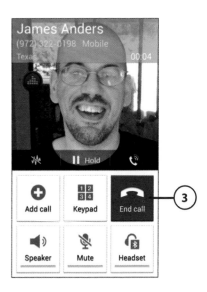

Working with Data

Any activity that transmits data to and from your phone over the cellular network counts toward your plan's data limit. The same data transmitted over Wi-Fi, on the other hand, doesn't count. By tapping icons in the Notification panel, you can manually control the method by which data transmissions occur, ensuring that the least expensive and fastest method is used. In this section, you learn how to enable and disable Wi-Fi, as well as how to connect your phone to a wireless (Wi-Fi) network.

Connection Methods

At any given time, only Wi-Fi or 2G/3G/4G can be the active data connection method. When Wi-Fi is enabled and you're connected to a network, 2G/3G/4G is automatically disabled. When Wi-Fi is disabled or unavailable and you perform a data-related activity, 2G, 3G, or 4G is automatically used (depending on what's available at your current location).

You can also use Bluetooth to exchange data directly between the phone and any Bluetooth-capable computer or laptop. For instructions on using Bluetooth for data transfers, see Chapter 15.

Manually Setting a Connection Method

1. Open the Notification panel by touching the status bar at the top of the screen and dragging downward.

2. The Wi-Fi icon toggles between a Wi-Fi and cellular (2G/3G/4G) data connection. Wi-Fi is enabled when the icon is green; a cellular connection is active when the Wi-Fi icon is dim. Tap the Wi-Fi icon to toggle its state.

3. Close the Notification panel by touching the bottom of the panel and dragging upward.

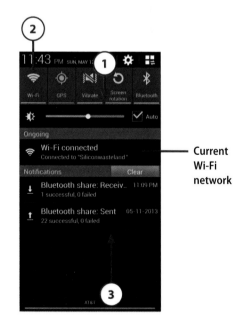

Current Wi-Fi network

Which Wi-Fi Network?

When you enable Wi-Fi, a notification in the Ongoing section of the Notification panel shows the network to which you're connected.

Monitoring Data Usage

If your data plan isn't unlimited, you can use the Data Usage setting to monitor your usage and warn when you're close to the limit. See "Managing Talk Time and Data Usage" in Chapter 19 for details.

Connecting to a New Wireless Network

Because it's free and often a faster connection than using a 2G, 3G, or 4G cellular connection, it's advantageous to use a Wi-Fi connection whenever it's available. After you successfully connect to a given network (such as your home network or one at a local coffee shop), your phone can reconnect without requesting the password again.

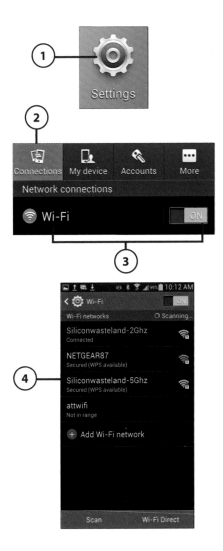

1. On the Home screen, tap Apps, followed by Settings.

2. Selection the Connections tab.

3. Enable Wi-Fi (if it's off) by dragging its slider to the On position and then tap the Wi-Fi text.

4. A list of nearby networks appears. If a network to which you've previously connected is found, the phone automatically connects to it. If no network is automatically chosen or you want to connect to a *different* network, tap the name of the network to which you want to connect.

5. Do one of the following:

- If the network is unsecured (open), tap the Connect button.

- If the network is secured (password protected), enter the requested password, and then tap the Connect button.

Show Password

When entering a lengthy or complex password, you may find it helpful to tap the Show Password check box. Otherwise, each character in the password is visible only as you type it and is immediately covered by a bullet (•) character.

6. If successful, the Settings screen shows you're connected to the network. While connected, this information also displays in the Notification panel.

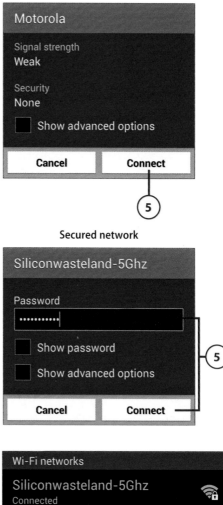

Unsecured network

Motorola

Signal strength
Weak

Security
None

☐ Show advanced options

Cancel   Connect

⑤

Secured network

Siliconwasteland-5Ghz

Password

••••••••••

☐ Show password

☐ Show advanced options

Cancel   Connect

⑤

Wi-Fi networks

Siliconwasteland-5Ghz
Connected

⑥

>>>Go Further

WI-FI NETWORK TIPS

If you have occasion to connect to more than one Wi-Fi network, here are a couple of tips you may find helpful:

- To *forget* a network to which you've previously connected, press and hold the network name in the Wi-Fi Networks list, and then tap Forget Network.

- To view information about the network to which you're connected, tap its name (shown in blue type) in the Wi-Fi Networks list. If there are multiple unsecured networks within range, you can connect to each one and compare their signal strength and speed.

Network properties

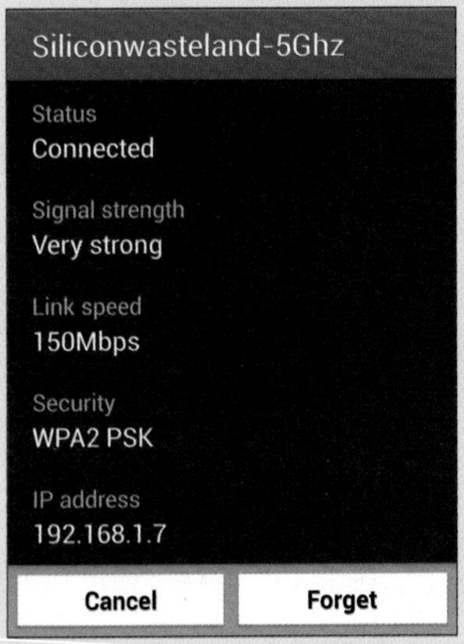

Siliconwasteland-5Ghz

Status
Connected

Signal strength
Very strong

Link speed
150Mbps

Security
WPA2 PSK

IP address
192.168.1.7

| Cancel | Forget |

Changing the Default Language

If English isn't your native language, you can change the phone's language to another supported language.

1. On the Home screen, tap Apps, followed by Settings.

2. Select the My Device tab, scroll down to the Input and Control section, and tap Language and Input.

3. Tap Language.

4. Tap the desired language.

5. Icon names, display text, prompts, dialog boxes, and other text change to reflect the selected language.

1

Settings

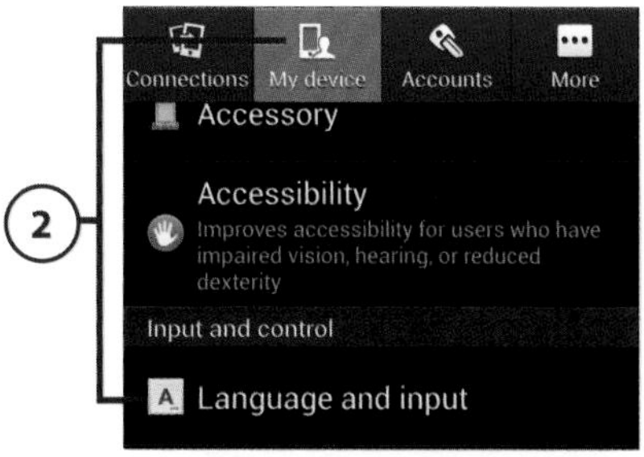

2

| Connections | My device | Accounts | More |

🖥 Accessory

Accessibility
Improves accessibility for users who have impaired vision, hearing, or reduced dexterity

Input and control

🅰 Language and input

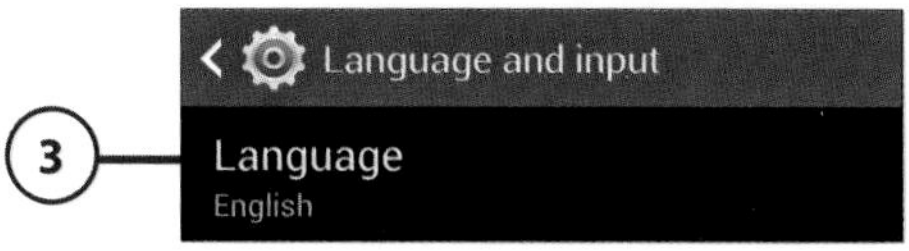

3

‹ ⚙ Language and input

Language
English

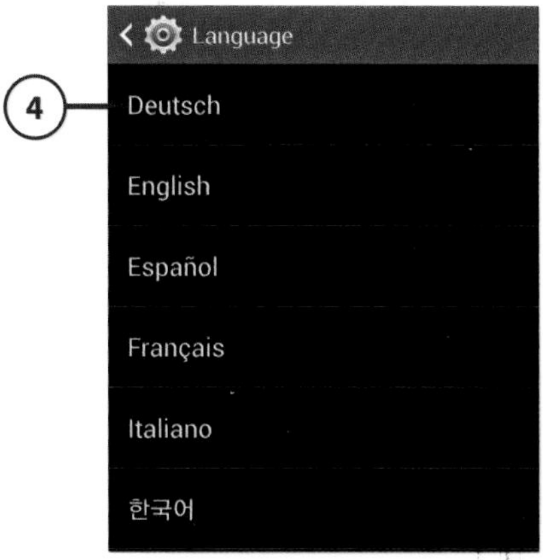

4

‹ ⚙ Language

Deutsch

English

Español

Français

Italiano

한국어

5

‹ ⚙ Sprache und Eingabe

Sprache
Deutsch

Tastaturen und Eingabemethoden

Standard
Samsung-Tastatur ⟩

☑ Google Spracheingabe
Automatisch ⚙

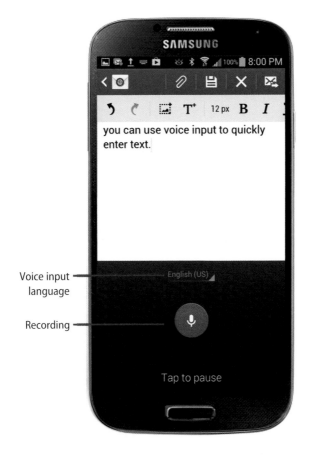

you can use voice input to quickly enter text.

Voice input language — English (US)

Recording

Tap to pause

In this chapter, you become familiar with the Samsung Galaxy S 4 interface and discover how to interact with it. Topics include the following:

→ Understanding the Home screen and its components

→ Using the three hardware keys below the touchscreen

→ Working with the Notification panel

→ Tapping and interacting with touchscreen elements

→ Using the onscreen keyboard and voice input to enter and edit text

Understanding the Android/TouchWiz Interface

The Galaxy S 4 has a touch-sensitive screen (or *touchscreen*) that can detect location, pressure, and motion on its surface. The Android operating system and Samsung's TouchWiz modifications to it determine how the phone and its applications react to the various touches. Even if you've previously owned an Android phone or another touch-sensitive device, such as an iPod touch or a tablet, you need to be familiar with the information in this chapter. Read on for the essential methods of interacting with the touchscreen and the hardware keys below the screen, as well as the techniques for entering and editing text.

The Home Screen

The Home screen is Command Central for your phone. You launch *apps* (applications) from this screen, view the latest information presented on widgets (such as the local weather from AccuWeather.com), and initiate phone calls and messaging sessions.

The important parts of the Home screen include the status or Notification bar, the main area (equivalent to a PC or Mac desktop), Home screen indicator, and icons for five primary shortcuts (Phone, Contacts, Messaging, Internet, and Apps).

Status or Notification bar

Main area

Home screen indicator

Primary shortcuts

The Status or Notification Bar

The status or Notification bar at the top of the screen serves two functions. First, icons on the right side of the bar show the active communication features (such as Wi-Fi, 3G/4G, Bluetooth, and GPS) and display status information (such as the current battery charge and Wi-Fi signal strength).

Second, the left side of the bar displays notification icons for important events, such as new email, new text messages, missed calls, and downloaded or uploaded items.

Although it might be tempting to do so, you can't interact with the bar; tapping its icons does nothing. To change the active features or respond to notifications, you use the Notification panel (described in "The Notification Panel," later in this chapter).

Notification icons ———  ——— 73% 6:37 PM

Service status icons

Main Area

The Home screen is yours to embellish as you like. As you can see, you can place widgets and shortcuts wherever you want, as well as choose a custom background (*wallpaper*) for it, as explained in Chapter 3.

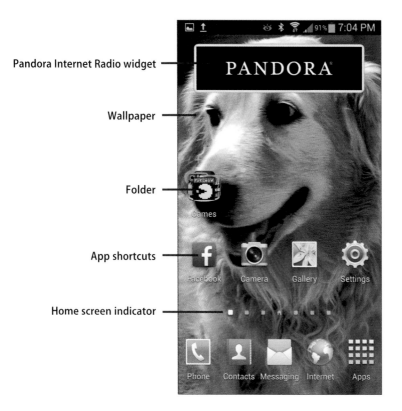

Extended Home Screen

The Home screen actually consists of up to seven different screens or pages, each represented by a Home screen indicator. As with the center Home screen page, you can add different widgets and shortcuts to each page. To move from one page to another, do any of the following:

- Press the Home key to go directly to the main Home screen page.
- Tap the Home screen indicator of the page that you want to view.
- Swipe left or right to flip to the desired page.
- Drag a Home screen indicator to the left or right to see a visual and numeric representation of each Home screen page.

Dragging an indicator

Home screen page number

As explained in Chapter 3, you can rearrange the Home screen pages, add new ones (up to the maximum of seven), and delete unwanted ones.

Setting the Home Screen Mode

To make it easier for new smart-phone (or Android smartphone) users to become comfortable with their Galaxy S 4, the Home screen can be changed from Standard mode (which is the focus of this book) to the simpler Easy mode. Easy mode provides:

- Three simple Home screen layouts with larger icons and text

- Large, easy-to-read text in important apps, such as Contacts, Calendar, and Phone

- Fixed shortcuts to 12 essential apps and the option to add 3 more of your choosing

- Three fixed widgets (time, date, and temperature)

- Access to all additional apps as a scrolling alphabetical list

You can switch between Standard and Easy mode whenever you like. Customizations that you've made to the Home screen pages in either mode are restored when you return to that mode. To change Home screen modes, follow these steps:

1. On the Home screen, tap Apps, followed by Settings.

2. Select the My Device tab, and tap Home Screen Mode.

Main Home screen (Easy mode)

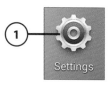

3. Select a mode (Standard or Easy), and tap Apply. Tap OK in the confirmation dialog box.

Other Screen Indicators

The indicator dots in Apps and Widgets work in the same manner as they do on the Home screen pages. Each dot represents a screen or page of icons. The lit dot indicates the screen or page that you're viewing.

Primary and Other App Shortcuts

Beneath the indicator dots on every Home screen page are icons for Phone, Contacts, Messaging, Internet, and Apps. These are known as the *primary shortcuts*. With the exception of the Apps shortcut, you are free to remove, reorder, or replace the first four. If, for example, you seldom use Messaging, you can replace its shortcut with one for Email, Settings, or another app that you constantly use, such as Angry Birds or Facebook. See "Repositioning and Removing Home Screen Items" in Chapter 3 for instructions.

Depending on your carrier, you may see additional app shortcuts *above* the indicator dots on some Home screen pages. Like the primary shortcuts—as well as other shortcuts that you add to any Home screen page—you can freely remove, reorder, or replace these shortcuts.

Primary shortcuts ——

Using the Hardware Keys

There are three ever-present hardware *keys* located directly below the touchscreen: Menu, Home, and Back. When pressed, each key performs a context-sensitive function related to the operating system (when viewing the Home screen) or the app that you're currently using.

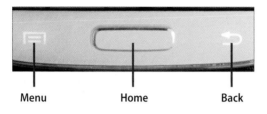

| Menu | Home | Back |

Menu Key

As its name implies, when you press the Menu key, a menu of options or commands may appear. When you press the Menu key on the Home screen, the menu presents options for creating a folder, setting preferences, and so on. When you press the Menu key within an app, the menu's contents are set by the developer and frequently vary depending on the part of the app that's active.

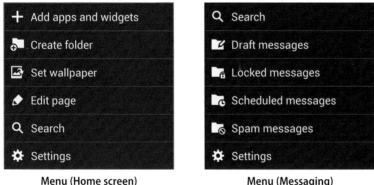

Menu (Home screen)   Menu (Messaging)

Home Key

The Home key has multiple functions, depending on whether you're on the Home screen or using an app. You can also use it in combination with the Power button to take screen shots (as described shortly).

Within an app. Press the Home key to exit the app and return to the most recently viewed Home screen page. Press and hold the Home key to display a list of recently run and active apps. You can tap any app thumbnail to launch or switch to that app.

Recently run and active apps

On the Home screen. When you press the Home key while viewing any Home screen page, it displays the main Home screen page. Press and hold the Home key to display a list of recently run and active apps. You can tap any thumbnail to launch or switch to that app or system component. If you quickly double-press the Home key, S Voice is activated. See "Using Voice Services" in Chapter 3 for information about using S Voice.

Within an app or on the Home screen. If you simultaneously press and hold the Home key and Power button, the phone performs a screen capture, creating a graphic image of the screen. All captures are saved in the Screenshots folder and can be viewed in Gallery. You can also perform a screen capture by dragging the side of your hand across the screen.

Number of items

Screenshots folder (Gallery)

Back Key

You use the Back key within apps to return to the previous screen or—if on the app's initial screen—to exit to the Home screen.

Within an app. Press the Back key to return to the previous screen. If you press it on the app's initial screen, you exit the app and return to the most recently viewed Home screen page.

Within Internet and Chrome. Press Back to display the previous web page. The Back key has the same function as pressing Backspace (Windows) or Delete (Mac) when using a web browser.

Within a dialog box or an options menu. Similar to pressing the Escape key in many computer programs, you can press Back to exit a dialog box or options menu without making a choice.

When typing. Press Back to dismiss the onscreen keyboard.

Within the Notification panel. Press Back to dismiss the panel.

The Notification Panel

When new notifications appear in the status bar announcing received email, text messages, software updates, and the like, you can display the Notification panel and optionally respond to or clear the notifications.

1. Open the Notification panel on the Home screen or within most apps by touching the status bar and dragging downward.

2. Tap a notification to respond to or interact with it. For example, tapping a New Email notification launches Email and displays the Inbox. When you respond to a notification, it's removed from the Notification panel.

3. To remove a notification without responding to it, drag it off the screen to the left or right. To simultaneously remove *all* notifications, tap the Clear button.

4. To close the Notification panel, touch the gray bar at the bottom of the screen and drag upward.

CONFIGURING QUICK SETTINGS

At the top of the Notification panel is a string of icons called *Quick Settings*. By tapping these icons, you can quickly enable or disable system features, such as Bluetooth, GPS, or Airplane Mode. When a feature is enabled, its icon is bright green. Swipe left or right to scroll through the icons until you find the one you need, and then tap the icon to toggle the feature's state. If you need to *configure* a feature (connecting to a new Wi-Fi network, for example), press and hold the Quick Setting icon to open its section in Settings. To display all the icons as an array, tap the grid icon.

>>Go Further

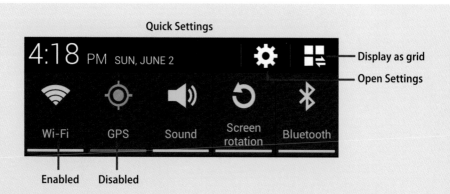

Quick Settings

4:18 PM SUN, JUNE 2 — Display as grid
— Open Settings

Wi-Fi   GPS   Sound   Screen rotation   Bluetooth

Enabled   Disabled

You can rearrange the Quick Settings icons, placing the ones you use most often earlier in the array or list. Open Settings by tapping its icon above the Notification panel, select the My Device tab, and tap Display, Notification panel. To move an icon, press and hold it, and then drag it to the new position.

Interacting with the Touchscreen

Your phone has a touch-sensitive screen that you interact with by tapping, touching, and making other motions with your fingers or hand. In addition, within many apps, the phone recognizes and responds to the angle at which it's being held or its proximity to nearby objects.

Using Your Fingers

You can interact with the touchscreen by doing any of the following:

- *Tap*. To launch an app, open a document, choose a menu command, select an item in a list, activate a button, or type characters on the onscreen keyboard, tap the item lightly with your fingertip. (A tap is equivalent to a mouse click on a computer.)

Tap a thumbnail to view a photo (Gallery)

- *Touch and hold (or press and hold).* You can interact with some items by touching and holding them. For example, touching and holding a person's record in Contacts causes a contextual menu to appear that enables you to do something with the record, such as edit or delete it. To move or delete a Home screen item (such as a shortcut or widget), you can touch and hold the item.

- *Flick.* Scroll up or down through a lengthy menu or any vertical list of items (such as a message list in Email) by making light, quick vertical strokes.

- *Swipe.* A swipe is the horizontal equivalent of a flick. Swipe to flip through images in a Gallery folder, view different Home screen pages, and move through the Apps and Widgets pages.

Try a Double Tap
In certain apps (Gallery, Internet, and Chrome, for example), you can also double-tap the screen to zoom in or out. Spreading and pinching, however, provide better control over the amount of magnification.

Touch and hold a song title in Music...

...to display this contextual menu

Flick up or down

Swipe left or right (Gallery)

Current image

- *Drag.* To move an item (such as a widget or app icon on the Home screen), press and hold the item, and don't release it until it's in the desired position—on the current screen page or a different one.

Drag a Home screen item to change its position

- *Spread/pinch.* To zoom in or out (increasing or decreasing the magnification) when viewing a photo or web page, place two fingers on the screen and spread them apart or pinch them together, respectively.

Rotating the Screen

In many apps, you can rotate the screen to change from portrait to landscape orientation and vice versa. It's extremely useful when viewing photos in Gallery that were shot in landscape orientation, when reading web pages in the Internet or Chrome app, and when you need to type on the onscreen keyboard, for example.

Landscape

Portrait

>>>Go Further

USING MOTIONS AND GESTURES

In addition to tapping, flicking, swiping, and pinching, you can perform certain actions using *motions* and *gestures*, such as shaking the phone, tilting the phone, or waving your hand over the phone. After mastering the basics of controlling the phone and apps via touch, you should explore the motion and air-based options (see "Enabling Motion and Palm Motion Settings" and "Enabling Air Gesture" in Chapter 3) and decide which ones, if any, you find helpful and want to enable.

Entering Text

In addition to simply viewing and listening to content on your phone, much of what you do involves entering text. You can enter text using the onscreen keyboard or by speaking into the phone.

Using the onscreen keyboard, there are two methods of typing. You're familiar with the first one in which you tap letter, number, and punctuation keys as you would on a computer keyboard or a typewriter. The second uses software called *Swype*, in which you drag your finger over the keyboard—touching the characters needed to spell each word.

Using the Keyboard: Tapping

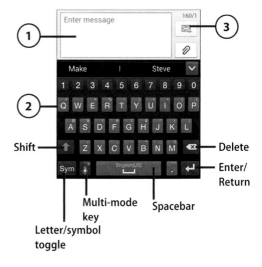

1. Tap to select a text field or box, such as the Internet address box, a password field, or the message area of a text message. The onscreen keyboard appears. A blinking text insertion mark shows where the next typed character will appear.

2. Tap keys to type.

Entering Nonalphabetic Characters

Tap the SYM key. The key above it is now labeled 1/2, and the layout displays numbers, currency symbols, and common punctuation. Tap this key again to cycle to the symbol (2/2) layout. To return to the alphabetic layout, tap the ABC key.

Restore alphabetic layout

3. To dismiss or hide the keyboard, perform the action necessary to complete your typing (such as tapping Send) or press the Back key. To restore the keyboard after pressing Back, tap in the text box or field again.

Restore alphabetic layout

Capitalization

When you begin entering text into a field or are starting a new sentence, the first character is typically capitalized automatically. Subsequent capitalization is determined by the state of the Shift key. Tap the Shift key to toggle it among its three states: lowercase, capitalize next letter only, and capitalize all letters.

| Lowercase | Capitalize next letter | Uppercase |

Using the Keyboard: Swype

1. Tap to select a text field or box, such as the Internet address box, a password field, or the message area of a text message. The onscreen keyboard appears. A blinking text insertion mark shows where the next entered character will appear.

2. To type each word, drag over its letters—in order. Complete the word by briefly lifting your finger from the screen and then drag over the letters needed to form the next word. A space is automatically inserted between each pair of words. Tap punctuation where it's needed.

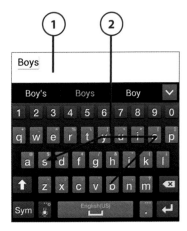

Duplicate Letters

If a letter is repeated in a word, such as l in follow, make a loop over the letter or scribble over it to indicate that it's repeated.

TYPING TIPS

Although the basics of typing are straightforward, the following tips can help you fine-tune this sometimes difficult process.

- *Try landscape mode.* To use a larger version of the keyboard, simply rotate the phone to landscape orientation. (For this to work, the phone's *auto-rotate* feature must be enabled. From the Home screen, press the Menu key, tap Settings, select My Device, tap Display, and ensure that Auto-Rotate Screen is checked.)

>>>Go Further

Landscape keyboard

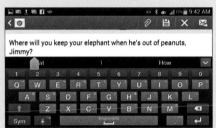

- *Change the input method.* The phone supports typed or traced text input (Samsung Keyboard and Swype) and voice input (Google Voice Typing). To switch from the current input method to the other while entering text, open the Notification panel, tap Select Input Method, and select the alternative method in the dialog box that appears.

Current input method ——

- *Explore the Language and Input settings.* Select the My Device tab in Settings and take time to browse the Language and Input options. You can configure Google Voice Typing (described in the next section) and set options for the Samsung Keyboard (tapping and Swype), such as whether to display predictive text or to support handwriting. You can view onscreen help for typing by tapping the Samsung Keyboard settings icon, followed by Help. For assistance using Swype, tap the Swype settings icon, followed by How to Swype.

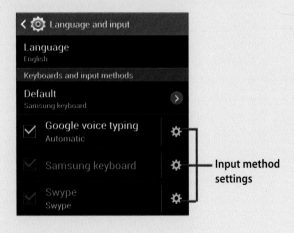

Input method settings

- *Change the language.* If English isn't your native or preferred input language, you can pick a different one. In the Language and Input settings, tap the Samsung Keyboard settings icon, followed by Input Languages. Select a language from the Downloaded Languages list. If the correct language isn't shown, press the Menu key and tap Update to update the list, and then download the language by tapping its name.

- *Use Predictive Text.* As you type or trace, the phone presents a list of suggestions (*predictive text*) for the word it thinks you're typing. If you see the correct one, tap it to use it as a replacement for the current word. You can also tap the down-arrow icon on the right to view other possible replacement words.

Predictive text ——————— Where   Ever   When   ∨ ——— More suggestions

Fine-Tuning Predictive Text

You can improve the predictive text suggestions by allowing it to study what you type in Facebook, Messaging, Contacts, and so on. When working in a text box, press and hold the multi-mode key (to the left of the spacebar), tap the Settings icon, tap Predictive Text, and review the options.

If you don't find predictive text helpful, you can disable it in the Language and Input settings. Tap the Samsung Keyboard settings icon and drag the Predictive Text slider to the Off position.

- *Character preview.* You can type certain secondary characters (such as the numbers above the top row of keys) without leaving the main alphabetic keyboard. If you press and hold any key, its secondary characters, if any, appear. Release the key to insert the secondary character into your text. If you press and hold longer on a key, every associated character, number, and symbol for the key appears in a pop-up menu. Slide your fingertip onto the one you want to insert. Note that different sets of characters are available for lowercase and uppercase keys.

Secondary characters for s ———— $ ß ś š ş

Press and hold

- *Other input options.* When entering text, you can switch input methods at any time, using any combination that you find convenient. To change methods, press and hold the multi-mode key and select the desired input method. Options include voice input (described in the next section), handwriting, inserting material from the Clipboard, text recognition using the camera, normal keyboard, and a floating keyboard that you can reposition by tapping its tab and dragging. The current method is marked with a green dot. Note that you can freely mix tapping and Swype without changing the input method.

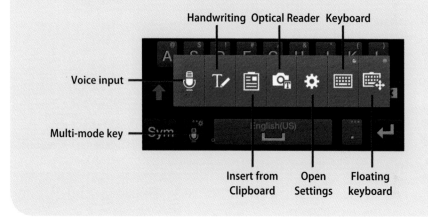

Using Voice Input

If you're abysmal at using the onscreen keyboard and are unwilling to take the time to master it, voice input (also called *voice typing*) may be more to your liking. You speak what you want to type, and it's translated into text.

1. To enable voice input, press and hold the multi-mode key and select voice input—the microphone. If the multi-mode key already displays the microphone, simply tap it.

Switch Using the Notification Panel

As explained earlier in the chapter, you can also switch input methods by opening the Notification panel, tapping Select Input Method, and selecting Google Voice Typing in the dialog box.

2. A recording indicator appears. Speak the text, saying punctuation (such as *comma*, *period*, *question mark*, and *exclamation point*) where it's needed. The text is transcribed as you speak.

3. When you finish recording, tap the recording icon and then tap the keyboard icon.

4. Any instance of questionable transcription is marked with a faint gray underline. To view and select possible corrections, tap the underlined text.

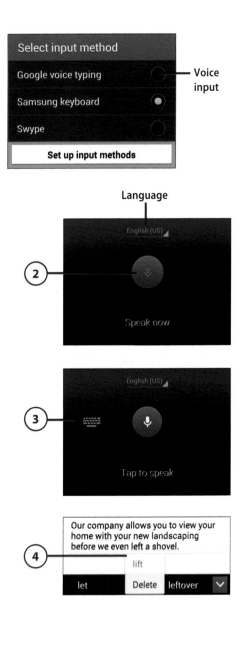

Voice input

Language

CHANGE THE VOICE INPUT LANGUAGE

>>>Go Further

Just as you can configure the keyboard to type in languages other than English (see Chapter 1), you can configure Voice Input in the same manner.

1. Tap the language indicator above the recording icon and select a language. If the desired language isn't shown, go to step 2.

2. Open Settings, select the My Device tab, and tap Language and Input.

3. Tap the Google Voice Typing settings icon, followed by Choose Input Languages.

4. Remove the check mark from Automatic, select the language(s), and return to step 1. (If you ever want to revert to the original language for voice input, check Automatic again.)

It's Not All Good

EXCELLENT, BUT NOT PERFECT

Voice input is great for converting straightforward, common speech to text—and every update includes some improvements. However, it still has some drawbacks that necessitate after-the-fact editing. For instance, if voice input doesn't understand a word, it frequently breaks it up into several short words that it *does* know, resulting in gibberish. Similarly, it occasionally fails to capitalize the first word of a sentence.

To determine if voice input will work for you, test it. Say some normal text and try reading a few sentences from a book or magazine. Whether it's a winner for you will be determined by how accurate it is and the amount of cleanup you need to do.

Editing Text

Typos, missing capitalization and punctuation, and bad guesses in Swype or voice input are common in entered text. Instead of just tapping Send and hoping your message recipient will *know* what you mean, you can edit the text by doing any of the following:

- At the blinking text insertion mark, you can type or paste new text or press the Delete key to delete the character to the left.

- To reposition the text insertion mark for editing, tap in the text. If the text insertion mark isn't positioned correctly, carefully drag the blue marker to the desired spot.

- To select a single word for deletion or replacement, double-tap or long-press the word. To delete it, tap the Delete key; to replace it, type over it.

- To select a specific text string (a word, sentence, or paragraph, for instance), start by selecting a word at the beginning or end of the text that you want to select. Drag the selection handles to highlight the desired text. Then select a command from the pop-up menu above the selection, press the Delete key, or overtype the selected text. (Note that the command icons, their appearance, and whether they're labeled varies from one app to another. If there are more icons than can be shown at once, they scroll horizontally.)

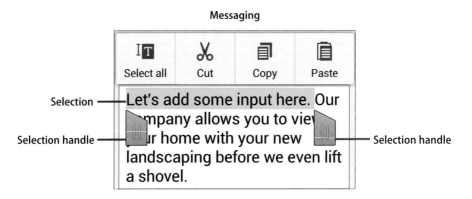

- To paste the most recently copied or cut text into a text box, set the text insertion mark, tap the blue marker, and then tap Paste in the pop-up that appears.

- When entering and editing text in Email or Gmail, you can tap icons on the toolbar above the message area to insert images, apply character and paragraph formatting, or undo the most recent change.

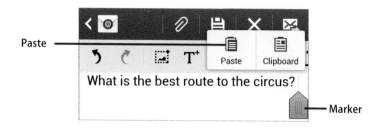

Paste

What is the best route to the circus?

Marker

Pasting Other Material

If you select Clipboard from the pop-up menu rather than Paste, you can paste *other* material—images, for example—that you recently copied or cut. Tap the item that you want to insert. To remove an unwanted item from the Clipboard, press and hold the item, and tap Delete from Clipboard.

Clipboard

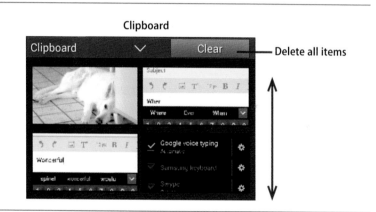

Delete all items

Copying Text from a Web Page

You can also use editing techniques to copy text from a web page. Press to select the first word, and then drag the handles to select the material to copy. In the toolbar that appears, tap Copy to copy the material so that you can paste it elsewhere, or tap Share to copy the material directly into a new email, text message, or Facebook post, for example.

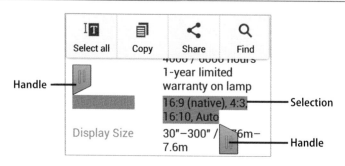

Handle

Handle

Selection

S Voice

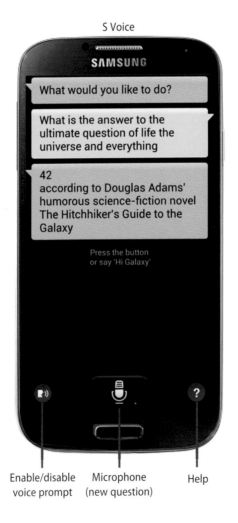

What would you like to do?

What is the answer to the ultimate question of life the universe and everything

42
according to Douglas Adams' humorous science-fiction novel The Hitchhiker's Guide to the Galaxy

Press the button
or say 'Hi Galaxy'

Enable/disable
voice prompt

Microphone
(new question)

Help

In this chapter, you find out how to customize your phone by populating the Home screen with widgets, shortcuts, and folders; change the default wallpaper; set default and contact-specific ringtones; issue voice commands and ask questions; and more. Topics include the following:

→ Customizing the Home screen with new wallpaper, shortcuts, folders, and widgets

→ Setting an Apps view

→ Changing system Settings

→ Setting default, contact-specific, and group ringtones

→ Configuring and using voice services (S Voice, Voice Control, and Google Voice Search) to find information and perform actions

Making the Phone Your Own

Nothing prevents you from using the phone exactly as it was when you first opened the box—keeping the default wallpaper, installing no additional widgets, downloading no new apps, and ignoring Settings for the operating system and apps. But the fun of having a powerful smartphone is in *customizing* it—personalizing the phone in ways that make it easier, more efficient, and fun to use.

Customizing the Home Screen

The easiest and most obvious way to personalize the phone is to customize its Home screen. In fact, many of the Home screen customization options, such as changing the wallpaper, adding widgets, and adding shortcuts to your favorite apps, are what users do first with their new phones.

Selecting Wallpaper

The simplest way to customize the phone is to change its Home screen background (called *wallpaper*) by selecting an image that's aesthetically pleasing, amusing, or touching. Wallpaper can be a static image or a *live,* moving image. The image you choose is applied to all Home screen pages.

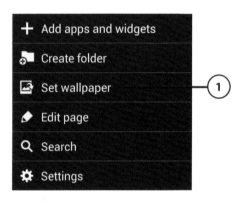

1. On the Home screen, press the Menu key and tap Set Wallpaper.

Wallpaper Shortcut

As an alternative, press and hold any empty spot on a Home screen page, and tap Set Wallpaper.

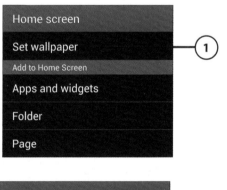

2. Tap Home Screen, Lock Screen, or Home and Lock Screens—depending on the screen(s) that you want to customize.

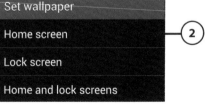

3. Select the type of wallpaper that you want to use. Options include Gallery (a cropped area of a photo or other image stored in Gallery), Live Wallpapers (images that move), and Wallpapers (static, full-screen images).

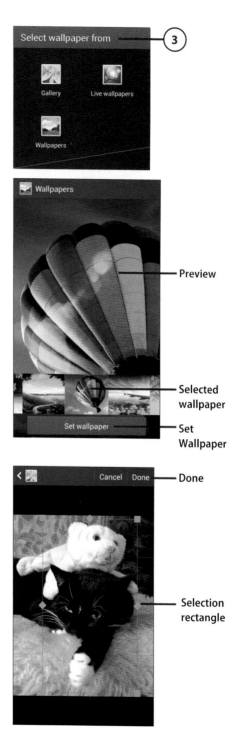

Carrier-Provided Wallpaper

Some carriers provide their own custom wallpaper. For example, Sprint phones include an ID Wallpapers category.

- *Wallpapers.* Tap a thumbnail in the horizontally scrolling list, and tap Set Wallpaper.

- *Gallery.* Open the folder that contains the image. Tap the image thumbnail, resize and move the selection rectangle to select the desired area, and tap the Done button.

- *Live Wallpapers.* Tap a wallpaper style to see a preview, and tap the Set Wallpaper button.

Static Versus Live Wallpaper

Live wallpaper contributes more to battery drain than a static Wallpaper or Gallery image. If you find that you're running out of power too quickly, consider replacing your live wallpaper with static wallpaper.

Rearranging, Removing, and Adding Home Screen Pages

The default Home screen has five horizontally scrolling pages. You can rearrange the pages, remove ones that you don't need, or add new pages (up to the maximum of seven).

1. On the Home screen, press the Menu key and tap Edit Page.

2. To change the position of a page, press and hold its thumbnail, and then drag it to a new location in the array.

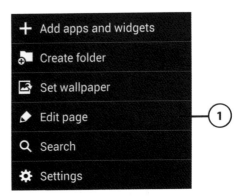

The Main Home Screen Page

If you rearrange Home screen pages, the main page (marked with a white up arrow) can be placed anywhere in the array—not just in the center. Whenever you're on the Home screen, pressing the Home button always takes you to this main page.

3. To delete a page, press and hold its thumbnail, and then drag it onto the Remove icon at the top of the screen. If the page contains one or more items, a confirmation dialog box appears. Tap OK to confirm the deletion.

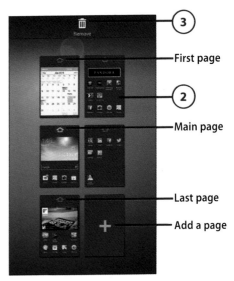

First page

Main page

Last page

Add a page

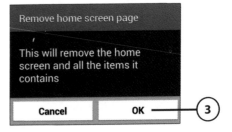

Effects of Deleting a Page

As indicated by the confirmation dialog, deleting a page also removes the items on that page, such as widgets and shortcuts. Of course, you can place those items on the remaining or new pages again.

4. To add a new page, tap any thumbnail that contains a plus (+) symbol (representing an available page). You can optionally change the location of the new page, as described in step 2.

5. When you finish editing, complete the process by returning to the Home screen—press the Back or Home key, or tap a Home screen page thumbnail.

Adding Shortcuts

You can place shortcuts to your favorite apps on the Home screen. When you tap an app shortcut, the app that it represents launches. An Android *shortcut* is the equivalent of a Mac alias or a Windows shortcut.

1. Navigate to the Home screen page to which you want to add the shortcut, ensure that it has an open space for the shortcut, and tap the Apps icon. (You can add the shortcut to any page, but the current one is initially offered as the destination.)

Fast Way to Add a Shortcut

To quickly add a new app short-cut to a Home screen page, press and hold any open spot on the page. The Home Screen dialog box appears. In the Add to Home Screen section, tap Apps and Widgets. Press and hold the app icon and drag it to its destination on the page.

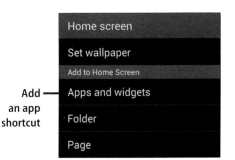

Add an app shortcut

2. Ensure that the Apps tab is selected. Locate the app for which you want to create a shortcut, scrolling horizontally as needed.

3. Press and hold the app's icon, drag it into an open spot on the current Home screen page and release the icon.

Repositioning or Removing a Shortcut

After creating a shortcut, you can reposition it on the current or a different Home screen page. Press and hold the shortcut, and then drag it to the desired position.

To remove a shortcut that you no longer need, press and hold it, and then drag it onto the Remove icon. Removing a shortcut doesn't affect the item that it represents.

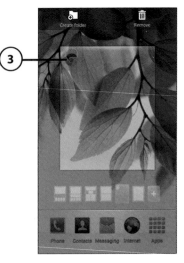

Creating a Bookmark Shortcut

You can also create shortcuts to your favorite web pages. In the Internet app, open the page or site for viewing. Press the Menu key and tap Add Shortcut. The bookmark is added to a Home screen page.

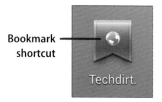

Bookmark shortcut

Adding Widgets

A *widget* is an application that runs on the Home screen. Many, such as Weather, aren't interactive or are only minimally so. For example, you can tap the refresh icon on the Weather widget to force an update of the weather info. Otherwise, such widgets simply provide continuously updated information. Other widgets, such as the Music widget, are designed for interaction. By tapping its buttons, you can pause or restart playback, and skip to the next or previous song.

You can add a widget in any free space on a Home screen page, as long as there's room for it. Widgets come in a variety of sizes, from one- or two-section widgets to full-screen ones. In addition to the widgets supplied with your phone, downloaded applications sometimes include their own widgets.

Widgets tab

To add a widget to a Home screen page, follow the steps listed in "Adding Shortcuts." In step 2 on the Apps screen, select the Widgets tab rather than the Apps tab. Under each widget name is the number of screen sections (horizontal × vertical) required by the widget.

>>>Go Further

WIDGET SHORTCUTS

Shortcuts in Android give you lots of flexibility because they can provide direct links to a variety of things: files, records, or operating system elements. For instance, you can create a Direct Dial shortcut that, when tapped, automatically dials a person's phone number. After adding the Direct Dial widget to a Home screen page, you tap the person's contact record to link it to the shortcut.

Here are some other widget-based shortcuts you might want to add:

- *Book.* Links to a favorite downloaded ebook that you can read with the Play Books app.

- *Bookmark.* Links to a web page selected from your stored bookmarks.

- *Contact.* Links to a person's record in Contacts, enabling you to easily call, message, email, or locate the person.

- *Direct Message.* Enables you to create a new text or multimedia message to a specific person in Contacts.

- *Settings Shortcut.* Opens a Settings category that you frequently access.

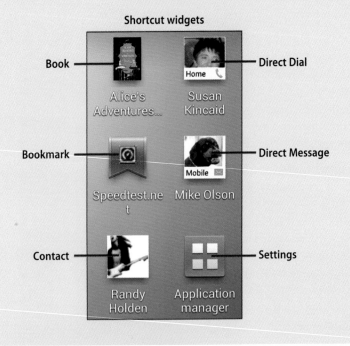

Shortcut widgets

Creating Folders

To help organize your Home screen items, you can add folders in which to store them.

1. On the Home screen, navigate to the page to which you want to add the folder, and do either of the following:

   - Press the Menu key and tap Create Folder.

   - Press and hold any open spot on the page. In the Home Screen dialog box, tap Folder.

2. Type a name for the folder in the Create Folder dialog box.

3. Tap OK.

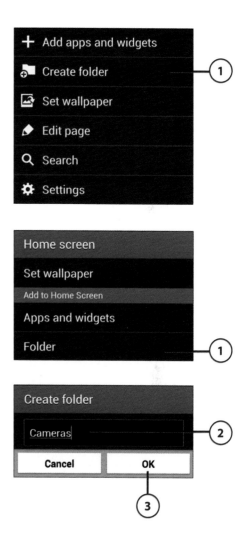

WORKING WITH FOLDERS

Of course, creating a folder is just the first step. Adding and organizing shortcuts within the folders is what makes them useful.

To insert an item into a folder, press and hold the item's icon, and then drag it onto the folder. Tap the folder to access its items. In the pop-out contents list that appears, tap an item to launch or open it.

To remove an item from a folder, tap the folder to open it, press and hold the item's icon, and then drag it to any location outside of the folder. (To delete an app shortcut that's in a folder, drag the shortcut out of the folder. Then press and hold the shortcut, and drag it onto the Remove icon.)

Finally, like other Home screen items, you can reposition a folder by pressing and holding its icon, and then dragging it to its destination on the current or a different page.

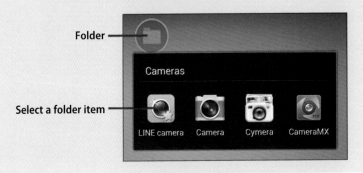

Folder

Select a folder item

Repositioning and Removing Home Screen Items

Part of the fun of setting up your Home screen pages is that you can freely rearrange items. And because many items are shortcuts, removing them from the Home screen has no effect on the actual items they represent. Follow these steps to reposition or remove Home screen items.

1. On the Home screen page, press and hold the item that you want to reposition or remove.

2. To *remove* the item, drag it onto the Remove (trash can) icon that appears at the top of the screen. When you release the item, it is removed.

3. To *reposition* the item, drag it to an empty or occupied spot on the current or another Home screen page. (If the destination is currently occupied, items will shift to make room—if possible.) When you release the item, the move is completed.

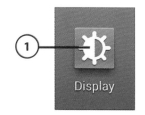

Moving Between Pages

When moving an item between Home screen pages, don't let up on the finger pressure until the destination page appears. If you inadvertently release the item on the wrong page or in the wrong spot, press and hold the item again and finish the move.

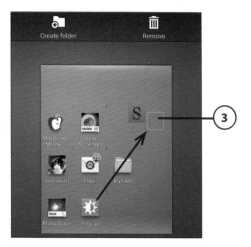

>>>Go Further

REARRANGING AND REPLACING THE PRIMARY SHORTCUTS

At the bottom of every Home page screen are the five primary shortcuts: Phone, Contacts, Messaging, Internet, and Apps. If desired, you can rearrange, remove, or replace any of the first four.

- To rearrange the primary shortcuts, press and hold the one that you want to move, drag it to the left or right, and then release it when it's in the desired position.

- To remove a primary shortcut, press and hold it, and then drag it to the Remove icon at the top of the Home screen page. If you want to remove the primary shortcut from the bottom of the screen but keep it on the page, drag it to any blank spot on the current Home screen page.

- To replace a primary shortcut (or add one, if you currently have less than four), find the replacement shortcut on a Home screen page, and drag it onto the primary shortcut you want to replace. (If the desired app shortcut isn't already on a Home screen page, you must first create a shortcut for it as described earlier in "Adding Shortcuts.")

New primary shortcut

Setting the Apps View

The default method of viewing your installed apps is an alphabetical, multi-page grid. Because you'll spend a lot of time in Apps, you may prefer to change this display to show your apps as an alphabetical scrolling list or as a custom grid arranged in any fashion and order that you like.

1. On the Home screen, tap the Apps icon.

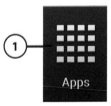

2. Select the Apps tab, press the Menu key, and tap View Type.

3. In the View Type dialog box, select one of the following:

- *Customizable Grid.* This option enables you to create additional grid pages and arrange the app icons however you like, such as putting all games together, placing the most frequently used apps on the first page, and creating folders in which to store certain apps.

- *Alphabetical Grid.* This is the default display style, presenting all app icons alphabetically on a series of 4×5 grid pages.

- *Alphabetical List.* Select this option to present the apps in an alphabetical, vertically scrolling list—like the contact list in Contacts.

4. If you chose Customizable Grid in step 3, you can customize the grid by pressing the Menu key and tapping Edit. (Be sure to choose the Edit command. Otherwise, changes made are to Home screen pages rather than the Apps pages.) Then do any of the following:

- To change an icon or folder's position, press and hold the item, and then drag it to a new position on the current page or another page. Surrounding icons move to make room for the item.

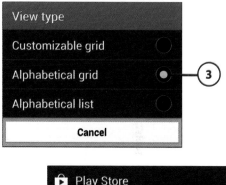

Drag the item to the Create Folder icon

- To create a folder, press and hold an icon that you want to move into the folder, and drag it onto the Create Folder icon at the top of the screen. Type a name for the new folder in the Create Folder dialog, and then tap the OK button. To add other apps to the folder, tap the folder, tap the plus (+) icon, select the check box for each app to add, and tap the Done button.

Name the folder

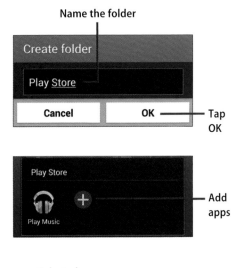

Tap OK

Add apps

Removing Apps from a Folder

To remove an app from a folder, tap the folder to display its contents, and then drag the app out of the folder.

Selected apps

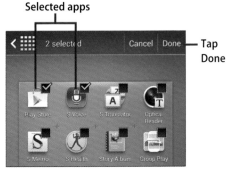

Tap Done

- To remove a folder, press and hold it, and then drag it onto the Remove icon at the top of the screen. Tap OK in the Remove Folder confirmation dialog. Apps within the deleted folder are restored to the Apps pages.

- To add a new Apps page, navigate to the page after which you want to insert the new page. Press and hold an icon that you want to add to the new page, and drag it onto the Create Page icon at the top of the screen.

When you finish making changes to the Apps pages, tap the Save button or tap Cancel to ignore all changes.

Remove

Create a new page

Save edits

Changing System Settings

By changing preferences in Settings, you can make the phone look and work to match your needs. Although system and app settings are discussed throughout the book, this section points out some settings that aren't mentioned elsewhere but are important in customizing your phone.

To access system settings, go to the Home screen, press the Menu key, and tap Settings. To access an app's settings (for those that provide them), launch the app, press the Menu key, and tap Settings.

Settings (System)

Settings (Internet)

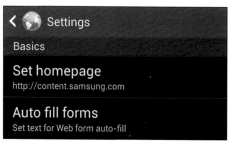

Setting the Date and Time

In Date and Time Settings, when the Automatic Date and Time and Automatic Time Zone settings are enabled, date, time, and time zone information is automatically obtained from the network. To change these settings, open Settings, select the More tab, and tap Date and Time.

If necessary, you can override this information by disabling the two Automatic settings and then making changes to the Set Date, Set Time, and Select Time Zone items. Tap Select Date Format if you want to change the format for displaying dates.

Date and Time Settings

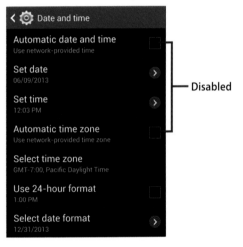

Enabling Motion and Palm Motion Settings

You can selectively enable Motion and Palm Motion settings to control phone features by tilting, shaking, or making special movements with the phone.

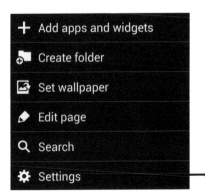

1. On the Home screen, press the Menu key and tap Settings.

2. Select the My Device tab. Scroll to the Input and Control section, and tap Motions and Gestures.

3. Move the sliders to On or Off to control the three categories of motions and gestures: Air Gesture, Motion, and Palm Motion. Tap Gyroscope Calibration to start a calibration routine for the phone's gyroscope.

4. Tap Motion to enable or disable the various Motion settings.

5. To use *any* of the motion features, you must set the Motion switch to On. Similarly, you can simultaneously disable all motion features by setting the Motion switch to Off.

6. When the Motion switch is On, the individual Motion settings work as follows:

   • *Direct Call.* When viewing a person's contact record, you can move the phone to your ear to place a call to the person.

   • *Smart Alert.* When you pick up the phone, you're notified of missed calls or messages.

   • *Zoom.* When viewing an image in Gallery or a web page in the Internet app, place two fingertips on the screen, and tilt the phone toward you to zoom in or away from you to zoom out.

   • *Browse an Image.* Press and hold an onscreen image in Gallery to pan within it by tilting the phone up, down, left, and right.

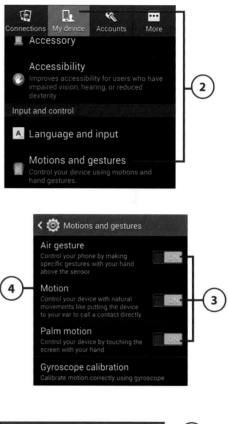

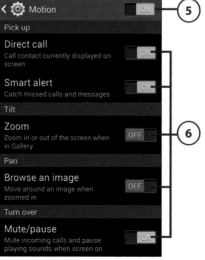

- *Mute/Pause.* Mute incoming call ringtones or pause playing media by turning the phone over so that it's face down.

7. Tap the Settings icon or press the Back key to return to the Motions and Gestures screen.

8. Tap the Palm Motion text to view the Palm Motion settings.

9. To use either of the Palm Motion features, you must set the Palm Motion switch to On. (You can turn both features off at once by setting the Palm Motion switch to Off.)

10. The Palm Motion settings work like this:

- *Capture Screen.* Create screen captures by placing the edge of your hand on the screen and dragging across it. Captured screens are saved in the Screenshots folder. (You can also create screen captures by simultaneously pressing the Home key and Power button.)

- *Mute/Pause.* Mute audio or pause video by covering the touchscreen with your palm.

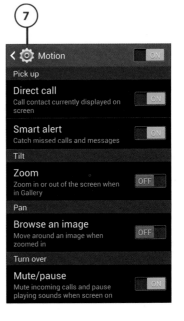

Enabling Air Gesture

The Air Gesture feature enables you to control your phone by gesturing over the sensor at the top of the screen—without touching the screen.

1. Tap the Air Gesture text on the Motions and Gestures screen.

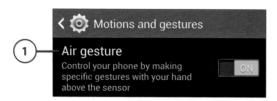

2. To use any of the Air Gesture features, you must set the Air Gesture switch to On. When you want to turn off all the Air Gesture features, move this switch to Off.

3. When the Air Gesture switch is On, the individual Air Gesture settings work as follows:

   - *Quick Glance.* When your phone's screen is off, move your hand over the sensor at the top of the screen to display information such as notifications, missed calls, unread messages, and battery level. To choose which information appears, tap the Quick Glance text and select check boxes in the scrolling More Information list.

   - *Air Jump.* When viewing a web page or an email message, wave your hand up or down over the sensor to scroll up or down by a screenful of text.

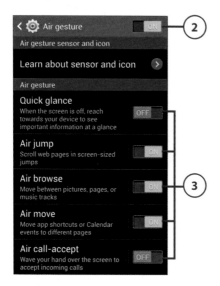

- *Air Browse.* When playing music, viewing pictures, browsing pages in the Internet app, or working in S Memo, move your hand left or right above the sensor to move to the next or previous item. To choose the apps in which Air Browse works, tap the Air Browse text, and then select check boxes in the scrolling Supporting Applications list.

- *Air Move.* When working on the Home screen, in the App list, or in Day or Week view in Calendar, tap and hold an item on screen with one hand, and then wave the other hand to the left or right over the sensor to move the item to another page.

- *Air Call-Accept.* When you receive an incoming call, wave your hand over the screen to accept it.

Where's the Air Gesture Sensor?

Tap Learn About Sensor and Icon to review some explanatory information about the sensor's location and the Air Gesture status bar icon.

Setting Ringtones

A *ringtone* is an audible event notification, such as a sound effect or
a snippet of music. You can specify
default ringtones for incoming calls
and text messages, as well as set
person-specific ringtones for anyone
with a Contacts record.

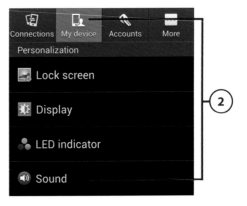

Setting the Default
Incoming Call Ringtone

Unless overridden by a personal or
group ringtone, the default ringtone
plays to notify you of an incoming
call.

1. On the Home screen, press the
   Menu key and tap Settings.

2. Select the My Device tab, and tap
   Sound.

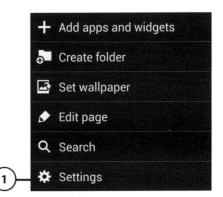

3. Tap Ringtones.

4. The Ringtones dialog box appears, showing a scrolling list containing all built-in, created, and downloaded ringtones. Tap a ringtone to play it. When you're satisfied with your choice, tap OK.

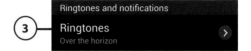

Setting the Default Notification Ringtone

Unless overridden by a personal or group ringtone, the default notification ringtone plays to signify new email, a text message, a missed call, a waiting voicemail, or an upcoming Calendar event. Unlike call ringtones, notification ringtones are brief and less intrusive.

1. Perform steps 1–2 from the previous task ("Setting the Default Incoming Call Ringtone").

2. On the Sound setting screen, tap Notifications.

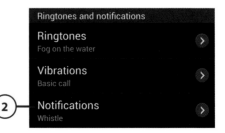

3. The Notifications dialog box appears, showing a scrolling list containing all the notification ringtones. Tap an entry to play it. When you're satisfied with your choice, tap OK.

Notifications
Join Hangout
Knock
On time
Opener
Postman
Pure bell
Sweet favour
Temple bell ●
Tickety-tock
Whisper
Whistle
Cancel   OK

— **3**

Assigning a Ringtone to a Contact

To make it easier to quickly recognize an incoming call from a person, you can associate a distinctive ringtone with his or her record in Contacts.

1. On the Home screen, tap the Contacts icon.

2. With the Contacts tab selected, find the person's record by scrolling or searching. Tap the record to open it.

3. Scroll to the Ringtone section of the record, and tap the ringtone entry.

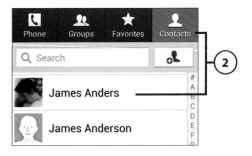

Contacts — **1**

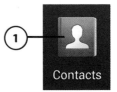

| Phone | Groups | Favorites | Contacts |

Q Search — **2**

James Anders

James Anderson

Ringtone
Default ⊙

— **3**

4. Select the ringtone that you want to use and tap OK. Select Default Ringtone (at the top of the list) only if you want to use the default ringtone for this contact.

Using Sound Files as Ringtones

If the ringtone you want to use does not appear in the Ringtones dialog box, tap Add. If the Complete Action Using dialog box appears, select the app that you want to use to locate the ringtone—for example, Choose Music Track or Sound Picker—and tap Just Once. When the app opens, navigate to the ringtone or sound file, select it, and tap OK.

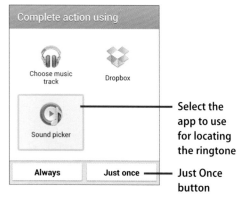

5. The selected ringtone is associated with the person's contact record.

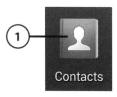

Select the app to use for locating the ringtone

Just Once button

Assigning a Ringtone to a Contact Group

You can also associate a distinctive ringtone with all members of a contact group. (To learn about groups, see "Working with Contact Groups" in Chapter 5.)

1. On the Home screen, tap the Contacts icon.

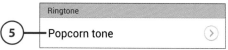

2. Tap the Groups tab to display the list of defined groups, and tap a group to show its members.

3. Press the Menu key and tap Edit.

4. Tap Group Ringtone and select a ringtone as described in step 4 of the previous task ("Assigning a Ringtone to a Contact").

5. Tap the Save button.

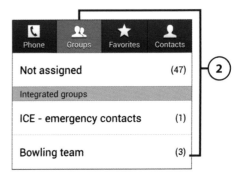

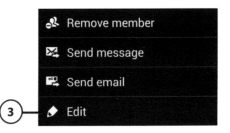

Current
ringtone

WHICH RINGTONE HAS PRECEDENCE?

After reading the material in this section, you might be wondering what happens when a person is associated with *multiple* ringtones. For instance, although Bob may have been assigned a personal ringtone, he may also be a member of a group that has a different ringtone associated with it. The answer is that *a contact record ringtone always has precedence.*

Thus, if a caller has no personal ringtone and doesn't belong to a group that has a ringtone, his calls are announced by the default ringtone. If the person belongs to a group with a ringtone and he doesn't have a personal ringtone, the group ringtone plays. Finally, if a person belongs to a group with a ringtone and he also has a personal ringtone, the personal ringtone plays.

Assigning a Default Messaging Ringtone

You can also select a ringtone to announce new text and multimedia messages.

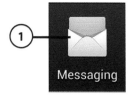

1. On the Home screen, tap the Messaging icon.

2. On the main Messaging screen, press the Menu key and tap Settings.

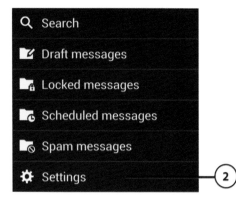

3. Scroll to the Notification Settings section, and tap Select Ringtone.

4. Select a sound effect from the scrolling list and tap OK. (If you'd rather not have a messaging ringtone, select Silent.)

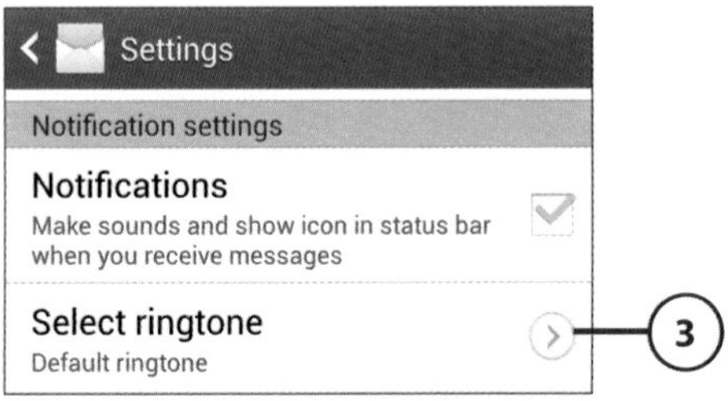

‹ ✉ Settings

Notification settings

Notifications
Make sounds and show icon in status bar when you receive messages ✔

Select ringtone
Default ringtone › ──3

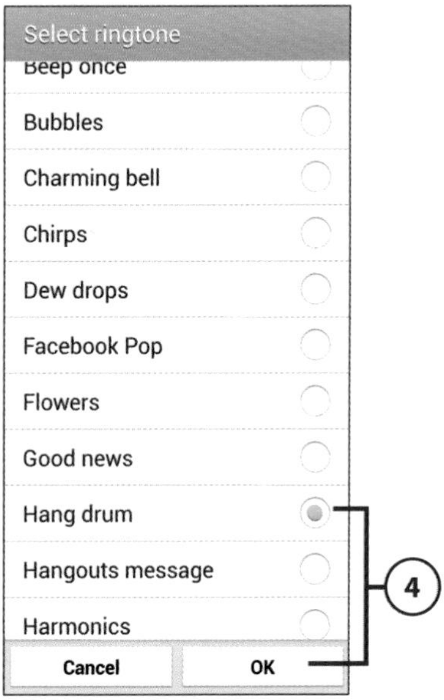

Select ringtone
Beep once
Bubbles ○
Charming bell ○
Chirps ○
Dew drops ○
Facebook Pop ○
Flowers ○
Good news ○
Hang drum ⦿
Hangouts message ○ ──4
Harmonics ○

Cancel | **OK**

CREATING RINGTONES FROM SONGS

>>>Go Further

You can also use a song that's stored on your phone as a ringtone.

1. Launch Music, and press and hold the song title.

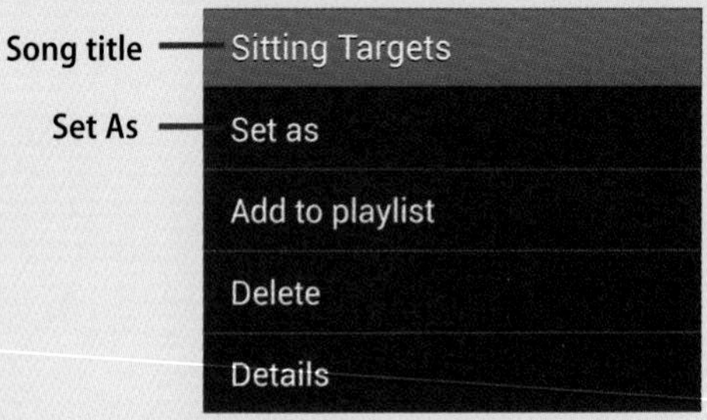

Song title —— Sitting Targets

Set As —— Set as

Add to playlist

Delete

Details

2. In the dialog box that appears, tap Set As.

3. Tap From the Beginning or Auto Recommendations to specify the part of the song to play as the ringtone.

4. In the Set As section, tap Phone Ringtone to use the song as the default ringtone for incoming calls. Tap Caller Ringtone to play the song whenever you receive a call from a particular person in Contacts. Tap Alarm Tone to use the song as the alarm tone for an alarm you're about to create in the Clock app.

5. Tap OK.

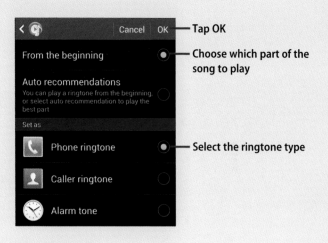

Personalize Your Call Sound

You can personalize the call sound by adjusting the sound balance. This enables you to compensate for hearing loss in one or the other ear or in the upper or lower ranges.

1. On the Home screen, tap the Phone icon.

2. In the Phone app, press the Menu key and tap Call Settings.

3. Tap Personalize Call Sound.

4. Do either of the following:

   - To set up a personalized sound balance, tap Adapt Sound and perform the remaining steps in this task.

   - Tap Soft Sound, Clear Choice, or Off, and skip the remaining steps.

5. Plug in your headphones, put them in or on your ears, and tap Start.

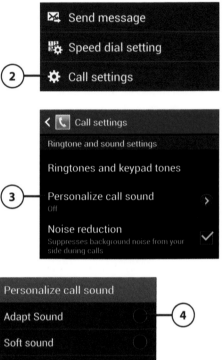

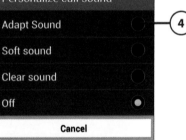

6. Listen for the tones your phone is playing. Tap Yes if you can hear each tone; tap No if you cannot.

7. On the Adapt Sound screen that appears at the end of the test, tap Left or Right to see a graph of the results for that ear.

8. Tap Preview Adapt Sound to hear audio with the adaptation applied. If the result isn't satisfactory, tap Retry to go back to step 5 and try again.

9. *Optional:* In the Adapt Sound Settings section of the screen, tap check boxes to indicate where you want to enable Adapt Sound—on phone calls and/or when playing music. If you tend to use one ear when you're on calls, tap Frequently Used Side and select your favored side.

10. Tap Done when you are satisfied with the results.

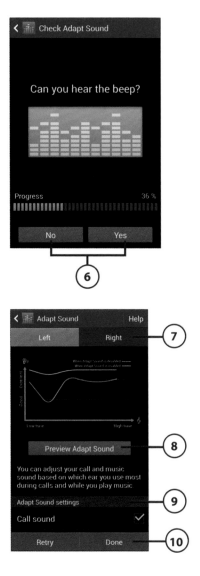

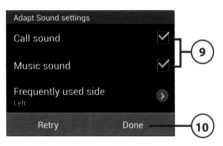

Using Voice Services

If you don't like tapping and typing (or are driving, making such activities dangerous and probably illegal), you can use S Voice, Voice Control, and Google Search/Voice Actions to control the phone. Note that Voice Control and Google Search run independently of S Voice.

S Voice and S Voice Driving Mode

S Voice is a voice app that enables you to ask questions in natural language ("Where can I find pizza?") and launch apps ("Open Calculator"). The result may be a direct answer, a web search, or the launch of an appropriate app, such as Maps. You can also turn on S Voice's Drive mode for hands-free navigation.

S Voice

1. *First Run Only:* Launch S Voice by tapping Apps, followed by S Voice.

Subsequent Launches
You can configure S Voice so that you can subsequently launch it by double-tapping the Home key, as well as by tapping the S Voice icon. With S Voice running and onscreen, press the Menu key, tap Settings, and enable Open Via the Home Key.

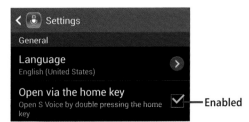

2. The S Voice screen appears. Say your first question or command. For example, you might ask, "What's the weather like today?" to see the weather forecast for your city. S Voice displays the information it finds.

3. To ask S Voice the next question or give it a new command, tap the microphone button or say the wake-up phrase. ("Hi, Galaxy" is the default phrase.)

S Voice Command Help

If you want assistance with question phrasing and app commands, tap the Help icon; say "Help"; or press the Menu key, tap Settings, and tap Help.

Be sure to check out the other settings, too. You can change the wake-up command, show or hide offensive words, and set your home address, for example.

Enable/disable voice prompt and feedback

S Voice Driving Mode

S Voice Driving mode is a hands-free mode in which you can control the phone with your voice. Driving mode has a simplified interface with larger text, so you can easily read the prompts when the phone is mounted on your dash. In Driving mode, your phone automatically speaks notifications to make you aware of them.

To switch to Driving mode:

1. To activate S Voice, press the Home key twice or tap Apps, followed by S Voice.

2. Say "Driving mode on."

3. The S Voice screen switches to Driving mode. Read the Driving Mode dialog box, and tap OK to dismiss it.

4. To give a command, say "Hi, Galaxy" (or the wake-up phrase you've set) and then speak the command. For example, say "Navigate to Phoenix, Arizona."

5. When you finish using Driving mode, say "Hi, Galaxy" to get S Voice's attention and then say "Driving mode off." S Voice restores its regular screen and announces that it has deactivated Driving mode.

Driving mode

You can disable Driving mode by saying "Driving mode off" in S Voice, or by changing the settings from Settings or the notification panel

☐ Do not show again

OK

Say
"Hi Galaxy"

📞 "Call"

✉ "Text"

◈ "Navigate"

▶ "Play"

☁ "Weather"

Voice Control

When Voice Control is enabled, you can use voice commands to control Phone, Clock, Camera, and Music. (Some carriers may also support voice control of other apps, such as ChatON.)

1. On the Home screen, press the Menu key and tap Settings.

⚙ Settings

2. Select the My Device tab.

3. Scroll to the Input and Control section. Enable Voice Control by moving its slider to the On position, and tap OK to dismiss the Voice Control dialog box that appears.

4. To specify the apps that you want to control, tap Voice Control.

5. On the screen that appears, add or remove check marks to enable/disable Voice Control in each app.

Supported Voice Commands

Review the screen for examples of supported voice commands, such as Pause, Play, and Next in Music. You must launch the appropriate app and make it active before saying commands; they don't work from the Home screen or within other apps.

Google Voice Search

Using the voice input feature of Google Search, you can perform a web search, find people in Contacts, or issue commands—called *voice actions*—to apps.

1. On a Home screen page that contains the Google Search widget, tap the microphone icon to its right. (From the Home screen, you can also tap Apps, followed by Voice Search.)

2. Say the search text, such as "Samsung Galaxy S 4," or issue a voice action command, such as "Listen to Talking Heads," "Call Jameson Auto Body," or say the name of a person or company in Contacts.

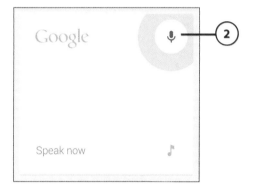

Reminders and Notes

A particularly useful voice command is "Note to self," followed by the note text. Whatever you say is automatically sent to your Gmail account as both an audio and a text note.

Voice Recorder

When you need to make a voice note or capture some audio, you can use the Voice Recorder app.

1. On the Home screen, tap Apps.

2. Tap Voice Recorder.

3. Tap the microphone icon to switch between Normal and High quality recording. When High quality is enabled, the icon has two white arcs above it.

4. Tap to start recording.

Recorded Files

5. Tap to stop the recording.

6. In the Recorded Files list, tap the recording to listen to it.

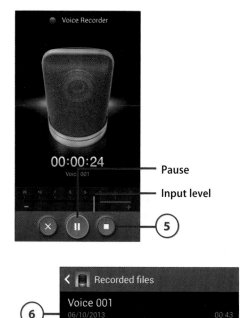

Pause

Input level

INTERESTING NEW APPS: S HEALTH, S TRANSLATOR, AND OPTICAL READER

Your Samsung Galaxy S 4 includes several new, special-purpose apps: S Health, S Translator, and Optical Reader.

- *S Health*. S Health is a health-monitoring app that includes a health diary and exercise-logging, weight-recording, and food-tracking features.

- *S Translator*. S Translator is a translation app that can translate text between English, French, German, Spanish, Japanese, Korean, and Simplified Chinese. You can either type the text or speak it. In addition to working as a standalone app, you can summon it from within Messaging and Email to translate incoming or outgoing messages.

- *Optical Reader*. Optical Reader is a handy app that uses your phone's rear camera to read text, such as words you want to look up, contact information you want to scan, or QR (Quick Response) codes that you want to follow.

In this chapter, you learn to use the phone to place and receive calls. Topics include the following:

→ Dialing calls manually and from contact records
→ Using the call logs to return calls, redial numbers, and reply to messages
→ Dialing from embedded numbers in email and messages
→ Placing an emergency call
→ Speed-dialing
→ Blocking your caller ID
→ Making a three-way call
→ Receiving incoming calls
→ Using call waiting and call forwarding
→ Using in-call options, such as the keypad, speakerphone, and Bluetooth headset
→ Checking your voicemail
→ Enabling Mute, Vibrate, and Airplane Mode
→ Configuring call settings

Placing and Receiving Calls

With all the functionality your smartphone provides, it's easy to forget that you can also use it to make and receive calls. But smartphone power often comes at a price. To optimize your use of the phone *as* a phone, you should learn the various calling procedures and the different options for performing each one.

Placing Calls

The Galaxy S 4 provides many convenient ways for you to make calls. You can manually enter numbers, dial a number from a contact record, use the call logs to return missed calls and redial numbers, call embedded numbers in text or email messages, create and use speed dial entries, and make three-way and emergency calls.

With or Without the 1

When dialing a number, you need to add the dialing prefix/country code only when you're calling a country that uses a *different* code. As a result, most numbers that you dial manually, as well as ones stored in Contacts, can either omit or include the dialing prefix.

Manual Dialing

You can use the Phone app's keypad to manually dial numbers. The procedure differs slightly if the number you're dialing is also associated with a record in Contacts.

Dialing Someone Without a Contacts Record

1. Tap the Phone icon at the bottom of the Home screen.

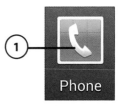

Phone

Launching Phone from the Lock Screen

If you're on the lock screen, you can go directly to the phone by dragging the Phone icon at the bottom of the screen upward (if the icon is present).

2. If the keypad isn't displayed, tap the Keypad tab. Then tap the digits in the phone number.

Dialing International Numbers

To make an international call, press and hold 0. A plus symbol appears as the first character in the number. Enter the country code, followed by the phone number.

Mistakes Happen

If you make a mistake, you can press the Delete key to delete the last digit entered. To remove the entire number and start over, press and hold Delete. You can also use normal editing techniques to position the text insertion mark within the number and make changes, such as inserting the area code.

3. *Optional*: To create a new contact record for this number or add the number to an existing contact record, tap Add to Contacts and select an option from the menu that appears.

4. Tap the green phone icon to dial the call. When you finish talking, tap the red End Call icon to disconnect.

Keypad tab

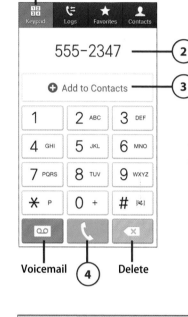

Voicemail ④ Delete

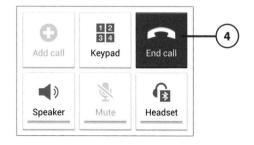

Dialing Someone with a Contacts Record

1. Tap the Phone icon at the bottom of the Home screen.

2. Tap the Keypad tab if it isn't automatically selected. Then tap any of the phone number's digits. You can start at the beginning or with any consecutive string of digits that you remember. As you enter the digits, potential matches from Contacts and from numbers you've previously dialed display.

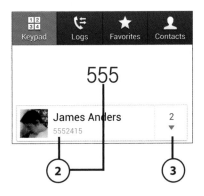

3. Do one of the following:

   - To select the main suggestion, tap the person or company's name.

   - To view additional matches, tap the numbered down arrow and select someone from the Search Results list.

   - Continue entering digits until the correct match is suggested, and then tap the person or company's name.

Dialing by Name

If you can't remember any part of a person's number but are sure he has a Contacts record, you can use the keypad to spell the person's name.

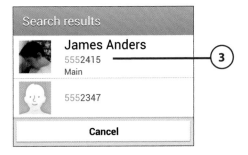

4. Tap the green phone icon to dial the call. When you finish talking, tap the red End Call icon to disconnect.

Dialing from a Contact Record

Many of your outgoing calls will be to people and companies that have a record in Contacts.

1. Open Contacts by tapping its icon at the bottom of the Home screen, tapping the Phone icon on the Home screen and then selecting the Contacts tab, or accessing Contacts from another app, such as Messaging.

2. If it isn't already selected, tap the Contacts tab at the top of the screen. Find the record by scrolling or searching, and then tap the entry to view the full record.

3. Tap a listed phone number or its green telephone icon to dial that number.

4. When you finish talking, tap the red End Call icon to disconnect.

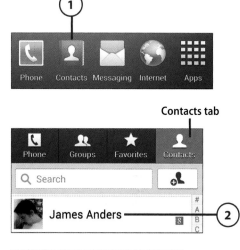

Contacts tab

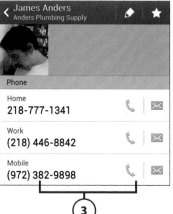

Dialing and Texting from the Call Logs

Every incoming and outgoing call and message is automatically recorded in the Logs section of Phone. By viewing the logs, you can quickly determine which calls and messages need to be returned, as well as initiate a call or the creation of a new message.

Returning and Redialing Calls

By selecting a particular log, you can see whom you've called and who has called you. You can also see people with whom you've exchanged messages. You can then dial or message any log entry.

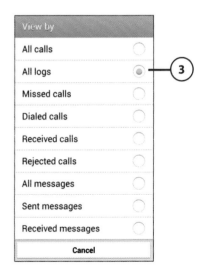

1. On the Home screen, launch Phone by tapping its icon.

2. Tap the Logs tab at the top of the screen.

Viewing the Logs from Contacts

You can also reach Logs from within the Contacts app. At the top of the screen, tap the Phone tab and then tap the Logs tab that appears.

3. To select a log to view (such as All Logs, Missed Calls, or Received Messages), press the Menu key, tap View By, and select an option from the View By menu. (If you don't select a log, the last one viewed displays.)

4. To call a person without leaving the current screen, swipe the log entry to the right. The number is automatically dialed.

5. To text a person, swipe the log entry to the left. A new message window in Messaging appears.

Tap Versus Swipe

If swiping isn't your thing or you want more control over what happens, tap the log entry. On the screen that appears, you can call the person by tapping the phone icon. To send a text or multimedia message to the person, tap the message icon.

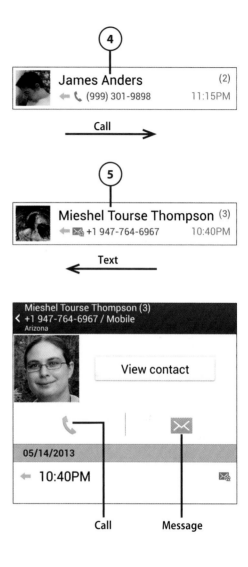

>>>Go Further

LOG ICONS

In each log entry, icons provide information about the call or message exchange (see Table 4.1). A phone or envelope icon denotes a call or message, respectively. The icon beneath the person or company's name indicates the type of call or message, as well as whether it was incoming or outgoing.

Table 4.1   Log Icons

Icon	Meaning
 ← ☎	Incoming call
 → ☎	Outgoing call
 ☎	Missed call
 ⊘ ☎	Rejected call
 Ⓐ ☎	Auto-rejected call
 ← ✉	Incoming text message
 → ✉	Outgoing text message
 ← ✉	Incoming multimedia message
 → ✉	Outgoing multimedia message

Other Log Options

Using the logs to return calls and messages is often more convenient than dialing manually or searching for the person's contact record. Here are some other actions you can take in Logs:

- Press and hold an entry to display a menu of commands specific to that person or company. Note the Delete command, which enables you to delete this single entry, as well as the Add to Reject List command. Future calls from any number in the Reject List are automatically sent to voicemail.

- You can clean up the logs by deleting old, duplicate, and unwanted entries. Press the Menu key, tap View By, and select the log that you want to manage. Press the Menu key again and tap Delete. Select the entries that you want to remove (or tap Select All), tap the Delete button, and tap Delete in the confirmation dialog box.

Pop-up menu

Mike Olson

Copy to dialing screen

Send number

View contact

Add to reject list

Delete

Select All   Delete

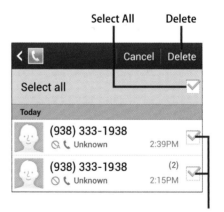

Cancel | Delete

Select all

Today

(938) 333-1938
Unknown   2:39PM

(938) 333-1938   (2)
Unknown   2:15PM

Selected items

Dialing a Number in a Text or Email Message

A phone number in an email or text message acts as a *link* that, when tapped, can dial the number.

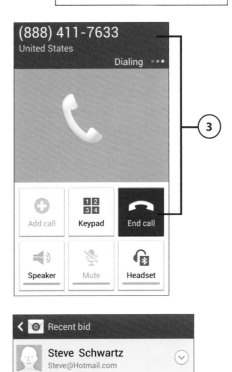

Text Message Links

1. In Messaging, display the received or sent message that contains the phone number, and then tap the number.

2. In the dialog box that appears, tap Call.

3. Phone launches and dials the number. When you finish talking, tap the red End Call icon to disconnect.

Email Message Links

1. In Email, display the received or sent email message that contains the phone number, and then tap the number.

2. The number appears in the Keypad section of Phone. If necessary, you can edit it (adding or removing the area code, for example) using normal editing techniques.

3. Tap the green phone icon to dial the number.

4. When you finish talking, tap the red End Call icon to disconnect.

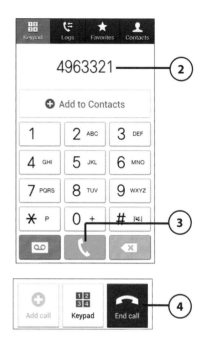

QUICK DIALING TECHNIQUES

For people and companies with a record in Contacts, you can also call them using a voice command, such as "Call Janice Gunderson." For information about using voice apps, see Chapter 3.

You can quickly call anyone with a Contacts record whose name appears in the Logs or Favorites list of Phone/ Contacts or with whom you've recently exchanged messages in Messaging. Locate the person or company in the Contacts, Logs, Favorites, or Messaging list and swipe the item to the right. The Phone screen appears, and the person or company's number is automatically dialed.

Emergency Calling

Where available, the Galaxy S 4 supports *e911* (Enhanced 911), enabling it to connect to a nearby emergency dispatch center regardless of where in the United States or Canada you happen to be. (The equivalent emergency number is different in other countries. In the United Kingdom, for example, it's 999.) When you place a 911 call, your position can usually be determined by the phone's GPS or by triangulating your position using nearby cell sites.

Calling 911

1. Do one of the following:

   • On the Home screen, tap the Phone app's icon.

   • If the lock screen is displayed and the phone is protected, you can go directly to the Phone screen by tapping the Emergency Call text at the bottom of the screen. (When you use this method to initiate an emergency call, an Emergency Dialer banner appears atop the Phone screen.)

2. Using the keypad, enter **911** (or your country's equivalent number) and tap the green phone icon to dial the number.

Lock screen (bottom)

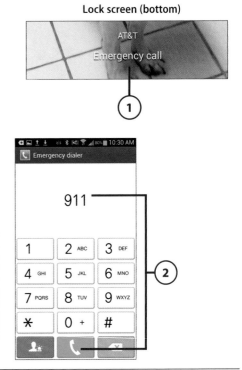

About the Emergency Call Text

Although tapping the Emergency Call text enables you to quickly make an emergency call without having to first unlock the screen and launch the Phone app, it has an important restriction. *Only calls to 911 and emergency responders (such as the police and fire department) are allowed; all others are blocked.* You cannot call your parents or spouse, for example. To emphasize this, the band at the top of the screen reads Emergency Dialer. If you need to call someone other than an emergency responder, you need to unlock the screen by supplying your pattern, PIN, or password; launch the Phone app; and then dial normally.

Emergency Calling Tips

Keep the following in mind when seeking emergency assistance:

- Even if you've disabled the phone's location/GPS functions for all other uses, these features remain available for 911 use.

- Not all emergency dispatch centers support e911. Instead of assuming they've determined your location based on GPS or triangulation, be prepared to give your location.

- Some emergency dispatch centers use an automated voice menu that prompts you to enter numbers. According to Sprint, for example, "If you encounter a prerecorded message instead of a live operator, wait for the appropriate prompt and say 'EMERGENCY' instead of pressing 1. Not all wireless phones transmit number tones during a 911 call."

Other Outgoing Call Options

The Galaxy S 4 also supports some additional outgoing call options: speed dialing, blocking your caller ID information, three-way calling, and inserting pause and wait commands.

Speed Dialing

To make it easy to dial your most important numbers, you can assign a *speed dial number* to anyone with a record in Contacts. The digits 2–100 are available as speed dial numbers; 1 is reserved for voicemail.

Accessing the Speed Dial Setting Screen

1. Launch Phone or Contacts by tapping an icon at the bottom of the Home screen.

2. To display the Speed Dial Setting screen, do either of the following:

   - With the Keypad tab in Phone selected, press the Menu key and tap Speed Dial Setting.

   - With the Contacts tab selected, press the Menu key and tap Speed Dial Setting.

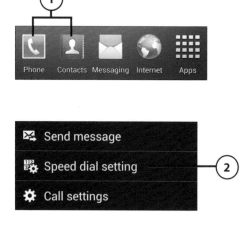

What Next?
When you reach the Speed Dial Setting screen, jump ahead to the section that describes the task you want to perform.

Assigning a Speed Dial Number

1. On the Speed Dial Setting screen, tap a currently unassigned number—that is, one that says Not Assigned.

2. In Contacts, select the person or company in the contacts list with which to associate this speed dial number.

3. If the contact record contains only one phone number, the number is automatically used. If the contact record contains more than one phone number, select the number to use.

4. The contact's phone number is assigned to the speed dial number.

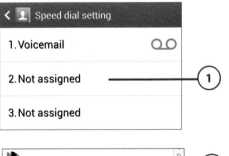

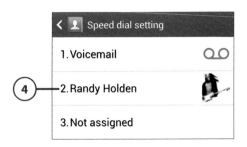

Replacing an In-Use Speed Dial Number

1. On the Speed Dial Setting screen, press and hold the number that you want to reassign.

2. In the dialog box that appears, tap Replace.

3. Select a person or company in the Contacts list.

4. If the contact record contains only one phone number, the number is automatically used. If the contact record contains more than one phone number, select the number to use.

5. The contact's phone number replaces the one previously assigned to the speed dial number.

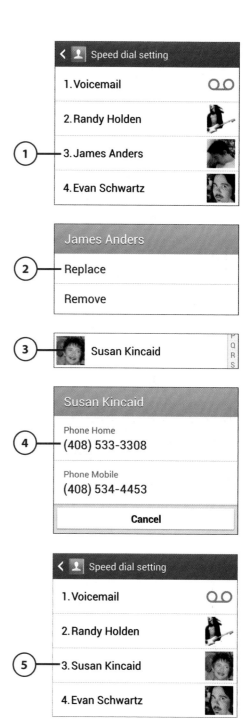

Removing Speed Dial Numbers

1. On the Speed Dial Setting screen, press the Menu key and tap Remove.

2. The Speed Dial list appears with an X beside each entry.

3. Tap each entry that you want to remove. The entry changes to Not Assigned.

4. When you finish, tap Done to complete the deletions or Cancel to retain the original speed dial assignments.

Removing a Single Speed Dial Number

If you want to clear only a single speed dial number, go to the Speed Dial Setting screen, and press and hold the number you want to remove. In the dialog box that appears, tap Remove. The contact previously associated with that speed dial number is instantly removed.

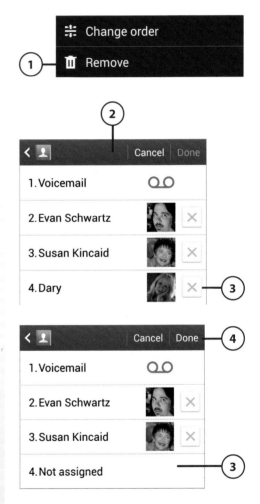

Rearranging Speed Dial Numbers

1. With the Speed Dial Setting screen displayed, press the Menu key and tap Change Order.

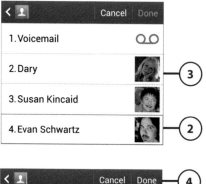

2. Tap the contact thumbnail to which you want to assign a new speed dial number.

3. Tap the destination slot—it can be empty or currently occupied. If empty, the contact is assigned the new speed dial number. If currently occupied, the contacts swap slots.

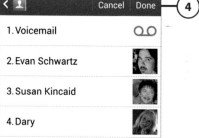

4. Repeat steps 2 and 3 for each additional pair of slots that you want to swap. When you finish, tap Done to accept the new arrangement or Cancel to restore the previous arrangement.

Dialing a Speed Dial Number

1. Launch Phone by tapping its icon at the bottom of the Home screen.

2. With the Keypad tab selected, enter the speed dial number. Press and hold the final digit.

3. The phone dials the person or company associated with the speed dial number. When you finish talking, tap the red End Call icon to disconnect.

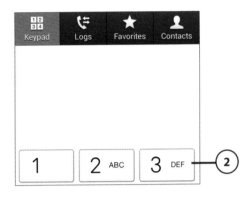

Dialing from the Speed Dial Setting Screen

If you can't remember a particular speed dial number, you can initiate a call or message from the Speed Dial Setting screen. Scroll to find the person or company's entry, tap it, and then tap Call or Message in the dialog box that appears.

Temporarily Blocking Your Caller ID Information

If you want to prevent your caller ID information from displaying on an outgoing call, precede the number with *67, such as *675591234 for a local call or *672925591234 for a long-distance call. The recipient's phone should display Private Number rather than your name, city, or number. Note that *67 is the correct prefix in the United States and Canada only; other countries have a different prefix.

If you want to prevent your caller ID information from displaying on *every* call, contact your service provider for assistance.

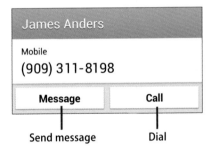

Send message   Dial

Three-Way Calling

By making a three-way call, you can talk to two people at the same time. (If you don't have an unlimited minutes plan, check with your service provider to determine how three-way calls are billed.)

1. Launch Phone, enter the first phone number or select it from Contacts, and tap the green phone icon to dial the number.

2. When the first person answers, tell him to wait while you call the second person. Tap the Add Call icon and dial the second number. The first person is automatically placed on hold.

3. When the second person answers, tap the Merge icon.

4. The display shows that you're all connected to a conference call. When the call is completed, tap End Call. Any person who is still connected will be disconnected.

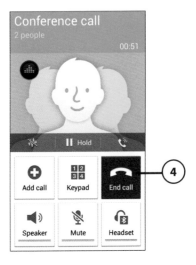

Inserting Pause and Wait Commands

If you're fed up with listening and responding to the convoluted automated answering systems used by banks, insurance companies, telephone companies, and cable systems, you might consider programming their Contacts record to automatically tap the correct keypad digits in response to their menus. For instance, 2148527777,,1,2,6310,,43 might take you to your Internet provider's technical support group.

In addition to digits, each phone number can contain commas (,) and semicolons (;). Each comma represents a 2-second pause (you can string together multiple pauses), and each semicolon instructs the phone to wait until you enter any number or press a key. Creating a number that responds correctly to voice prompts requires trial and error. For example, if you don't wait long enough (using pauses) before the next number is entered, the process fails.

As you enter or edit a phone number, press the Sym key to insert a pause or wait. The best numbers in which to use pauses and waits are the simple ones, such as those for which the initial prompt is for an extension. Complex, multilayered menus take much longer to program, and your efforts will "break" if the answering system's menu structure changes.

WI-FI CALLING (T-MOBILE)

>>>Go Further

T-Mobile Galaxy S 4 users can optionally make calls over a Wi-Fi network rather than using normal cellular service. This can be very useful when you live or work in a place that has a weak cell signal and, hence, poor call quality. Note that Wi-Fi calling doesn't cost extra, but it does use plan minutes. And if you want to make out-of-country calls, you still must have an international plan.

To turn on Wi-Fi calling, ensure that Wi-Fi is enabled and that you're connected to an available network. Then open Settings, select the Connections tab, tap More Networks, and move the Wi-Fi Calling slider to the On position. If you want to set calling preferences, tap Connection Preferences and make a selection (such as Wi-Fi Preferred).

Receiving Calls

The other half of the phone call equation is that of receiving and responding to incoming calls.

Responding to an Incoming Call

1. When a call comes in, the caller is identified by name and number (if she has a Contacts record), by number (if there's no matching Contacts record), or by Private Number (if she has blocked her caller ID).

2. You can respond in any of the following ways:

- *Accept call.* Drag the green phone icon in any direction.

- *Reject call.* Drag the red phone icon in any direction, sending the caller to voicemail.

- *Ignore call.* Do nothing; let the phone ring. After a number of rings, the caller is transferred to voicemail.

- *Reject with explanation.* Drag Reject Call with Message upward and select a text message to transmit to the caller. (Note that if the caller doesn't have a messaging plan or is calling from a landline, the text message might not be delivered.)

3. When the call concludes, tap the End Call icon.

Air Call Accept and Muting the Ringtone

When Air Call Accept is enabled, you can accept an incoming call and switch to the speakerphone by merely waving your hand over the sensor at the top of the phone. To learn about enabling Air Call Accept and other air gestures, see "Enabling Air Gesture" in Chapter 3.

Accept call   Reject call

Send text message

If you've enabled Mute/Pause in Motion Settings, you can turn the phone over to mute the ringtone that accompanies an incoming call. For instructions, see "Enabling Motion and Palm Motion Settings" in Chapter 3.

Incoming caller's info

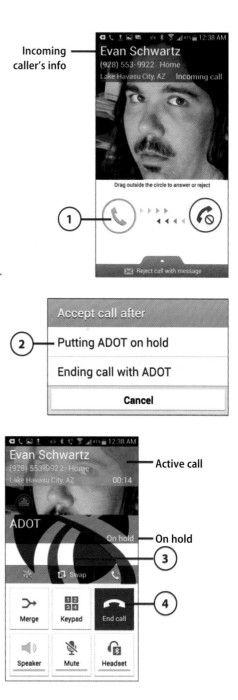

Call Waiting

Call waiting enables you to answer an incoming call when you're already on a call.

1. Answer the incoming call by sliding the green phone icon in any direction.

2. In the Accept Call After dialog box, tap Putting *current caller* On Hold.

3. The initial call is automatically placed on hold while you speak to the new caller. To switch between callers, tap the Swap icon. The active call is always shown in green at the top of the screen.

4. To end the active call, tap the End Call icon. The other call automatically becomes active.

Active call

On hold

Call Forwarding

You can have all or particular kinds of calls that your cell phone would normally receive forwarded to another number automatically. Forwarding works even when the Galaxy S 4 is turned off. To restore normal calling, deactivate call forwarding when you're finished. (Check with your service provider or review your plan to determine the cost of using call forwarding.)

Phone

1. Tap the Phone icon on the Home screen.

2. Press the Menu key and tap Call Settings.

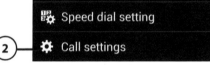

3. Tap Additional Settings (at the bottom of the first section).

4. Tap Call Forwarding.

First Use

Before making any changes to call forwarding, be sure to write down the default phone number listed on the Call Forwarding screen. It's the number for your carrier's voicemail, where calls are normally forwarded when you miss or reject a call, for example. You may need this number later if you elect to temporarily forward calls to a different number, such as a friend's landline.

5. To enable *unconditional forwarding* of all calls (regardless of type), tap Always Forward. When Always Forward is enabled, all other forwarding options are disabled.

6. Enter, edit, or review the phone number to which all calls will be forwarded, and tap Enable. You can manually enter the number or select it from a Contacts record. When you're ready to restore normal call handling, see "Ending Call Forwarding" at the end of this task.

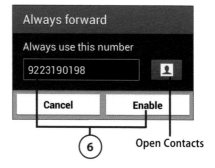

Dialing Prefix

It isn't necessary to enter the +*country code* (such as +1) at the beginning of the number. It's entered for you when you tap Enable.

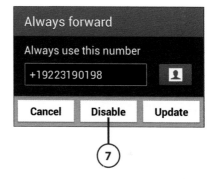

7. To enable *conditional forwarding* (selective forwarding based on call type), you must first disable Always Forward—if it's currently enabled. Tap Always Forward, and then tap the Disable button in the Always Forward dialog box.

About Forwarding

One forwarding state or the other is always active. Either all calls are automatically routed to a single number (Always Forward) or selected calls (Busy, Unanswered, or Unreachable) are routed to one or multiple numbers, depending on the type of call. Unless you change it, the forward-to number is your voicemail number.

8. To enable forwarding for selected conditions, tap any of the following options:

  • *Forward when busy.* Forward only when you're already on a call.

- *Forward when unanswered.* When you ignore a call, it is forwarded.

- *Forward when unreachable.* Forward calls only when it's determined that you're out of your provider's service area or the phone is turned off.

9. In the dialog box that appears, enter, edit, or review the phone number to which calls will be forwarded. You can manually enter the number or select it from a Contacts record. Tap the Enable, Update, Disable, or Cancel button. Repeat steps 8 and 9 for other forwarding options that you want to enable or change.

Ending Call Forwarding

To restore normal call handling, perform steps 1–5. In the Always Forward dialog box, tap the Disable button. Be sure to reset all conditional formatting options to the voicemail number. This happens automatically when you tap the option name and click Disable in the dialog box that appears.

In-Call Options

While on a call, you can access common in-call options by tapping various icons. (The first icon in the section at the bottom of the screen—variously labeled Add Call or Merge—was discussed in previous sections.) Additional options are available via hardware controls and the Notification panel.

Icon Options

During any call, you can tap icons to enable or disable options. In general, when an in-call option is enabled or active, its icon is green.

Personalize Call Sound

Hold/unhold

Noise reduction

Speakerphone

Mute/unmute

Extra Volume

- *Personalize Call Sound.* Tap this icon to choose an equalizer setting for the current call. Before you can use this feature, you must set it up as described in "Personalize Call Sound," later in this chapter.

- *Noise Reduction.* When enabled (green), this feature can improve call quality by reducing ambient noise. Tap the icon to toggle Noise Reduction on or off.

- *Hold/Unhold.* Place the current call on hold. Tap the icon again to reactivate the call.

- *Extra Volume.* You can boost in-call volume above the normal maximum by tapping the Extra Volume icon. Tap it a second time to disable the volume boost.

- *Keypad.* If you need to enter information to respond to a voice prompt system or enter an extension, for example, tap the Keypad icon to display the dialing keypad. The Keypad icon's label changes to Hide. To dismiss the keypad, tap the Hide icon or press the Back key.

- *Speaker.* To toggle the phone between normal and speakerphone modes, tap the Speaker icon. When the speakerphone is active, the icon is green.

Keypad

Hide keypad

- *Mute.* To temporarily turn off the phone's microphone so that the other party can't hear you, tap the Mute icon. When muting is active, the icon is green.

- *Headset.* To use a Bluetooth headset on the current call, tap the Headset icon. When Bluetooth is active, the icon is green. To return to a normal, non-Bluetooth call, tap the icon again.

- *End Call.* Tap End Call to "hang up," disconnecting from the other party.

Other In-Call Options

Two other important options are available during calls that aren't represented by icons:

- *Volume adjustment.* To change the volume, press the volume control on the left side of the phone. An onscreen volume indicator appears. Press the top half of the hardware volume control to raise the volume; press the lower half to lower the volume. You can also adjust the volume by dragging the onscreen slider.

- *Notification panel controls.* You can drag down the Notification panel to access the Mute, Speaker, and End options. This is especially useful if you leave the Phone screen during the call to run other apps.

Volume indicator

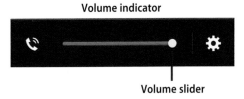

Volume slider

Notification panel in-call controls

Phone Call Multitasking

You can run other apps while on a call. Return to the Home screen by pressing the Home key and then launch the apps, or press the Menu key while on the Phone screen to launch Contacts, S Memo, or Messaging. The status bar turns neon green to indicate that a call is in progress. When you're ready to end the call, launch Phone again or tap the End icon in the Notification panel.

Status bar

Email app

Using Voicemail

Using your service provider's voicemail, people can leave messages for you when you're unavailable or the phone is turned off. See Chapter 1 for instructions on setting up voicemail.

You can check your voicemail in two or more ways. First, you can tap a received New Voicemail entry in the Notification panel. Second, you can launch the Phone app, and then press and hold 1 (the speed dial number assigned to voicemail) or tap the Voicemail icon on the keypad. Finally, your service provider may include a separate voicemail app with which you can listen to and manage your voicemail.

When voicemail messages are waiting, a notification icon appears in the status bar. Note that if you set up voicemail to require a password, you'll be asked to enter it each time you contact voicemail. When prompted, tap each digit in the password and end by tapping the pound sign (#)—or follow whatever instructions your carrier provides.

1. Connect to your carrier's voicemail service by doing either of the following:

   - Drag down the Notification panel and tap the New Voicemail entry. The carrier's voicemail is automatically dialed.

   - Launch the Phone app and open the Keypad by tapping its tab. Press and hold 1 (the speed dial number assigned to voicemail) or tap the voicemail icon. The Phone app dials the carrier's voicemail.

2. You connect to your carrier's voicemail system. Because the voicemail menus require you to enter numbers to choose options, tap the Keypad icon to reveal the keypad (if it's currently hidden). Listen to the menu options and tap numbers to indicate your choices.

3. When you finish using voicemail, tap the End Call icon.

Changing Voicemail Settings

You can change your voicemail settings (such as your greeting, password, and notification methods) whenever you want. Connect with voicemail and respond to the prompts.

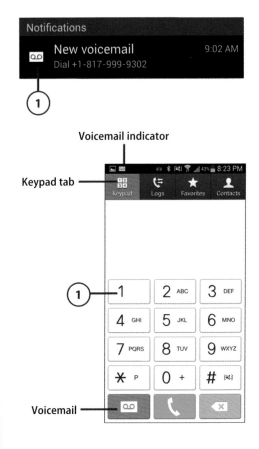

Voicemail indicator

Keypad tab

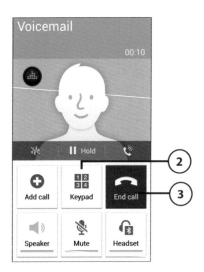

Enabling Mute, Vibrate, or Airplane Mode

Your phone has three special settings that you'll occasionally find useful: Mute, Vibrate, and Airplane Mode. Enable Mute when your phone *must* remain silent, such as when you're in a meeting or place of worship. Vibrate also silences notifications, but denotes them by vibrating the phone. Enable Airplane Mode during flights to quickly make your phone compliant with government and airline regulations by disabling the ability to place or receive calls, as well as transmit data.

Mute and Vibrate

When Mute is enabled, all sounds except media playback and alarms are disabled. Incoming calls cause the Phone app to launch—even when the screen is dark—but no sound or vibration occurs. Vibration has the same silencing effect as Mute, but important events are signaled by vibration.

Device Options menu

Volume control

1. To enable muting or vibration, do one of the following:

   • Press and hold the Power button until the Device Options menu appears, and then tap the Mute or Vibrate icon.

   • On the Home screen, press and hold the Volume down key until the onscreen volume control shows that Mute or Vibrate is enabled. (Lower the volume all the way to enable Mute. When the Mute icon is shown, you can quickly switch to Vibrate by tapping the Volume up key once.)

- Open the Notification panel. Repeatedly tap the Sound icon to toggle between its three states: Mute, Vibrate, and Sound.

2. When Vibrate or Mute is active, a matching indicator displays in the status bar.

3. To restore normal sound, select Sound in the Device Options menu or the Notification panel, or increase the volume.

Airplane Mode

When flying, you can quickly set your phone to Airplane Mode, disabling its capability to place or receive calls and to send or receive data. Other functions operate normally.

1. To enable Airplane Mode, do one of the following:

   - Open the Notification panel, scroll to the right, and tap the Airplane Mode icon. When enabled, the icon is green.

   - Press and hold the Power button until the Device Options menu appears. Tap Airplane Mode.

   - Open Settings, select the Connections tab, tap More Networks, and tap the Airplane Mode check box.

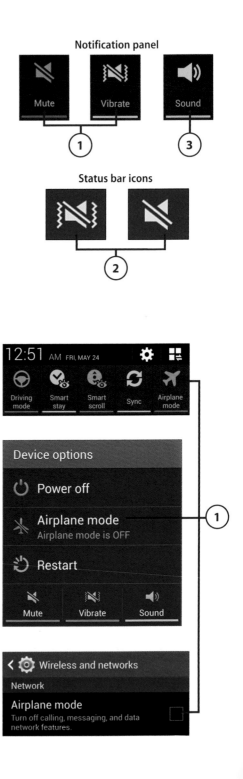

2. In the Enable Airplane Mode dialog box, confirm by tapping OK. The Airplane Mode indicator appears in the status bar; 3G/4G, Wi-Fi, and Bluetooth are automatically disabled.

3. To restore normal calling and data transmission functionality, disable Airplane Mode by reversing any of the actions described in step 1. Tap OK in the Airplane Mode dialog box.

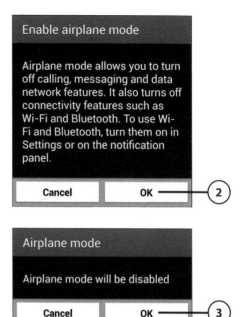

Configuring Call Settings

You can set preferences for many phone operations in Call Settings. Although the default settings will suffice for most calling situations, here are some settings that you might want to examine.

1. Within Phone, press the Menu key and tap Call Settings.

2. The Call Settings screen appears. Here are some of the more common, useful settings:

- *Call Rejection.* Tap Call Rejection to enable/disable Auto Reject Mode for blocked callers (or to temporarily reject *all* incoming calls), as well as add or remove numbers from the Auto Reject List. Rejected calls are sent straight to voicemail.

- *Set Up Call Rejection Messages.* Add or delete text messages that you can send when manually rejecting an incoming call by dragging Reject Call with Message upward.

- *Answering/Ending Calls.* Add methods to quickly answer incoming calls or end calls. (Answer calls by pressing the Home key or by saying "Answer" or "Reject." End calls by pressing the Power button.)

- *Turn Off Screen During Calls.* When enabled, the proximity sensor determines when you're on a call and the display is automatically turned off to reduce battery consumption.

- *Call Alerts.* Specify whether the phone vibrates when the call recipient answers and when the call ends, whether tones denote each call connection and end, and whether alarm and new message notifications are active during calls. When Minute Minder is enabled, the phone beeps twice whenever another minute of connect time passes.

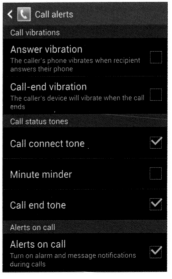

Call Alerts Settings

Missed Call Notification

If you miss a call, a missed call icon appears in the status bar and a message is displayed on the lock screen. If you tap the lock screen message, you're taken directly to the call log, enabling you to return the call or delete the log entry.

Missed call icon

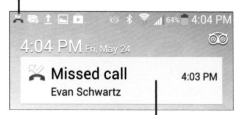

Missed call notification

- *Call Accessories.* Configure the phone for a Bluetooth headset, enabling the headset to automatically answer incoming calls and specify a delay period prior to answering.

- *Additional Settings.* Two settings that you might want to examine are Caller ID (specifies how calls from your phone are identified to others) and Auto Redial (instructs the phone to automatically redial whenever your call can't connect or is cut off).

- *Ringtone and Sound Settings.* These specify the sounds that announce an incoming call and govern sound quality during calls. Tap Ringtones and Keypad Tones to select or create a ringtone for incoming calls (see "Setting Ringtones" in Chapter 3), change the vibration pattern, enable or disable vibration when ringing, and enable or disable the playing of tones when touching numbers on the keypad. Tap Personalize Call Sound to adapt the call audio to your needs (see "Personalize Call Sound" at the

Ringtone and Sound Settings

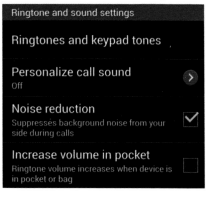

end of this section). Enable Noise Reduction to suppress background/ambient noise during calls. When Increase Volume in Pocket is enabled, the ringtone volume is boosted when the proximity sensor detects that the phone is in a pocket or bag.

Voicemail Settings

Voicemail	
Voicemail service My carrier	❯
Voicemail settings	
Sound Default ringtone	❯
Vibrate	☐
TTY mode TTY Off	

- *Voicemail Settings.* Tap Sound to change the sound effect that announces new voicemail. Tap Vibrate to enable or disable vibration when new voicemail is available.

3. When you finish viewing and changing settings, press the Back key to return to the main Phone screen.

PERSONALIZE CALL SOUND

>>>Go Further

To improve audio quality during phone calls or while listening to music, you can enable the Adapt Sound feature. Based on a hearing test, the phone adjusts the sound to ensure that it is optimal for you.

1. In Phone, press the Menu key and tap Call Settings.

2. Scroll down and tap Personalize Call Sound.

3. Plug in your earphones and, following the instructions, take the audio test.

4. At the test's conclusion, tap icons to compare unaltered (Original) audio in the left, right, and both ears with that of the Adapt Sound (Personalized) audio. When you finish listening, press the Back key or tap the Back icon at the top of the screen.

5. Set options in the Adapt Sound Settings section of the screen. To enable Adapt Sound during calls and listening to music, tap their check boxes. Tap Frequently Used Side to specify the side of your face that you typically use when speaking on the phone.

6. Tap Done.

Adapt Sound setup

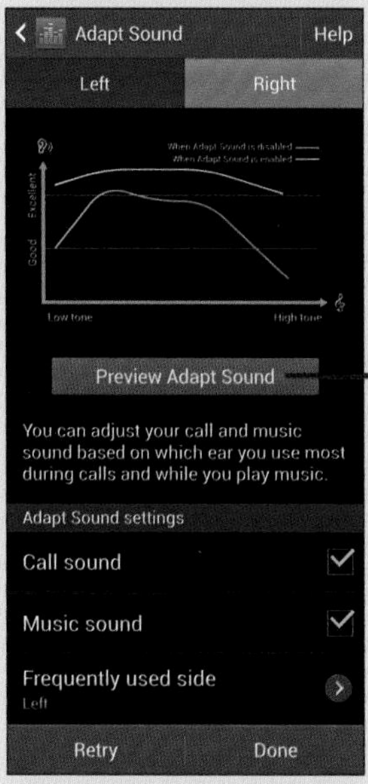

Preview

Personalize Call Sound menu

During a call, tap the Personalize Call Sound icon to disable or enable the feature, and then choose Adapt Sound (for your personalized setting) or one of the other audio options. When Personalize Call Sound is enabled, the icon is green. When using earphones to listen to songs in Music, you can enable or disable Adapt Sound by pressing the Menu key, tapping Settings, and then tapping Adapt Sound. (Without earphones, Adapt Sound is automatically disabled.)

Tabs

Search

Create a contact

Owner's contact record

Index letters

Section letter

Contact record

In this chapter, you find out how to use the Contacts app to create and manage your business and personal contacts. Topics include the following:

→ Understanding the Contacts interface
→ Creating, viewing, and editing contact records
→ Joining multiple contact records for the same person
→ Defining and working with contact groups
→ Backing up your contacts to the SIM card, built-in memory, or a memory card
→ Exporting Outlook (Windows) and Contacts/ Address Book (Mac) contacts and importing them into Google Contacts
→ Setting display options for the Contacts record list

Managing Contacts

Contacts is the Galaxy S 4's built-in address book app. It's populated by contact records created on the phone, in your Google Contacts account on the web, and in other information sources that you sync to it, such as Facebook, LinkedIn, and Exchange Server accounts. The Contacts app links to Phone for dialing numbers, Email for selecting email recipients, and Messaging for selecting text and multimedia message recipients.

The Contacts Interface

Contacts has four sections, each represented by a tab at the top of the screen. Here's what you can do in each section:

Section tabs

Groups tab

Group name   Number of members

Favorites tab

Favorites list

Frequently Contacted list

- *Phone.* Tap the Phone tab to switch to the Phone app to make a call. (Phone and Contacts are linked; you can quickly switch between them by tapping the appropriate tab. Chapter 4 covers the Phone app.)

- *Groups.* Groups are contact record subsets whose members share some common element. Some groups, such as Family and Friends, are predefined or automatically created as you use the Galaxy S 4. You can also define your own groups, such as members of your bowling team or a committee on which you're serving. To see the members of any group, tap the Groups tab and then tap the group name. To learn more about using and creating groups, see "Working with Contact Groups," later in the chapter.

- *Favorites.* Tap this tab to view a list of only those contact records that you've marked as favorites. To add or remove someone as a favorite, open the person's record for viewing in any list and tap the star icon to the right of the name. Beneath your favorites are other people and companies that you frequently call or message but have not marked as favorites. For more information about favorites, see "Marking Contacts as Favorites," later in this chapter.

Grid Versus List View

If you've added photos to your favorite contacts, press the Menu key and tap Grid View to display favorites as photo thumbnails. (To restore the Favorites scrolling list, tap List View.)

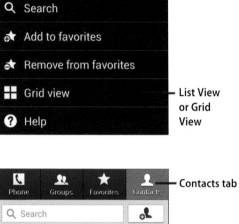

List View or Grid View

- *Contacts.* This is the default Contacts tab. It displays a scrolling list of your contact records. You can tap a person's name to view her contact record. This section of Contacts can optionally be displayed by Phone, Email, and Messaging to enable you to select a call, email, or message recipient. The Contacts section is discussed throughout this chapter.

Contacts tab

Contacts list

Creating a Contact Record

In addition to creating contacts in Google Contacts or another address book utility that you're syncing with your phone, you can create new contact records directly on the phone.

1. To launch Contacts, tap its Home screen icon or select it in Apps.

Other Contacts Launch Options

You can also launch Contacts by tapping the Contacts tab in the Phone app or the Contacts icon in Email or Messaging when selecting message recipients.

2. If it isn't automatically selected, tap the Contacts tab.

3. To create a new contact record, tap the plus (+) button to the right of the search box.

4. The screen for creating a contact appears, ready for you to enter the person or company's contact information.

5. The top entry shows where the contact will be created and shared. To change this setting, tap its text. Select Device for a contact that will reside only on the phone. Select Google, Microsoft Exchange ActiveSync, or Samsung Account to share this record with the specified contact list. (These options appear only after you add accounts of these types.) Select SIM to store the contact on your SIM card; only the name, email address, and phone number are stored.

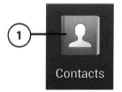

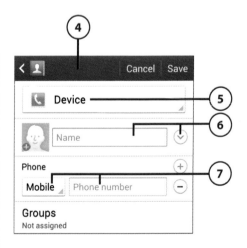

6. Enter the person's name. You can type the full name in the Name field or—to enter more detailed name information, such as a prefix, suffix, or middle name—tap the expand/collapse icon beside the field. When you finish entering the name components, you can collapse the name by tapping the same icon.

7. Enter a phone number for the person in the first Phone field. If the label (Mobile, for example) is incorrect, tap the label and select the correct one from the dropdown list. (Select Custom, at the bottom of the list, if you want to create your own label.)

To add more numbers, tap the Phone field's plus (+) icon. To remove an unwanted or blank number, tap its minus (–) icon.

Text Messaging
If you intend to send text or multimedia messages to this person, you must enter at least one number that's designated as Mobile.

8. To add fields that aren't currently shown, tap Add Another Field at the bottom of the screen. As an example, steps 9–11 explain how to add Email and Address fields to the record.

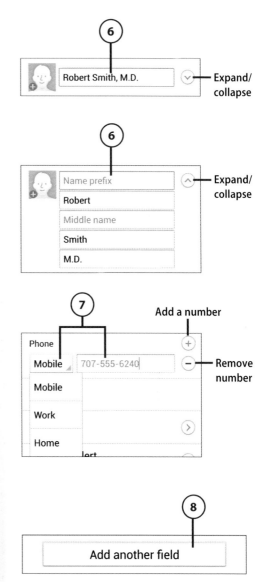

9. In the Add Another Field dialog box, tap Email.

10. Use the method described in step 7 to add one or more email addresses to the contact record. As with phone numbers, you can select a label for each email address from the drop-down list.

11. You can record one or more physical addresses for the person by tapping Add Another Field and then selecting Address in the Add Another Field dialog box. Use the same method that you used to enter Phone and Email information. Address is a composite field with separate entries for Street, City, State, and ZIP Code. To add other elements, such as P.O. Box or Country, tap the expand/collapse icon.

Adding Other Fields

To add other fields to the contact record, tap Add Another Field and select a field from the Add Another Field list. Only fields that you haven't already added to the record are displayed.

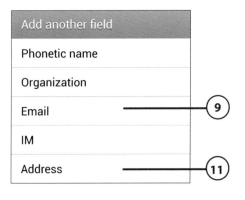

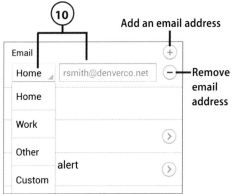

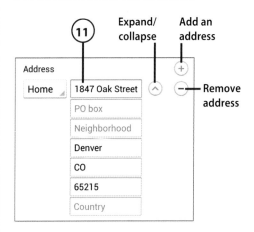

12. *Optional:* You can assign the person to one or more contact groups. The advantage of using groups is that you can text or email all members of the group by addressing a message to the group rather than to each member. To assign the person to groups, tap the Groups field, select the check box of each appropriate group, and tap Save. (To learn how to create and use groups, see "Working with Contact Groups," later in this chapter.)

13. *Optional:* To specify a distinctive ringtone that will announce calls from this person, tap Ringtone, select an option in the Ringtones dialog box, and tap OK.

Specifying a Ringtone

You can select ringtones from those provided with the phone (Ringtones) or use any audio file—such as a downloaded ringtone or a complete song—that you've stored on the phone. To assign such a custom ringtone to the record, tap the Add button and locate the audio or music file. Ringtones are discussed in greater detail in "Setting Ringtones" in Chapter 3.

14. *Optional:* To choose a distinctive alert for messages from this contact, tap Message Alert, select an alert tone in the Message Alert dialog box, and tap OK.

15. *Optional:* To assign an identifiable vibration pattern to the contact, tap Vibration Pattern, select a pattern in the Vibration Pattern dialog box, and tap OK. To create a custom vibration pattern, tap Create, and then drum the pattern on the Create Pattern screen.

16. When you finish entering the initial information for this contact, tap the Save button at the top of the screen or tap Cancel to discard the record.

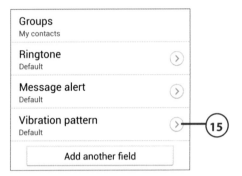

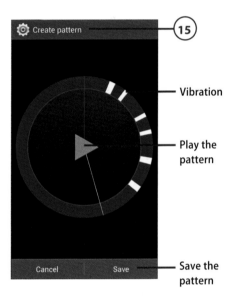

Vibration

Play the pattern

Save the pattern

Adding a Photo to a Contact Record

To help identify a contact, you can add a photo to the person's record. You can use any photo that's stored on the phone or use the phone's camera to shoot the picture.

1. To associate a photo with the contact, tap the photo placeholder in the upper-left corner while creating or editing the contact record. (If the record already has a photo, you can tap it to replace it with a new photo.)

2. In the Contact Photo dialog box, select the appropriate option. Tap Image to use a photo stored on the phone. Tap Pictures by People to use a previously shared image. Tap Take Picture to use the phone's camera to shoot the picture now. Tap S Memo to use an item you've stored in the S Memo app.

3. If you tapped Image or Pictures by People in step 2, Gallery launches. Tap the folder that contains the photo, tap the photo's thumbnail, and go to step 6.

① Robert Smith, M.D.

② Contact photo

Image

Pictures by people

Take picture

S Memo

Image (Gallery app)

③ Cancel

4. If you tapped Take Picture in step 2, Camera launches. Tap the Camera button to take the person's picture. If you don't care for the shot, tap Discard and try again; otherwise, tap Save and go to step 6.

5. If you tapped S Memo in step 2, S Memo launches. Select the memo that you want to use.

6. On the cropping screen, move and resize the blue cropping rectangle to select the area of the photo that you want to use, and then tap Done. The cropped photo is added to the contact record.

7. If you're done creating or editing the record, tap the Save button at the top of the screen.

Take Picture (Camera app)

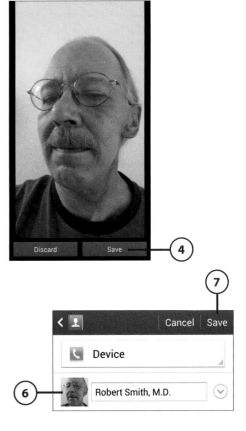

Viewing Contacts

The bulk of what you do in Contacts involves finding and viewing individual contacts so you can call, email, or text them.

1. Launch Contacts by tapping its Home screen icon.

2. With the Contacts tab selected, contacts are displayed in an alphabetical scrolling list. By default, all contacts from all sources are listed. You can restrict contacts to a single source (LinkedIn, for example) and set

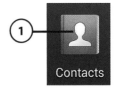

other display options by following the instructions in "Setting Display Options" at the end of this chapter.

3. To find a particular contact, you can use any of the following techniques:

   - Flick up or down to scroll the list.

   - Tap an index letter on the right edge of the screen to go to that approximate spot in the alphabetical list.

   - Press and drag in the index letter list. As you drag, a large version of each index letter appears. Remove your finger when the correct letter is shown. For example, to find a person whose last name is Jones, release your finger when J appears.

   - To search for someone, tap the Search box and begin entering any element of the person's record, such as first or last name, street name, or email address. As you type, a list of likely matching contacts appears. When you see the correct record, tap the person's entry.

4. When you find the contact, tap it to view the person's record. Depending on the information recorded for the contact, you can dial any listed number by tapping the green phone icon, send a text message to the person by tapping a mobile phone number's envelope icon, or address a new email to the person by tapping an email address' envelope icon.

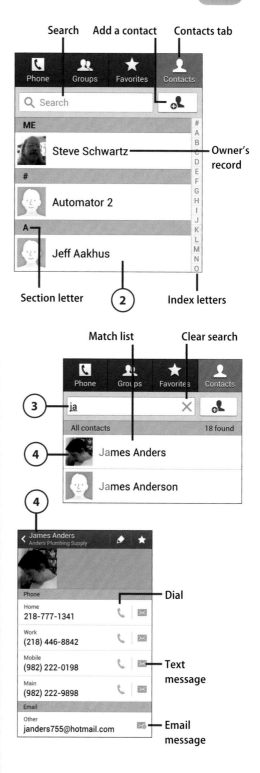

Search Add a contact Contacts tab

ME

Steve Schwartz ——— Owner's record

\#

Automator 2

A

Jeff Aakhus

Section letter (2) Index letters

Match list Clear search

(3) — ja

All contacts 18 found

(4) — James Anders

(4) — James Anderson

(4) — James Anders
Anders Plumbing Supply

Phone

Home
218-777-1341

Work
(218) 446-8842 ——— Dial

Mobile
(982) 222-0198 ——— Text message

Main
(982) 222-9898

Email

Other
janders755@hotmail.com ——— Email message

Editing Contact Records

Contact records sometimes require editing. You might have to add or change an email address or phone number, or you may want to substitute a better picture. Editing a contact employs the same techniques that you use to create contact records. In this section, you discover several ways to edit records, as well as delete them.

Editing Contacts

When changes to a record are necessary to bring it up to date, here's what you need to do:

1. In Contacts, select the record that you want to edit.

2. The complete record displays. Tap the Edit icon, or press the Menu key and tap Edit.

3. Using the techniques described in "Creating a Contact Record," make the necessary changes to the person's information.

4. Tap Save to save your edits, or tap Cancel if you decide not to save the changes.

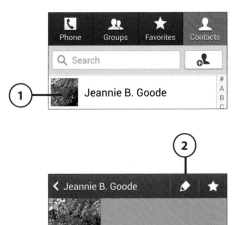

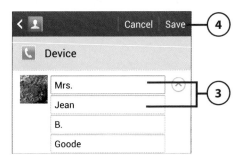

Setting Defaults for a Contact

Several contact fields can have multiple entries. For example, a record can have several phone numbers, email addresses, IM usernames, and mailing addresses. For some of these fields, you can optionally specify a *default entry*—that is, one that you want to treat as primary.

1. In any Contacts list, select the record for which you want to view, set, or change defaults.

2. The complete record displays. Press the menu key and tap Mark as Default.

3. All items for which you can set a default are displayed. To set an entry as a default, tap its radio button. If necessary, scroll to see any additional items.

4. Tap Done to set the new defaults for the record.

5. Whenever you view the record, default entries have a blue check mark.

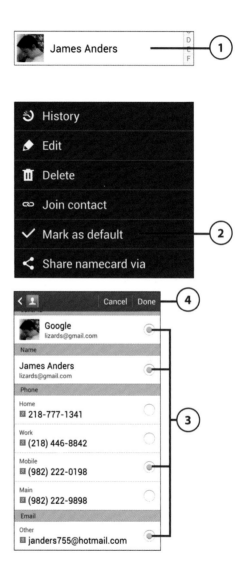

Joining and Separating Contacts

Your contact records probably come from multiple sources. Some are created on the phone; others might originate in Google Contacts, LinkedIn, an Exchange Server account, or a social networking site. As a result, when you scroll through the entries in Contacts, you may find some duplicates. You can use the Join Contact command to merge the duplicates for a person into a single contact record.

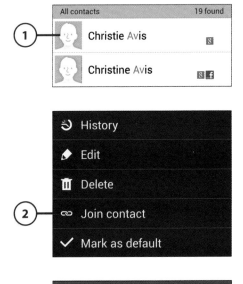

1. In the Contacts list, locate a pair of records for the same person by browsing or searching. Tap one of the entries to open the record.

2. Press the Menu key and tap Join Contact. (You can also press and hold the person's name in the Contacts list and choose Join Contact from the menu that appears.)

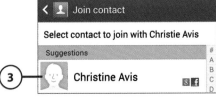

3. A Suggestions list appears. If it includes the person's other record, tap to select it. Otherwise, scroll down to look for the record in the All Contacts section, and then tap to select it.

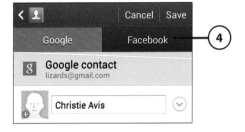

4. The two records are joined to create a single record. If you edit the record (display the record, and then either tap the Edit button or press the Menu key and tap Edit), you can see the sources of the joined records—in this example, Google and Facebook. If still more records exist for this person, you can join those as well by using the Join Contact command again.

Separating Joined Contacts

If necessary, you can separate joined records, re-creating the original, individual records. Open the joined record, press the Menu key, tap Separate Contact, and tap the minus (–) sign beside one of the listed records.

Marking Contacts as Favorites

To make it easy to quickly find people with whom you're in regular contact, you can mark records as *favorites*. Doing so adds those people to the contacts in your Favorites list.

1. In a Contacts list, press and hold the contact's name until the menu appears.

2. Tap Add to Favorites. If you subsequently need to remove the contact from Favorites, open the menu again and tap Remove from Favorites.

Marking and Removing Favorites in an Open Contact Record

With a contact record open, you can mark it as a favorite by tapping the star icon to the right of the person's name, turning the star gold. To remove the person from your favorites, tap the gold star, removing the color.

Simultaneously Adding or Removing Multiple Favorites

To add or remove *multiple* contacts from Favorites, select the Favorites tab, press the Menu key, and tap Add to Favorites or Remove from Favorites. Tap the check box of each person that you want to add or remove, and then tap Done. (When removing favorites, you can also remove people from the Frequently Contacted list by tapping their check boxes.)

Done

Remove from Favorites

Deleting Contacts

People leave your personal and business life for many reasons. When you're certain that you no longer need their contact records, you can delete them.

1. To delete a record while viewing any Contacts list, press and hold the record, tap Delete in the menu that appears, and tap OK in the Delete Contact confirmation dialog box.

2. To delete a record while viewing it, press the Menu key, tap Delete, and tap OK in the Delete Contact confirmation dialog box.

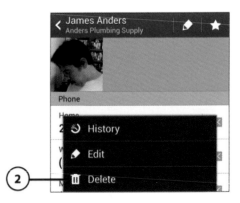

3. To simultaneously delete *multiple* records, display the Contacts list, press the Menu key, and tap Delete. Tap the check box beside each record that you want to delete, tap the Delete button, and tap OK in the Delete Contact confirmation dialog box.

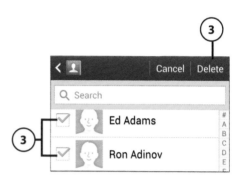

Working with Contact Groups

A *group* is a collection of contacts that have something in common, such as membership in a parents' organization, employees in a company department, or high school friends. Because each group is a subset of Contacts, you can use groups to quickly find every important person of a particular type. You can also use a group as the recipient for an email or text message, automatically sending it to all members. You can create groups and define their memberships from scratch, as well as use the built-in groups (Family and Friends, for example) and ones created for you by social media sites, such as LinkedIn and Facebook.

Creating a Group

1. In Contacts, select the Groups tab.

2. Press the Menu key and tap Create.

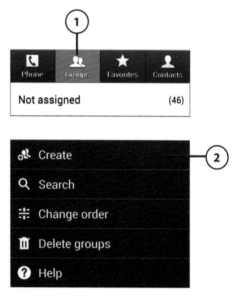

3. *Optional:* If you've registered more than one Google account, you can specify the account of which this group will be a subset by tapping the Create Group In entry.

4. Enter a name for the group.

5. *Optional:* Specify a ringtone that will announce calls from group members.

6. *Optional:* Specify an alert for text messages from group members.

7. *Optional:* Specify a vibration pattern that will announce calls or text messages from group members.

8. *Optional:* Tap Add Member to set the initial group membership. Select members by tapping their names and then tap Done. (Note that you can add members at any time.)

9. Tap the Save button to save the group name, membership, and settings. The group name is added to the Integrated Groups list. Whenever you want to view the group's membership, select the Groups tab and tap the group's name in the list.

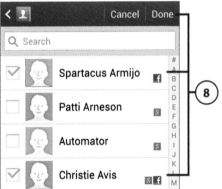

Changing a Group's Definition or Membership

You can quickly change a group's settings or membership. Select the Groups tab, press and hold the group name, and select Edit Group in the menu that appears. When you finish making changes, tap Save.

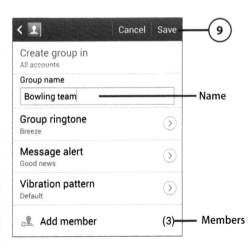

Adding or Removing a Person from Group Membership

1. With the Contacts tab selected, tap a person's name to open her record.

2. Tap the Groups entry.

3. Add or remove check marks to assign or remove the person from the listed groups. Tap Save to save the changes. (Note that a person can be a member of multiple groups.)

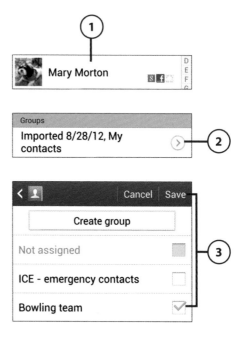

Quickly Removing Members from a Group

In addition to adding new members to a group, you can easily remove one or more members. On the Groups tab, tap the group name to display its membership. Then press the Menu key and tap Remove Member. Select the members that you want to remove from the group and tap Done.

Emailing or Texting a Group

1. In Email or Messaging, tap the Compose icon.

2. Tap the Contacts icon to select email or message recipients.

3. In Contacts, select the Groups tab and then tap the group that you want to email or message.

4. Tap the names of the group members that you want to email or message, or tap Select All to include the entire group as recipients.

Multiple Choice

If a selected individual has multiple email addresses or mobile phone numbers, a dialog box appears in which you must select the correct address or number.

5. Tap Done to transfer the selected members' email addresses or mobile numbers to Email or Messaging, respectively. Complete your email or compose your message as you normally do.

Start an Email or Text Message from Contacts

You can also initiate a group email or text message from within Contacts. Select the Groups tab, press and hold a group name, and tap either Send Email or Send Message. Select the members and tap Done. (You can also start this procedure when viewing a group's membership. Press the Menu key and follow the same steps.)

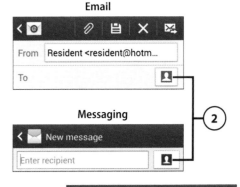

Email

Messaging

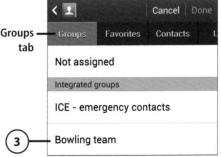

Groups tab

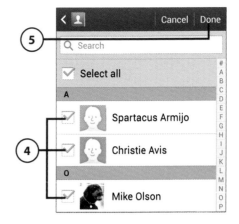

Group

Group message

Group email

Reordering the Groups

1. With the Groups tab selected, press the Menu key and tap Change Order.

2. To change a group's position, drag the group up or down by the dot pattern on its right edge. Release the group when it's in the desired spot. Repeat for other groups whose positions you want to change.

3. Tap Done to save the new group list order.

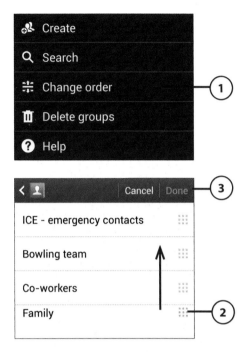

Deleting a Group

1. With the Groups tab selected, press the Menu key and tap Delete Groups.

2. Select the groups you want to delete by tapping check boxes, and then tap the Delete button.

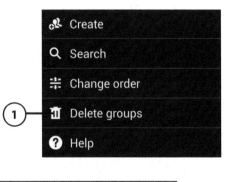

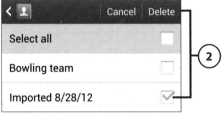

3. In the Delete Group dialog box, indicate whether you want to delete only the selected group(s)—leaving the associated contact records intact—or the group(s) *and* member contact records.

4. Confirm the deletion(s) by tapping OK or tap Cancel if you've changed your mind.

Deleting a User-Created Group

To quickly delete a group that you created, press and hold its entry in the groups list and tap Delete in the dialog box that appears.

Backing Up/Restoring and Exporting/ Importing Contact Records

As security against phone-related disasters or in preparation for switching to a new phone, you can back up your Contacts data to a memory card, built-in memory, or SIM card, or you can merge the data with your Google or Samsung account.

You can also use export/import procedures to manually move copies of contact records from your computer-based email and address book utilities into Contacts. For information about and strategies for syncing your contact data with its various sources, see Chapter 16.

Carriers Differ

Each carrier decides the Contacts backup and restore procedures that it supports, as well as the steps each requires. However, regardless of which carrier you have, you should find several procedures in this section—occasionally with small variations—that are applicable to *your* phone.

Backing Up Contact Data

You have multiple options for backing up your Contacts data.

Merging with Google Contacts or Your Samsung Account

1. With the Contacts list displayed, press the Menu key and tap Merge Accounts.

2. In the Merge Accounts dialog, tap Merge with Google or Merge with Samsung, as appropriate.

3. Tap OK in the confirmation dialog box.

4. When you view the full contact list, you see that all records are now marked as Google contacts or as Samsung contacts.

Only the Device (Phone) Records Merge

If you merge your phone's contacts with the Samsung account that you created during the phone's setup, only those contacts created with Device as the source are merged; Google contacts are left unchanged.

To Merge or Not to Merge

Think carefully before performing a Merge with Google or—to a lesser degree—Merge with Samsung Account, especially if your contact records have many different sources and you want to keep those sources intact. Unlike the other backup and export procedures described in this section, the Merge commands modify the records by changing their creation source. Thus, use Merge with Google only if you're committing to using Google/Gmail as the repository of *all* your contact data.

Copying Contacts to the SIM Card

1. With the Contacts tab selected, press the Menu key. Depending upon your carrier, do one of the following:

   • Tap Import/Export, followed by Export to SIM Card.

   • Tap SIM Management, followed by Copy Contacts to SIM.

SIM Backup Limitations

Some carriers do not support backing up to or restoring from the SIM card. In addition, SIM card backups only include names, email addresses, and phone numbers—ignoring all other information entered in the records.

2. Select the contacts that you want to export and tap Done.

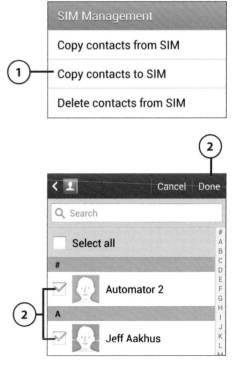

Selecting All or Most Contacts

If you want to copy most of your contacts but intend to leave a few out, scroll to the top of the list and tap Select All. Then tap the check boxes of only those records that you want to *omit*.

3. Tap OK in the confirmation dialog box. A dialog box informs you that the selected contacts were copied to the SIM card.

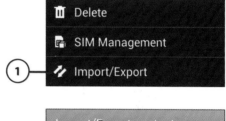

Backing Up to a Memory Card

1. With the Contacts tab selected, press the Menu key and tap Import/Export. (Note that you *must* have a memory card installed in the phone to export your Contacts data using this procedure.)

2. Tap Export to SD Card.

3. Tap OK in the Confirm Export dialog box. The data is exported to the displayed vCard filename and location. (The extSdCard in the file pathname indicates that your add-in memory card is the destination.)

Multiple Backups

As time passes, you can export *multiple* backups of the Contacts database to your memory card. Each new backup increments the filename by 1 over the highest-numbered backup on the card. For example, if there's already a Contacts_002.vcf, the next backup will be Contacts_003.vcf.

Exporting to USB (Built-In Memory)

If you don't have an add-in memory card, you can export your contacts to a vCard file in the phone's built-in memory. From there, you can copy the file to your computer or store it in an online storage service.

In the Import/Export Contacts dialog box, tap Export to USB Storage, and then tap OK in the Confirm Export dialog box.

BACK UP *EVERYTHING!*

>>>Go Further

Before you begin experimenting with contact importing/exporting or syncing, it's extremely important to have current backups of *all* your contact data sources on your computer, the web, and company servers, as well as the Contacts data on your phone. If you're a Mac user, for example, that might mean backing up Microsoft Outlook contacts, Address Book or Contacts, and Google Contacts. If something goes wrong (such as ending up with duplicates of every contact), you can delete all contacts in the affected applications and then restore the original data from the backups.

Restoring Contacts from Backups

If something happens to the Contacts database on your Galaxy S 4 or you switch to a new phone, you can restore the data from one or more backups.

Restoring Contacts from the SIM Card

1. With the Contacts tab selected, press the Menu key. Depending upon your carrier, do one of the following:

   - Tap Import/Export, followed by Import from SIM Card.

   - Tap SIM Management, followed by Copy Contacts from SIM.

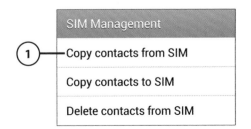

2. When the contacts are imported from the SIM card, they must be associated with an account. Select an account from the dialog box.

3. Select the contact records that you want to restore—or tap Select All—and then tap Done.

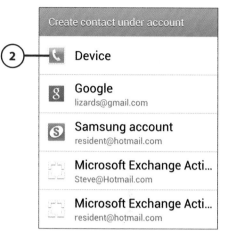

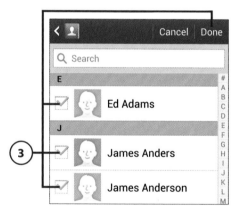

Restoring Contacts from a Memory Card Backup

1. If this is a new phone, install the memory card in the phone to which you want to restore your Contacts database. (See "Adding a Memory Card" in Chapter 19 for instructions.) Launch the Contacts app.

2. With the Contacts tab selected, press the Menu key and tap Import/Export.

3. Tap Import from SD Card.

4. When the contacts are imported, you must associate them with an account. Select an account from the Save Contact To dialog box.

Beware of Duplicates

When restoring a backup from a memory card, the procedure doesn't check for duplicate records. Thus, it's safest to restore to a device that contains no contact records or only new, unique records that you've created on the phone. Remember, too, that if you have any contacts that you previously created or synced with Google Contacts, those contacts will automatically be restored on your first sync. In other words, restoring from the SD card might be unnecessary.

Restoring a USB (Built-In Memory) Backup

If you've stored your Contacts backup in the phone's built-in memory, you can restore it by tapping Import from USB Storage in the Import/Export Contacts dialog box. In the Save Contact To dialog box, choose an account to associate with the restored contacts.

If you've only exported to USB once, your contacts are immediately imported. On the other hand, if you've created multiple USB backups, the Select vCard File dialog box appears. Select the file or files that you want to import, and then tap OK.

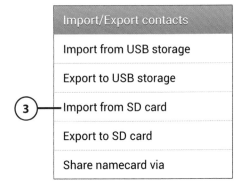

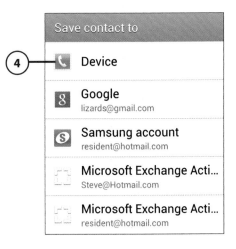

It's Not All Good

PROBLEMS WITH RESTORES

Although the steps required to restore most types of backups are straight-forward, the results might not be what you expect. In my experience, getting a clean restore that doesn't require hours of deleting duplicates and joining records from multiple sources is something of a rarity. Perhaps your best bet—and the simplest approach—is to use Google Contacts as the repository of all contact records and just allow it to restore the Contacts database on the first sync.

Importing Contact Data from Other Sources into Google Contacts

Although Google Contacts (Gmail's address book) is the *de facto* source for Android contact data, it's *not* the place in which many of us have chosen to store our contacts. You may already have years of contacts stored in email clients and address book utilities on your computer. You can also sync Outlook 2011 (Mac) and Address Book/Contacts (Mac) directly with Google Contacts, as explained in Chapter 16.

Exporting Your Computer's Data

Here's how to export your data from your existing contact-management application on your Mac or PC:

- *Address Book or Contacts (Mac).* Select the contacts to export and then choose File, Export, Export vCard (or Export Group vCard). Alternatively, drag the contacts out of the Address Book or Contacts window to your Desktop or a convenient Finder window.

- *Outlook 2010 or 2013 (Windows).* Click the File tab, click Options, and then click Advanced. Click the Export button to launch the Import and Export Wizard, click Export to a File, and click Next. Select the Comma Separated Values (Windows) option and click Next. Select the Contacts folder and click next. Click Browse, select the folder in which to place the exported file, and click Next. Finally, click Finish to export the data.

Importing the Exported Data into Google Contacts

1. In your browser, go to mail.google.com or gmail.com and log into your account. Open the Gmail menu and click Contacts.

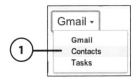

Just in Case…

As a safety measure, you might want to back up the Google Contacts data by choosing More, Export. If the import described in this task doesn't go as planned, you can restore your original Google Contacts data by choosing the More, Import command or by choosing More, Restore Contacts. The former command restores from your backup file, whereas the latter restores from one of several Google-provided backups.

2. To replace all current data in Google Contacts with the new data, you must delete all the records. From the first Contacts menu, choose All to select all visible records. Then from the More menu, choose Delete Contacts.

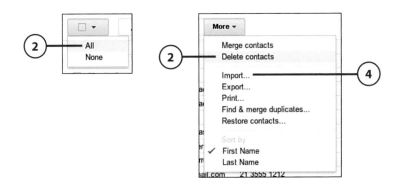

Caution: Selective Deletions

If Google Contacts contains records that do not exist in the imported data, you may want to delete all records *except* those.

3. If still more records exist, repeat step 2. Continue until all records have been deleted.

4. Choose More, Import.

5. To select the data file to import, click the Choose File button in the Import Contacts dialog box.

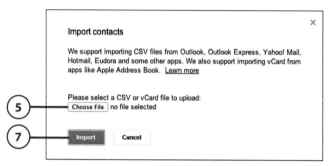

6. In the file dialog box that appears, select the exported data file and click the Choose button.

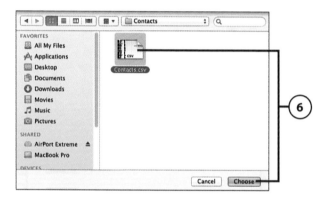

7. In the Import Contacts dialog box, click the Import button. The exported data appears in Google Contacts.

Odds and Ends

Contacts has a couple of other commands that you may occasionally find useful.

The Send Email and Send Message Commands

While viewing the Contacts list, you can select recipients for a new email or text message. Press the Menu key, tap Send Message/Email, and then tap Send Message or Send Email in the Send Message/Email dialog box. Select the Contacts, Groups, Favorites, or Logs tab; select recipients; and then tap Done to address the new email or text message.

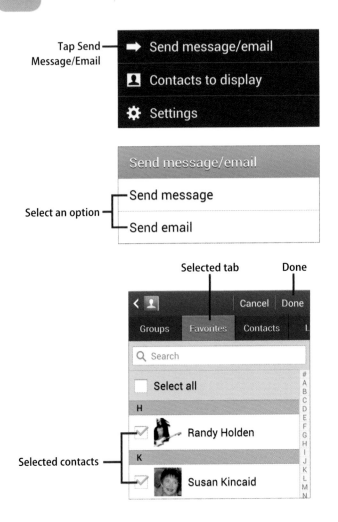

Tap Send Message/Email

Select an option

Selected tab

Done

Selected contacts

Setting Display Options

With the Contacts tab selected, you can set a variety of useful options that determine which records are shown and the order in which they appear.

1. Press the Menu key and tap Settings. The Settings screen appears.

2. Tap the Only Contacts with Phones check box to hide contact records that don't include a phone number. (To restore the full contacts list, tap it again to remove the check mark.)

3. You can sort contacts alphabetically by first name or last name. To change the current sort order, tap List By and then select an option in the List By dialog box.

4. Regardless of the List By order specified in step 3, you can display each contact as first name first (Bob Smith) or last name first (Smith, Bob). Tap Display Contacts By, and then select an option in the Display Contacts By dialog box.

5. When you finish making changes, tap the Back icon or press the Back key.

Specifying Contacts to Display

There's also an option to view only those contacts associated with a particular account. For instance, you can view only your Facebook friends or LinkedIn colleagues. With the Contacts tab selected, press the Menu key, tap Contacts to Display, and select the account that you want to view. (To create a custom view that combines several accounts, tap the Settings icon to the right of the Customized List option.)

SAMSUNG
10:20 PM
Today
Calendars
+
Apr
May 2013
Jun
Year
Month
Week
Day
List
Task
Sun Mon Tue Wed Thu Fri Sat
Cinco de Mayo
Money to New..
Mother's Day
Memorial Day
Josh to Kmart
7:00PM – 8:00PM
Kids return with furniture
8:00PM – 9:00PM

In this chapter, you find out how to use Calendar to create, view, and edit events and tasks. Topics include the following:

→ Adding Calendar accounts to display events and tasks from your Gmail, Microsoft Exchange ActiveSync, and other account calendars

→ Creating events and tasks, viewing the calendar, and managing events and tasks

→ Responding to reminders for upcoming events and tasks

→ Setting Calendar preferences

Using the Calendar

Similar in design to a full-featured calendar application (such as the one in Microsoft Outlook), the Calendar app enables you to record upcoming events, meetings, and tasks and then receive reminders for them. If you already maintain calendars in Google, Facebook, Hotmail (Microsoft Exchange ActiveSync), or a corporate Exchange Server account, you can synchronize your Calendar app data with that of your other calendars.

Adding Calendar Accounts

If you've used a Google/Gmail account on your phone to access any Google service, Calendar has two calendars that it can immediately associate with new events and tasks: your Google/Gmail Calendar and My Calendar, a phone-specific calendar created by the Calendar app. In addition to these sources, Calendar can use data from and sync with Samsung, Facebook, and Microsoft Exchange Server calendars. Thus, before you experiment extensively with Calendar, decide which external calendar sources you want to use and keep in sync with Calendar (adding other accounts as needed). You can find instructions for automatically and manually synchronizing your calendar data in Chapter 16.

1. To add a Facebook, Microsoft Exchange Server, Samsung, or Gmail calendar account (only these account types support calendar syncing with your phone), go to the Home screen and tap Apps, followed by Settings.

2. On the Settings screen, select the Accounts tab.

3. At the bottom of the My Accounts list, tap Add Account.

Multiple Accounts of the Same Type

Account types that are marked with a green dot have already been added. You can have multiple Exchange and Google accounts, but only one instance each of Samsung and Facebook accounts.

4. Select one of these account types: Sync Apps with Facebook, Microsoft Exchange ActiveSync, Google, or Samsung Account.

5. Follow the instructions to add the account. At a minimum, you need to supply your username and password (or use the provided option to create an account).

6. If offered as an option, ensure that Sync Calendar is enabled.

7. You can add other accounts by repeating steps 3–6. When you finish, press the Home key to return to the Home screen.

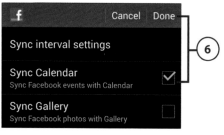

Working in Calendar

Within Calendar, you can create events and tasks, set a view (Year, Month, Week, Day, List, or Task), and edit or delete events and tasks.

Creating Events and Tasks

In addition to events and tasks that are pulled from your Gmail/Google, Facebook, Exchange, and Samsung accounts, you can also create new items within the Calendar app. These new items can be synced with your accounts automatically, manually, or not at all (as explained in Chapter 16).

Every Calendar item is either an *event* (a scheduled item for a specific date, with or without a start time) or a *task* (an unscheduled item with or without a due date). An event can be an all-day occurrence, such as a vacation day or birthday, or have a defined start and end time.

Creating an Event

1. Launch the Calendar app by tapping its Home screen shortcut or by tapping Apps, followed by Calendar.

2. *Optional:* On the calendar, select the date or time when you want to schedule the event. (Selecting the start date or time saves you the trouble of specifying this information when you create the event.) To change the Calendar view so that you can pick a start date or time, tap the Month, Week, or Day tab.

3. Tap the plus (+) icon to create a new event.

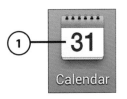

Be General or Specific

The more specific your selection (start date or date/time), the more information is prefilled for the event. On the other hand, regardless of the currently selected date or start time, you can still set a different date or time when you create the event.

Another Plus Icon Option

You can also create a new event or task by tapping the plus icon in a Calendar widget.

Create event or task

Calendar (Mini Today) widget

4. The scheduling screen appears. Ensure that the Add Event tab is selected. (When selected, the tab is dark.)

5. To associate the event with a different calendar, tap Calendar and select an account to use. (My Calendar is the phone-specific calendar.)

Associated calendar

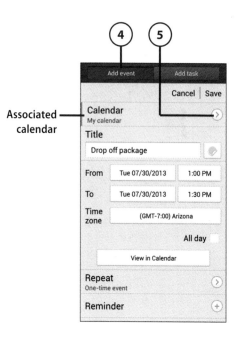

Using Multiple Calendars

The calendar you specify for each new item is very important. When you sync calendars, it's the calendar that records the event. If you choose your Google/Gmail calendar, for example, the event will also be available to you from Google's website using any browser. On the other hand, if you choose My Calendar, the event will be available only on your Galaxy S 4. To use other account calendars with Calendar, see "Adding Calendar Accounts" at the beginning of this chapter.

6. Enter a title for the event.

7. *Optional:* Select a *sticker* (icon) or color that signifies something about or helps classify the event.

8. Do one of the following:

   - If this is an all-day event or one with no specific schedule other than the day on which it occurs, tap the All Day check box. The From and To times are removed, as well as the time zone. Go to step 9.

   - If the From (starting) date or time is incorrect, tap the date or time item and correct it. Tap arrow icons to increment or decrement a component (such as the hour) by one unit. Alternatively, you can select the item you want to change and type the new value. Tap Set to accept the corrected date or time. Repeat this process for the To (ending) date and time.

9. *Optional:* Tap the Time Zone entry to specify a different time zone to use for scheduling this event.

10. If the event will repeat at regular intervals (such as a weekly staff meeting on Monday at 1:00 p.m.), tap Repeat and select a repetition interval. Then specify a duration or end date, and tap OK.

11. *Optional:* You can set a *reminder* (alarm) for the event by tapping the Reminder plus (+) icon. To specify an interval other than the default (15 mins before), tap the interval box, and select a new one from the scrolling list. (Select Customize if none of the intervals is correct.)

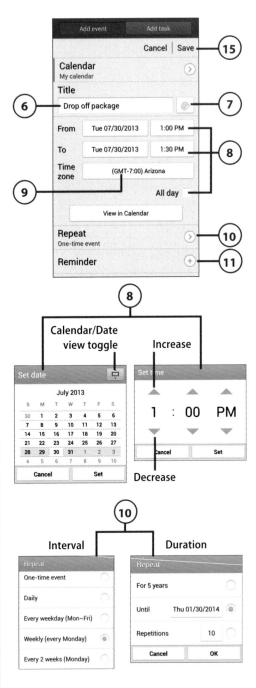

More About Reminders

You can optionally set *multiple* reminders for an event. Tap the plus (+) icon to add a new reminder. To remove a reminder, tap the minus (–) icon to its right. If the Calendar account with which this event is associated has an email address (such as your Google/Gmail account), you can elect to be notified via email rather than by the usual methods. Tap the box to the right of the reminder interval and choose Email.

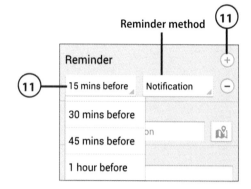

Reminder method

12. *Optional:* Enter a location for the event by typing in the Location box, or by tapping the Location icon, performing a search, and tapping Done.

13. *Optional:* In the Description text box, enter a detailed description of or notes related to the event.

14. You can attach existing or new S Memos or photos to the event by tapping the Memos or Images plus (+) icon.

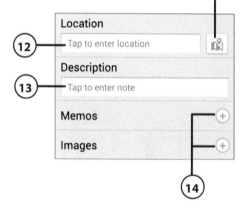

Location icon

Advanced Calendaring

To maintain compatibility with events created in Google/Gmail and Microsoft Exchange ActiveSync accounts (or created in Calendar and designated as either of these account types), additional fields (Participants, Show Me As, and Privacy) appear when you create, edit, or view such events. The fields are normally used to manage attendance at corporate meetings and can—or should—be skipped when creating standard Calendar events. When you save an item with designated

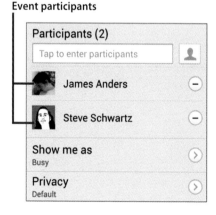

Event participants

participants, each person is automatically emailed an invitation when you save the event.

15. Tap the Save button to add the event to the calendar or tap Cancel to discard it.

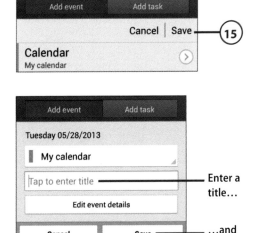

The Minimalist Approach

Unless you're a stickler for detail, it's quickest to enter only the essential information for each new event or task: the Title and the scheduled date/time. In addition to following the steps in this task, you can use the following shortcut.

In Month, Week, or Day view, tap to select a date, date/time, or time slot, respectively. Tap the selected period again to open a basic Add Event dialog box. Select the Add Event or Add Task tab (displayed in Month view only), enter an event or task title, and tap Save. If you need to enter more details, tap Edit Event Details, enter the necessary information, and then tap Save.

Creating a Task

1. Launch the Calendar app by tapping its Home screen shortcut or by tapping Apps, followed by Calendar.

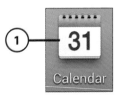

2. *Optional:* On the calendar, select the due date for the task's completion. (Selecting the date saves you the trouble of specifying it when you create the task.) To change the Calendar view so that you can select a due date, tap the Month, Week, or Day tab.

3. Tap the plus (+) icon.

4. The scheduling screen appears. Ensure that the Add Task tab is selected. (When selected, the tab is dark.)

5. To associate the task with a different account, tap Task and select the account to use. (My Task is the phone-specific account.)

6. Enter a title for the task.

7. Do one of the following:

   • If there's a particular date on or by which the task must be completed, tap the Due Date button, specify the date in the Set Date dialog box, and tap the Set button.

   • If the task is open-ended, tap the No Due Date check box.

8. *Optional:* You can set a *reminder* (alarm) for the task by tapping the arrow icon. In the Reminder dialog box, select either On Due Date or Customize (to specify a different date). The selected date and the current time are set as the reminder. To change the time, tap its entry, specify the time in the Set Time dialog box, and tap the Set button.

Selected view

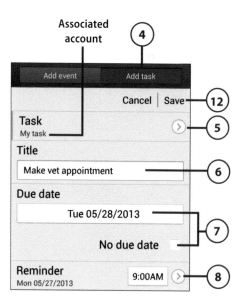

Associated account

9. *Optional:* Specify a completion priority (high, medium, or low) by tapping the arrow icon.

10. *Optional:* In the Description text box, enter a detailed description of or notes related to the task.

11. You can attach existing or new S Memos or photos to the task by tapping the Memos or Images plus (+) icon.

12. Tap the Save button to add the task to the calendar or tap Cancel to discard it. (When added to a calendar, a task is preceded by a check box.)

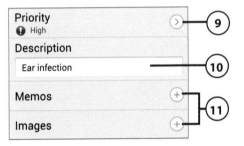

Viewing the Calendar

Calendar has six *views:* Year, Month, Week, Day, List, and Task. You interact differently with Calendar in each view.

1. When you launch Calendar, the last displayed view appears. To change views, tap a different view tab. The tab for the current view is beige.

2. *Year view.* You can't view events or tasks in Year view. Its purpose is to enable you to easily select a month for viewing—in this or another year. Scroll to previous or future years by tapping the arrow icons or by swiping the screen horizontally. When the target month and year appear, tap the month to view it in Month view.

Other Year View Options

To immediately return to the current year, tap the Today button. Today's date is encircled in blue.

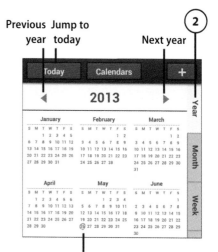

Previous year | Jump to today | Next year

Today's date

3. *Month view.* In Month view, the event/task text is color-coded to match the calendar account with which the item is associated. For example, bright blue text is used to show My Calendar items, dark blue for Facebook events, and purple for Google Calendar items. Select a date to display events and tasks for that date at the bottom of the screen or in a pop-up window (depending on a Calendar Settings option). To move forward or back one month, tap a month name or flick the screen vertically or horizontally.

Jump to today

Previous month | Next month

Today's date | Selected date

Events and tasks on selected date

4. *Week view.* In Week view, items are colored-coded to match the calendar with which they're associated. Tap an item to view its details, edit, or delete it. Scroll to the previous or next week by tapping an arrow icon or flicking horizontally.

Alternative Styles for Week and Month Views

There are two different styles for displaying events and tasks in Week view and Month view. To switch view styles, press the Menu key, and tap Settings, View Styles, Week View (or Month View Styles). See "Setting Calendar Preferences" at the end of the chapter for more information.

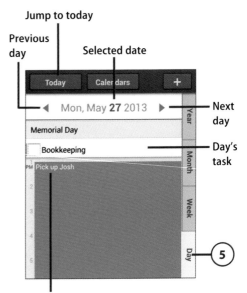

Previous week   Selected date
Jump to today   Next week

Event

Task   Today's date

5. *Day view.* Use Day view to see scheduled items and their duration for a selected date. Items are colored-coded to match the calendar with which they're associated. Tap an item to view its details, edit, or delete it. Press and hold a time slot to create a new item with that start time. You can scroll the day's time slots by flicking vertically and switch days by tapping arrow icons or swiping horizontally.

Jump to today

Previous day

Selected date

Next day

Day's task

Scheduled event

6. *List and Task views.* Select these views to see a chronological list of events or tasks, respectively. Items are color-coded to match the calendar with which they're associated. Tap an item to view its details, edit, or delete it. Scroll through the list by flicking vertically. In List view, you can display additional older or future events by tapping Tap to Look for More at the top or bottom of the list, respectively. You can search for events or tasks by entering search text in the box and choosing a filter (All, Event, Task, or Sticker).

Searching in Other Views

To display the search box in other views, press the Menu key and tap Search.

Sorting Tasks

You can change the sort order in Task view by pressing the Menu key, tapping Sort By, and making a selection.

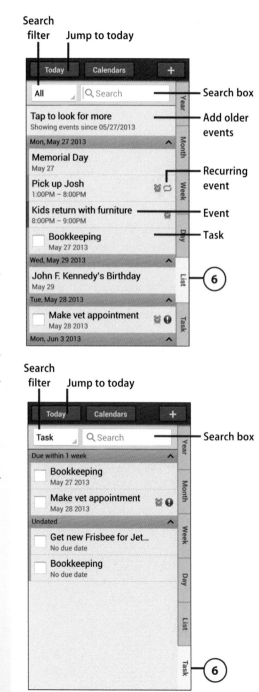

Search filter Jump to today

Search box

Add older events

Recurring event

Event

Task

Search filter Jump to today

Search box

7. To go to a specific date (in any view except Task), press the Menu key and tap Go To. In the Go To dialog box, specify the target date and tap Done.

8. You can display events and tasks from one or multiple calendar accounts. To select accounts to show, tap the Calendars button at the top of the current view, select the calendar and task accounts to display, and tap Done.

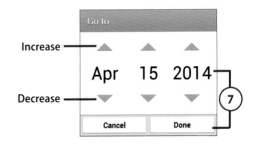

Increase

Apr 15 2014

Decrease

Done

Select all

>>>Go Further

CONSIDER CALENDAR WIDGETS

You can do much of your Calendar viewing on the Home screen by installing Calendar widgets. They draw their data from Calendar and enable you to view upcoming events and tasks, as well as create new ones.

- *Briefing.* In addition to listing events for today and tomorrow, you can tap the Settings icon to configure this Yahoo!-based widget to show news headlines, stock quotes, and recent Facebook status updates. The display automatically switches between content types, but you can manually move from one to the next by flicking vertically. Tap an event to view, edit, or delete it in Calendar; tap a news article or stock quote to view additional information from Yahoo!'s website; tap the speech icon to have your event list and other content read aloud; and tap Refresh to force an immediate content update.

Calendar widgets

- *Calendar.* This resizable events-only widget displays upcoming events in a scrolling list. Tap an event to view, edit, or delete it in Calendar. Tap the main date to view that day in Calendar.

- *Calendar (Mini Today).* This widget displays a day's events and tasks. Tap any item to view, edit, or delete it in Calendar; tap an arrow icon to move one day forward or backward; tap a task's check box to toggle its completion status; and tap the plus (+) icon to create a new event or task.

- *Calendar (Month).* This full-screen Calendar widget shows the same information as Calendar in Month view. Select a date with scheduled items and tap it to see the events and tasks in Calendar. Select any date and tap the plus (+) icon to create a new event on that date in Calendar. You can switch months by clicking an arrow icon, return to the current month by tapping Today, or switch to Calendar in Month view by tapping the month name.

For help with adding, moving, and removing widgets, see "Adding Widgets" and "Repositioning and Removing Home Screen Items" in Chapter 3.

Managing Events and Tasks

After creating an event or task, you can delete or edit any aspect of it, such as the title, start date, start time, description, reminder interval, or completion status.

1. Open the Calendar app and, in any view, tap the item that you want to delete or edit. The item opens in detail view.

Faster Editing, Deleting, and Rescheduling

If you press and hold an item on the calendar, a menu appears that enables you to go directly into edit mode or delete the item without first switching to detail view. In Week and Day views, you can change the date/time or duration of an event by dragging in the Calendar. To reschedule the event, press and drag it to a new date/time slot. To change its duration, drag the event's bottom edge down or up. When examining an event in detail view, you can tap the item title to immediately switch to edit mode.

2. Press the Menu key and do one of the following:

   • To delete the item, tap Delete and then tap OK in the confirmation dialog box. (If multiple items are displayed for a date, you can delete all or only selected ones by tapping their check boxes.)

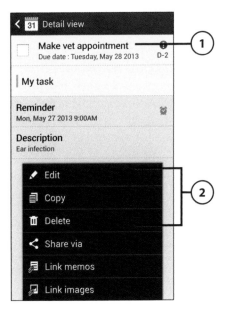

- To modify the item, tap Edit. Make the changes and tap the Save button.

Task Completion

To mark a task complete, tap its check box.

Editing a Repeating Event

When you edit a repeating event, a dialog box appears that enables you to change only this occurrence, all occurrences forward, or every occurrence. A dialog box with similar options appears when deleting a repeating event.

Edit a repeating event

Details
Only this event
This & future events
All repetitive events

Responding to Reminders

When an event or task reminder is triggered, a message appears briefly in the status bar and is replaced by a number (denoting the number of current alerts) or a separate alert screen appears. A distinctive ringtone may also play. The notification methods used are determined by Event Notification settings, as explained in "Setting Calendar Preferences," later in this chapter. You can respond to a reminder by *snoozing* (requesting that it repeat later), dismissing, or ignoring it.

Clock app

Simple Alarms

If you just need an alarm to remind you that it's time to wake up or do *something*, you don't need to schedule a Calendar event. You can create alarms in the Clock app.

5:12 PM
Alarm

Dismiss ———— ⊗   zZ ———— Snooze

1. If the Set Alerts and Notifications setting is *Status Bar Notification*, an icon showing the number of waiting reminders appears in the status bar. Pull down the Notification panel and tap the reminder that you want to handle.

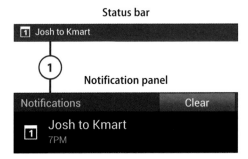

Status bar

Notification panel

2. If the Set Alerts and Notifications setting is *Alert* (or you tapped the reminder in the Notification panel in step 1), an icon showing the number of reminders appears in the status bar and the Event Notifications screen appears. One or multiple waiting reminders may be presented at a time.

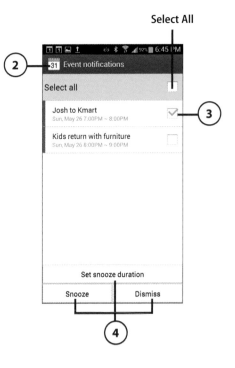

Select All

3. Specify the reminders to which you want to respond by doing one of the following:

   • If there's only one waiting reminder, skip to step 4.

   • To respond the same way to all listed reminders, ensure that they're all checked. (Tap Select All to simultaneously check or uncheck all reminders.)

   • To respond the same way to multiple—but not all—reminders, ensure that only the reminders to which you want to respond are checked.

4. Do one of the following:

   • To repeat the selected reminder(s) after the current snooze duration (such as 5 minutes) has passed, tap the Snooze button.

   • To snooze the selected reminder(s) for a custom duration, tap the Set Snooze

Duration button, select the duration and tap OK, and then tap the Snooze button.

- To cancel the selected reminder(s), tap Dismiss.

- To ignore the reminders for now, press the Back key. You can return to them when it's convenient by opening the Notification panel, as explained in step 1.

Dismissing a Reminder

Dismissing an event or task's reminder doesn't delete the item from Calendar; it merely eliminates the reminder. To *delete* the event or task, you must perform the procedure described in "Managing Events and Tasks," earlier in this chapter.

5. *Optional*: To respond to other waiting reminders, repeat steps 3 and 4.

Responding to a Lock Screen Reminder

A full-screen notification appears when the screen is dark; that is, when the lock screen is active. To respond, press and drag the Dismiss (X) or Snooze (zZ) icon. If you elect to snooze, the reminder is snoozed for the default duration.

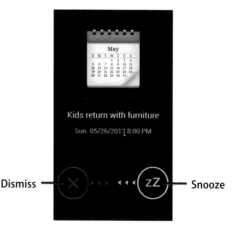

Dismiss ——   —— Snooze

Setting Calendar Preferences

You can set options on Calendar's Settings screen to customize the way the app works.

1. Launch the Calendar app. (On the Home screen, tap the Calendar shortcut, or tap the Apps icon and then the Calendar icon.)

2. Press the Menu key and tap Settings to view the Settings screen.

3. *View Styles.* Choose a display option for Month view (Calendar View + List or Calendar View + Pop-up) and Week view (Analog or Timeline).

4. *First Day of Week.* Specify whether calendar weeks should start on Saturday, Sunday, Monday, or match local customs.

5. *Hide Declined Events.* When enabled, event invitations that you've declined aren't shown in Calendar.

6. *Lock Time Zone.* When Lock Time Zone is disabled (unchecked), all event times reflect the phone's current location. When enabled (checked), event times always reflect the time zone specified in Select Time Zone (see step 7).

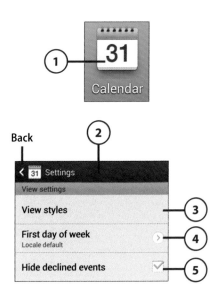

Back

Month view (Calendar View + List)

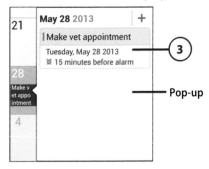

List

Month view (Calendar View + Pop-up)

Pop-up

A Lock Time Zone Recommendation

This is one of the most confusing aspects of Calendar. In general, the easiest way to use Lock Time Zone is to leave it disabled. When you're home in California, for example, all event times reflect Pacific time. If you travel to New York, the events display Eastern times. Finally, when you return home, events automatically change to show Pacific times again.

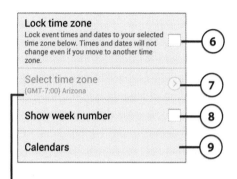

Current time zone

7. *Select Time Zone.* To force all event times to reflect a particular time zone (when you're traveling or if you want events to always reflect the home office's time zone, for example), enable Lock Time Zone (see step 6) and tap Select Time Zone to choose a time zone.

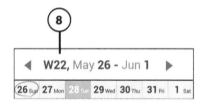

8. *Show Week Number.* When enabled, Week view also displays the week number (1–52).

9. *Calendars.* Tap Calendars followed by the Display button to specify the account calendars from which events and task are shown, as well as whether birthdays in Contacts records are listed as events. Tap Done when you finish making changes.

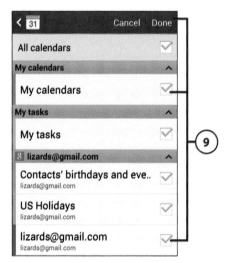

Synchronizing Calendar Data

To quickly perform a manual Calendar sync based on your current account settings, press the Menu key and tap Sync. To learn more about synchronizing data, see Chapter 16.

10. *Event Notification settings.* These settings determine the manner(s) in which reminders for upcoming events and tasks are presented.

- Tap Set Alerts and Notifications to specify whether a reminder will display as a status bar icon (Status Bar Notification), as a full screen pop-up (Alert), or not at all (Off).

- Tap Select Ringtone to associate a ringtone with reminder alerts. Select Silent if you want to disable this option.

- Enable Vibration if you want Calendar reminders to cause the phone to vibrate. Like other notification settings, you can set Vibrate as the sole notification method or use it in combination with other methods.

- Tap Quick Responses to view, edit, add, or delete brief email responses that you can send in response to event invitations.

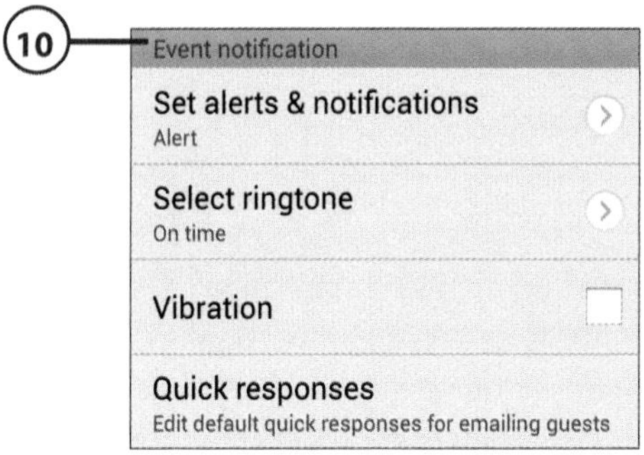

Event notification

Set alerts & notifications
Alert

Select ringtone
On time

Vibration

Quick responses
Edit default quick responses for emailing guests

Back —

Forward —

Bookmarks —

Windows —

In this chapter, you learn how to use the Internet app, one of the web browsers on the Galaxy S 4. Topics include the following:

→ Launching the browser
→ Visiting web pages
→ Setting options for viewing pages
→ Creating and organizing bookmarks
→ Configuring the browser

Browsing the Web

You're probably already familiar with the basics of using a web browser. Making the transition from browsing on a computer to doing so on your phone is relatively easy. As with a desktop browser, you can enter page addresses by typing, tapping links, and selecting bookmarks for your favorite sites.

Note that the Galaxy S 4 ships with a second browser: Google Chrome. Although this chapter focuses on using the Internet app as your browser, you might also want to check out Chrome. You can use whichever browser you prefer, as well as switch between them when you like.

Launching the Browser

You can launch the Internet app in several ways. The most common are as follows:

- On the Home screen, tap the Internet icon at the bottom of the screen. The browser opens to its home page.

- On the Home screen, tap Apps, followed by Internet. The browser opens to its home page.

- Tap a web link in an email message. Links can be blue underlined text, images, or other objects. If the item you tap is indeed a link, the linked page appears in the browser.

Home screen

Internet app

Complete Action Using

Because there *are* two browser apps installed on the phone, whenever you perform an indirect action that requires a browser (such as tapping a link), a Complete Action Using dialog box appears that asks which browser to launch. Tap a browser icon (Internet or Chrome), and then tap Just Once. After familiarizing yourself with both browsers, you can specify a *default browser* to use for all future indirect launches by tapping Always.

If you ever want to reverse your decision, open Settings, select the More tab, and tap Applications Manager. Select the All tab, scroll to find the browser that you previously set as the default (Internet or Chrome), and tap its name. In the Launch by Default section of the app's page, tap the Clear Defaults button.

Link in an email message

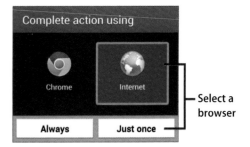

Select a browser

- Tap a blue underlined link in a text or multimedia message. In the dialog box that appears, tap Open URL to open the page in the browser or press the Back key if you change your mind.

If you want to see the list of my published books, go to:

www.siliconwasteland.com /misc.htm

12:38PM

Link in a text message

Unexpected Web Redirections

Apps and certain documents can contain links that automatically redirect you to web pages, causing the browser to launch if it isn't currently running. For example, if you tap text, an icon, or a button in some apps when searching for instructions, a help file or manual might open in the browser.

www.siliconwasteland.com/ misc.htm

Open in browser —— Open URL

Add to Bookmarks

Copy message text

Visiting Web Pages

You can go to a particular web page (called an *address* or *URL*) using the same methods that you use with Internet Explorer, Safari, Firefox, and other popular desktop web browsers. The most common methods are typing the address, tapping a link on the current page, choosing a bookmarked or recently visited (History) site or page, and searching for a site or page with one of the popular search engines.

Typing the Address

1. If the browser isn't currently running, go to the Home screen and tap the Internet icon.

2. Tap the Address field. The current page's address is selected.

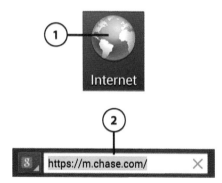

Internet

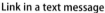

https://m.chase.com/

3. Enter the new address and tap Go. (Because the current address is already selected, typing anything immediately replaces the address.) The web page loads.

Fast Address Selection

As you type, a list of possible addresses appears. If you see the one you want, you can tap it instead of completing the address.

Suggested site

Delete

Go

Following a Link

In the browser, if you tap an object, graphic, or text that represents a web link, the link briefly turns blue and the linked page appears.

Page link

Not Every Link Leads to a Page

Other than special *mobile* versions of web pages (designed for viewing on cell phones), the pages displayed in the Internet app are identical to those you see in Internet Explorer, Safari, and other desktop browsers. That means that they also contain links designed to download PC and Mac applications, device drivers, and the like. Of course, such programs and drivers can't be used by your phone, but you may not be prevented from downloading them.

To remove these downloads, go to the Home screen and tap Apps, followed by Downloads. Tap the check box for each inappropriate download and then tap the Delete button.

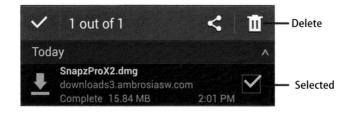

Delete

Selected

Visiting a Bookmarked, Recent, or Saved Page

1. Scroll the page up until the Address field is visible, and tap the star icon on the right.

2. To visit a *bookmarked* page (one whose address you stored), expand sections and open folders as necessary, and then tap the page's thumbnail or name. (For information about creating and managing bookmarks, see "Working with Bookmarks," later in this chapter.)

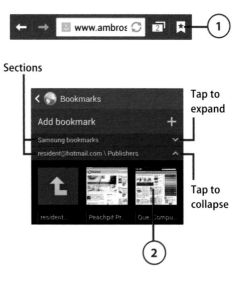

Sections

Tap to expand

Tap to collapse

Display Options

You can view bookmarks as a thumbnail grid or a scrolling list. To switch views, press the Menu key and tap List View or Thumbnail View. To expand or collapse bookmark sections, tap the arrow icon on the right side of the section name.

You can change the order of your personal bookmarks by pressing the Menu key and tapping Change Order. If you've created multiple or nested folders, you'll be asked to select the parent folder whose contents you want to rearrange. In Thumbnail View, press and hold any thumbnail and drag it to a new location. In List View, select a bookmark by pressing the dot grid to its right, drag it up or down in the list, and release when it's in the desired position. When you're satisfied with the changes, tap Done—or tap Cancel to ignore the changes.

3. To go from the current page to a *saved* page (one that you saved for later or offline reading), press the Menu key, tap Saved Pages, locate the page in the scrolling list, and tap its thumbnail.

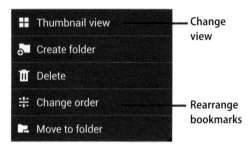

Thumbnail view — Change view

Create folder

Delete

Change order — Rearrange bookmarks

Move to folder

Saving a Page

To store a copy of the current page in Saved Pages, press the Menu key and tap Save Page. Use this command for any page that you want to read later or that might not be readily available online, such as a receipt for an online purchase.

Saved pages

Today   06/07/2013

The New York Times - NYTi...
The New York Times Search
SUBSCRIBE LOG IN June 7,...

Collapsed

4. To return to a recently viewed page, press the Menu key and tap History, locate the page in the scrolling list, and tap its name. To make it easier to find the page, you can *expand* (show) or *collapse* (hide) selected page-view periods (Today, Last 7 Days, and so on) by tapping section heads.

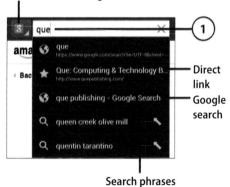

History

Today

Last 7 days

cnn - Google Search
https://www.google.co...-us&source=android-b

Video - Breaking News Videos from...
www.cnn.com/video/standard.html

Expanded

Searching for a Site or Page

1. Enter your search phrase in the address box, such as "exercise machines" or "trimming a parrot's beak." As you type, the search engine builds a list of possible sites and search topics. (The search links take you to your default search engine's site and perform the search; other entries go directly to the specified page.)

Current search engine

que

que
https://www.google.com/search?ie=UTF-8&client=

Que: Computing & Technology B... — Direct link
http://www.quepublishing.com/

que publishing - Google Search — Google search

queen creek olive mill

quentin tarantino

Search phrases

2. Do one of the following:

- Tap a direct link in the suggestion list to load that page.

- Tap a search entry—that is, an entry preceded by a magnifying glass or one that includes the word *Search*—to perform that search in the default or specified search engine's site.

- Tap the Go key on the keyboard to perform a search using the exact wording and spelling of your search phrase.

Changing Search Engines

The active search engine's icon is shown to the left of the address box. To switch search engines, tap the icon and choose a different one.

Tap to choose a
search engine

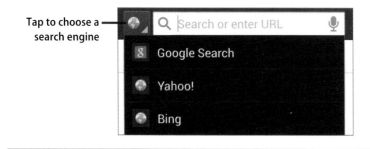

Viewing Pages

Similar to your computer's browser, the Internet app provides several ways for you to view pages, such as viewing in portrait or landscape mode, scrolling the page, changing the magnification, reloading the page, and displaying multiple pages in separate windows.

Portrait or Landscape View

Depending on the direction that you rotate the phone, you can view any page in *portrait* (normal) or *landscape* (sideways) mode. You can change the phone's orientation whenever you want; the page adjusts automatically. (If the orientation doesn't change when you rotate the phone, launch Settings, select the My Device tab, tap Display, and enable Auto-Rotate Screen.)

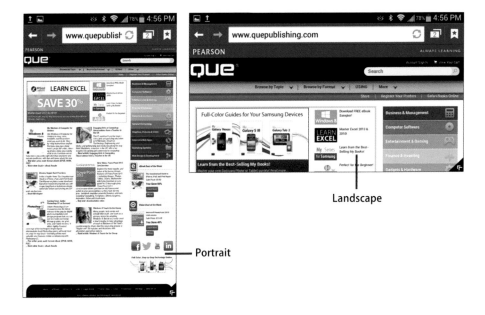

Landscape

Portrait

Scrolling the Page

Many pages don't fit entirely onscreen. To view parts that are off-screen, flick or drag up, down, right, or left, depending on the direction you want the page's material to scroll. If you want to take advantage of some new tricks, you can scroll by tilting your head up and down (*Smart Scroll*) or by waving your hand up and down over the sensor at the top of the phone (*Air Jump*).

- To activate Smart Scroll, open Settings, select My Device, tap Smart Screen, and enable Smart Scroll.

- To activate Air Jump, open Settings, select My Device, tap Motions and Gestures, enable and then tap Air Gesture, and enable Air Jump.

Magnification (Zoom)

You can increase the magnification of the current page to make it easier to read (*zoom in*) or reduce it to get a bird's-eye view of the entire page (*zoom out*).

- To *zoom in* (making everything on the page larger), put your thumb and forefinger on the page and spread them apart.

- To *zoom out* (making everything on the page smaller), put your thumb and forefinger on the page and pinch them together.

Zoomed in

Zoomed out

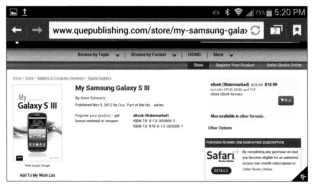

Zoom by Tapping, Tilting, or Almost Touching

You can quickly zoom in or out by double-tapping the screen. Repeat to reverse the zoom. If you've enabled Zoom (a Motion setting), you can place two fingertips on the screen and tilt it toward you to zoom in or away from you to zoom out. If Webpage Magnifier (an Air View setting) is enabled, you can create the effect of a magnifying glass by hovering your fingertip over text that you want to magnify.

- To activate Zoom, open Settings, select My Device, tap Motions and Gestures, enable and then tap Motion, and enable Zoom.

- To activate Web Page Magnifier, open Settings, select My Device, enable and then tap Air View, and enable Webpage Magnifier.

Refreshing the Page

If the current page didn't load correctly or you think the content might have changed while you were viewing it, you can refresh the page. Tap the Reload icon in the address box.

Reload

If a page is loading slowly, you can stop it by tapping the X icon in the address box.

Stop loading

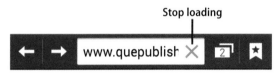

Working with Windows

The tabbed interface of current computer browsers enables you to keep several web pages open simultaneously and easily switch among them. The Internet app mimics this feature by enabling you to open multiple *windows*. Each window is the equivalent of a new browser and operates independently of other open windows.

- To create a new window, press the Menu key and tap New Window. You can also tap the Windows icon to the right of the address box and then tap the plus (+) icon in Window Manager. A window opens, displaying your home page.

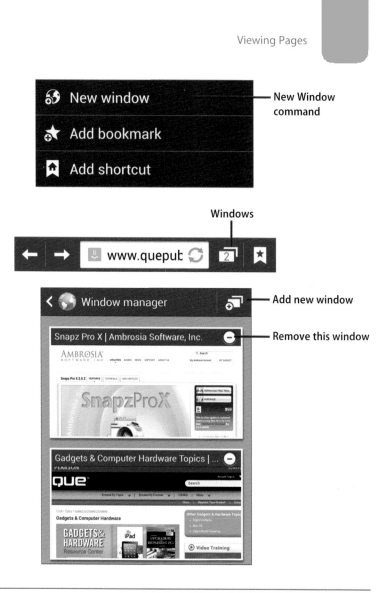

Another Way to Create a New Window

If you press and hold a site's name in Bookmarks or History, you can tap Open in New Window in the menu that appears. Doing so opens the website or page in a new window.

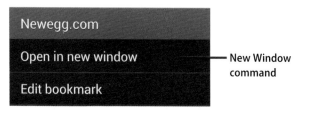

- To navigate among or manage the open windows, tap the Windows icon to open the Window Manager and then scroll up and down. To switch to one of the windows, tap its thumbnail. To remove a window that you no longer need, tap its minus (–) icon or swipe the window horizontally off the screen.

Page Navigation

As you replace the current page with new ones by entering new addresses, tapping links, and selecting bookmarks, you can tap icons to move through the stack of pages. To return to the previous page, tap the Back icon or press the Back key. You'll go back one page for each tap or key press. If you've gone back one or more pages, you can move forward through the stack by tapping the Forward icon.

Back   Forward

Incognito Browsing

The Internet app supports *incognito browsing* in which entries aren't recorded in History, searches aren't recorded, and cookies aren't stored. Rather than make this a general browser setting, Internet enables it only for pages loaded into a designated incognito window.

1. Tap the Windows icon at the top of any browser page.

2. In Window Manager, press the Menu key and tap New Incognito Window.

3. Review the text in the Incognito Mode dialog box, and tap OK to dismiss it.

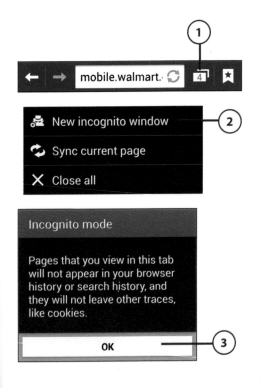

4. A new incognito window appears. Web activities performed in this window are secure; activities performed in *other* Internet windows are recorded normally.

Quickly Switching to Incognito Mode

In addition to creating a new window for incognito mode, you can initiate it in the page you're currently viewing by pressing the Menu key and tapping Incognito Mode.

Incognito icon

5. To restore normal browsing, open the Window Manager, find the incognito page, and delete it by tapping the minus (–) icon in its upper-right corner.

Which One Is the Incognito Window?

Although there's no visible indication that you're working in an incognito window, there are two ways to tell. First, press the Menu key. If Incognito Mode is grayed out, it's an incognito window. Second, when examined in Window Manager, an incognito window has a special icon in its upper-left corner.

Working with Bookmarks

As explained earlier in this chapter, *bookmarks* are stored addresses of websites and pages that you regularly visit. The purpose of creating a bookmark is to enable you to view the site or page again by simply tapping its entry in the Bookmarks grid or list rather than having to reenter the address.

Creating a Bookmark from the Current Page

It's common to decide to bookmark a page while you're viewing it.

1. Tap the star icon at the right of the address bar.

A Bookmark Shortcut

With the page that you want to bookmark onscreen, you can jump to step 3 by pressing the Menu key and tapping Add Bookmark.

2. Tap Add Bookmark.

3. Edit the bookmark name, if necessary.

4. Specify the folder in which to store the bookmark. By default, new bookmarks are stored in the Bookmarks folder.

Get Organized

If you've created other folders (see "Moving Bookmarks into Folders," later in this section), you can tap the arrow icon to select a subfolder in which to store the bookmark.

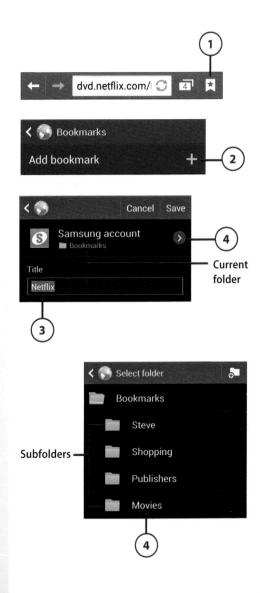

Current folder

Subfolders

5. Tap Save to store the new bookmark.

Folder

Bookmark title

Creating a Bookmark from the History List

If you've recently visited a page, the quickest way to add it as a new bookmark is to locate it in the History list.

1. With any web page onscreen, press the Menu key and tap History. (You may have to scroll the menu to find the History command.)

2. In the History list, locate the page that you want to bookmark. Press and hold the entry, and tap Add Bookmark.

3. Perform steps 3–5 from the previous task: editing the name, selecting a storage location, and saving the new bookmark.

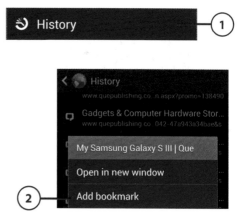

Folder

Bookmark title

Editing Bookmarks

You can edit a bookmark's title, its address (setting it for a site's main page or another specific page), or the folder in which it's stored.

1. In the Bookmarks list, find the bookmark that you want to edit.

2. Press and hold the bookmark until the menu appears, and tap Edit Bookmark.

Other Options
The same menu enables you to set the current bookmark as your home page, share it with a friend, create a desktop shortcut from it, or delete it.

3. In the Edit Bookmark dialog box, make the desired changes to the title, address, and/or folder, and then tap Save.

Editing the Address
Although you normally won't want to edit a page's address if it requires a lot of typing, it's relatively simple to change a page-specific URL to one that goes to a site's main page. In the example shown in step 3, I changed the reference from a promotions page to the site's main page by deleting the extraneous material to the right of http://m.newegg.com/.

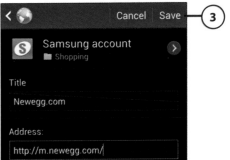

Using Bookmark Folders

After amassing more than a handful of bookmarks, you can optionally create additional folders in which to organize your bookmarks—rather than storing them all in Bookmarks, the main folder. When creating a new bookmark or editing an existing one, you can move it into the most appropriate folder.

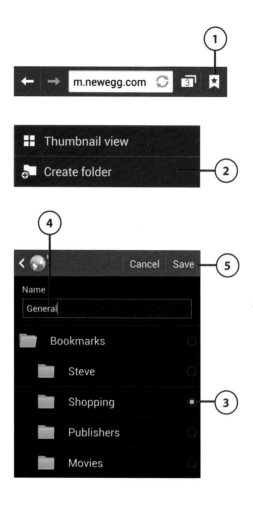

Creating a Bookmark Folder

1. Tap the star icon at the right of the address bar.

2. Press the Menu key and tap Create Folder.

3. Select a *parent* (containing) folder for the new folder.

4. Enter a name for the new folder.

5. Tap Save. The new folder is created within the selected folder and added to the Bookmarks list.

Moving Bookmarks into Folders

1. Tap the star icon at the right of the address bar.

2. Press the Menu key and tap Move to Folder.

3. As necessary, open folders to expose the bookmarks that you want to move. (Note that the bookmarks to be moved must all have the same destination folder.) Select each bookmark by tapping its check box (in List View) or its thumbnail (in Thumbnail View), and then tap Done.

4. Select the destination folder by tapping it. The selected bookmarks move into the folder.

Deleting Bookmarks

You can delete any bookmark that you no longer use.

1. Tap the star icon at the right of the address bar.

2. Expanding sections and opening folders as necessary, press and hold the bookmark that you want to delete.

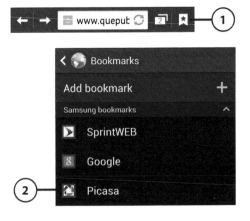

3. Tap Delete Bookmark in the menu that appears.

4. Confirm the deletion by tapping OK.

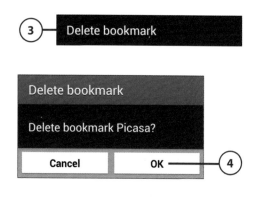

Deleting Multiple Bookmarks

When deleting a single bookmark, the method described in this task is very efficient. If you want to clean house, though, you can simultaneously delete as many bookmarks as you want.

With the Bookmarks list displayed, press the Menu key and tap Delete. Scroll through the bookmarks and tap the check box of each bookmark that you want to delete. (If necessary, you can open folders by tapping their names.) You can also delete an entire bookmark folder and its contents by selecting the folder. When you finish making selections, tap Delete. Deletions are *immediate*; no confirmation dialog box appears.

More Menu Commands

The main menu contains additional useful commands that haven't been discussed so far. Here's an explanation of what the remaining ones do.

1. With any web page displayed, press the Menu key to reveal the scrolling menu. Other than Saved Pages, History, Desktop View, Brightness, Settings, and Help (in the lower half of the menu), each command applies only to the current page.

2. *Homepage.* Display your home page in the current window.

3. *Add Shortcut.* Create a Home screen shortcut for the current page. When you tap the shortcut, the Internet app launches and displays the web page.

4. *Share Via.* Share the page with another person or device using a variety of methods.

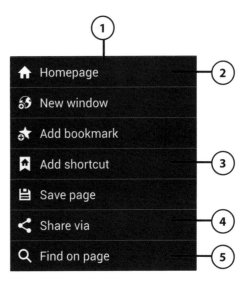

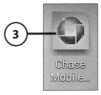

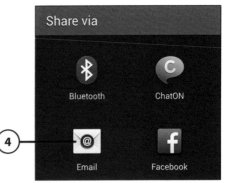

5. *Find on Page.* Search the current page for a text string. Each match (if any) is highlighted. To move between matches, tap an arrow key. The page scrolls as necessary to display each match.

6. *Saved Pages.* Displays the pages that you previously saved for later or offline reading using the Save Page command. Tap a page to open it. To manage a saved page, press and hold it, and then select a command from the menu that appears. To manage *all* saved pages, press the Menu key, and tap Delete or Sort By.

7. *Desktop View.* Display all pages as though they were being viewed in a desktop browser.

8. *Print.* Print the current page on a compatible Samsung Wi-Fi printer.

9. *Settings.* View and modify Internet app preferences (see "Configuring the Browser," in the next section).

10. *Help.* Get help using the Internet app.

Configuring the Browser

As is the case with a Mac or PC browser, you can configure the Internet app to match your preferred way of working and perform common browser actions, such as clearing the cache and managing cookies.

1. With any web page displayed, press the Menu key and tap Settings.

2. The Settings screen appears, divided into six categories:

   - *Set Homepage.* Specify a new home page.

   - *Auto Fill Forms.* Enable web form auto-fill.

   - *Privacy.* Remember form data and passwords; delete a variety of cached data types.

   - *Accessibility.* Zoom control and full-screen mode; text size and scaling.

   - *Content Settings.* Accept cookies; enable/disable location information access and JavaScript; block pop-ups; specify the default storage location; and reset browser settings to defaults.

   - *Bandwidth Management.* Preload pages; disable image downloads.

   To view or modify settings, tap a category, make the necessary changes, and press the Back key repeatedly until the browser screen reappears.

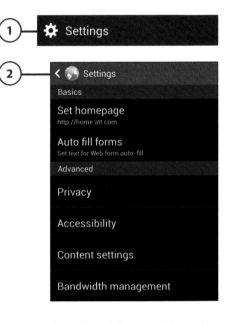

Delete selected data types (Privacy)

Select account or folder

Unread message
(light background)

Read message
(gray background)

Expand/collapse group

Favorite message

Compose
message

Refresh

In this chapter, you add important email accounts to the phone so that you can send and receive email and attachments. Topics include the following:

→ Adding and configuring email accounts
→ Automatically and manually checking for new email
→ Reading mail and working with attachments
→ Composing new messages, replying to messages, and forwarding messages
→ Adding attachments and inserting material into messages
→ Managing email

Sending and Receiving Email

You can easily configure your phone to send and receive mail for your POP3, IMAP, and Exchange Server email accounts. In addition, the Email app supports many web-based accounts—as long as they also provide POP, IMAP, or Exchange support. If you aren't sure what types of email accounts you can set up, contact your *Internet service provider* (*ISP*), call your information technology (IT) department, or review the Help information for your web-based accounts. (For information on creating and adding *Gmail accounts*, see Chapter 1.)

Adding Email Accounts

You can add accounts to your phone in two ways: automatically or manually.

Automatically Adding an Account

1. On the Home screen, tap the Email icon. (If the icon isn't present, you can tap Apps and then Email.)

Setting Up Your First Account in the Email App

If you haven't set up an account in the Email app, when you open the app, the Set Up Email screen automatically appears. Skip steps 2 and 3 and go to step 4.

2. On Email's main screen, press the Menu key and tap Settings.

3. Tap Add Account.

4. Enter your full email address and account password. If you have difficulty using the onscreen keyboard, tap the Show Password check box to ensure that you enter the password correctly.

5. *Optional:* If you want the phone to treat this as your main, default account from which email is normally sent, tap the Send Email from This Account by Default check box. This check box appears only when you set up a second or subsequent account; when you set up your first email account, Email assumes this account is the default and doesn't give you the choice.

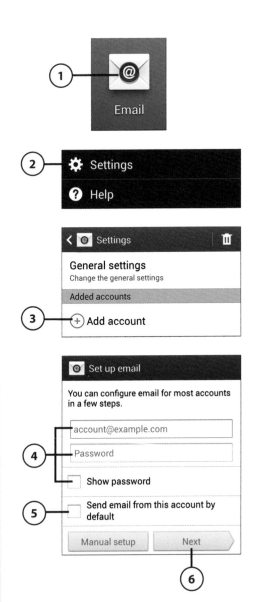

6. Tap the Next button.

7. Email attempts to verify the account and determine the correct Internet standard protocol to use: POP3, IMAP, or Exchange.

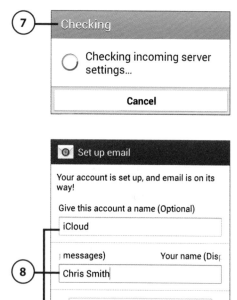

8. If successful, you're given an opportunity to name the account and specify the name that displays on outgoing mail from the account. Make any necessary changes and tap Done.

No Option to Set the Display Name

Certain account types, such as Hotmail, automatically take the display name from your current account information.

9. The account's Inbox appears, and email is downloaded to the account.

Try Manual Setup

Automatic setup can fail for a variety of reasons. If there's a problem, an error dialog appears. Tap the Edit Details or Continue button, check your username and password for errors, and try again. If automatic setup fails *repeatedly*, use the manual setup method described in the next task.

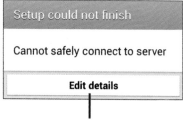

Edit Details button

Manually Adding an Account

1. Perform steps 1–5 of the previous task ("Automatically Adding an Account") and tap the Manual Setup button.

Continuing from Automatic Setup

If you just performed an automatic setup and it failed with an error in step 7, you can also begin a manual setup here.

2. On the Add Email Account screen, specify the Internet standard protocol for sending and receiving account email by tapping its button. If you aren't sure which protocols are supported, contact your ISP or IT department for the correct option(s).

Multiple Protocols

If your ISP supports multiple protocols—such as POP3 and IMAP—performing a manual setup is sometimes the only way to ensure that your preferred protocol is used.

3. Check the proposed settings on the Incoming Server Settings screen, and make any necessary changes. Tap the Next button.

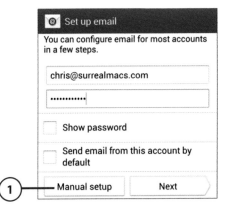

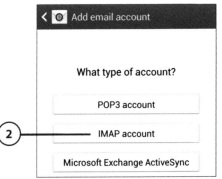

Entering Your Username

Depending on the account provider, the *username* may be the part of the name that precedes the @ symbol, or it may be the complete email address. If this step fails and an error dialog appears, tap the Edit Details button, enter the username the other way, and try again.

Delete Mail from Server (POP3 Only)

If you're adding a POP3 account, scroll to the bottom of the screen and you'll see a Delete Email from Server option. Normally, POP3 email is deleted from the mail server immediately after it's delivered. If this account is also on other devices, such as your computer or tablet, leave this option set to Never to ensure that the messages are also delivered to the other devices. If this is your *only* device, choose When I Delete from Inbox.

This option isn't available for IMAP accounts. Because IMAP is designed to synchronize across all your devices, if you delete an email message on *any* device, it's simultaneously deleted from all devices. Otherwise, the message remains on the server indefinitely.

4. The Outgoing Server Settings screen appears. Check the details, make any necessary changes, and tap Next.

5. On the Account Options screen, specify settings and tap Next.

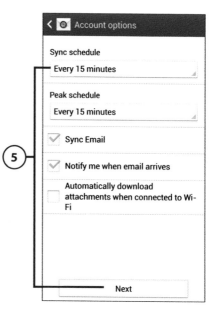

6. Name the account, and specify the name to display on outgoing mail from the account. Tap Done.

7. The account's Inbox appears, and email is downloaded to the account.

Set up email
Your account is set up, and email is on its way!
Give this account a name (Optional)
Work
Your name (Displayed on outgoing messag
Chris Smith
Done

6

It's Not All Good

TIPS FOR ADDING ACCOUNTS

Adding an email account doesn't always go smoothly. In my recent attempts, for example, success was sporadic. Here are some actions to take when adding an account fails:

- *Try, try again.* When using automatic setup, if you're certain that the username and password are correct, wait awhile and try again. Because of the vagaries of the Internet and the fact that mail servers aren't available 100% of the time, you may simply have been unlucky on the initial attempt—or three.

- *Switch to manual.* When repeated automatic attempts fail, it's time to switch to manual. If you try manual setup immediately after an automatic failure, much of the correct information is already filled in. Leave it as is, but try the username as the full email address and as only the username—with *@domain* stripped off. Some mail servers have specific requirements for the username and will accept it only in one form. (In automatic mode, you must use the full email address—even if only the username portion is all that's normally accepted.)

- *Contact your ISP or IT department.* When all else fails, contact your ISP or network administrator, find out the exact settings needed, and—in manual mode—override the proffered settings with the ones you're given.

Configuring Email Accounts

With the exception of General Settings, the settings for each email account can differ. After adding each email account, check its settings to ensure that the default choices are satisfactory. (To view or change the General Settings, display any message list, press the Menu key, tap Settings, and then tap General Settings.)

Editing Account Settings

You can change a variety of settings to ensure that your messages are retrieved on a reasonable schedule, display proper identifying information, and so on. Note that an Exchange ActiveSync account (such as a Hotmail or a corporate Exchange Server account) has some additional options that aren't available for POP or IMAP accounts.

1. Within Email, press the Menu key and tap Settings.

2. The Settings screen appears. Tap the account whose settings you want to review or change.

3. *Email Notifications.* Select this check box if you want an email icon to appear in the status bar whenever new mail arrives.

4. *Select Ringtone.* Change the notification sound that plays when new mail arrives. In the Select Ringtone dialog box, tap a ringtone to hear it. When you've made your selection, tap OK.

No Ringtone

Select Silent if you don't want an audible notification of new mail.

5. *Vibrate.* Select this check box if you want the phone to vibrate when it receives mail.

6. *Sync Email.* Select this check box to instruct Email to sync this account using the schedules specified in Sync Schedule.

7. *Sync Schedule.* Tap to display the Sync Schedule screen, on which you can specify how often the phone automatically checks for new, incoming email to this account.

8. *Set Sync Schedule.* Tap to display the Set Sync Schedule dialog box, and select a frequency with which to sync the account's email. Your choices are Never or a specifiic interval, such as Every 5 Minutes or Once a Day.

9. *While Roaming.* To control how your phone syncs email when you roam on other networks, tap While Roaming and choose Manual or Use Above Settings.

10. *Peak Schedule.* To sync email on a different schedule during peak hours, select this check box. You can then tap Set Peak Schedule and select a frequency. Tap the Peak Days buttons to apply or remove the green bars that indicate peak days. Tap Peak Start Time and Peak End Time to set the start and end times for the peak days.

11. Tap the Back icon or press the Back key to return to the Settings screen for the email account.

12. *Size to Retrieve Emails.* To avoid data charges when out of range of a Wi-Fi network, you can specify the maximum size message that will automatically be delivered to the phone. Larger messages—primarily those with attachments—must be manually retrieved by tapping the message header.

Size to retrieve emails ⊘	⟵(12)
All including attachments	
Common settings	
Signature ON	⟵(13)
Sent from my Sprint phone	
Default account ✓	⟵(14)
Send email from this account by default	
More settings	⟵(15)

13. *Signature.* To automatically add a personal *signature* (static text) to the end of each outgoing message, set the Signature switch to the On position. To change the signature, tap Signature, edit the current signature, and tap OK.

14. *Default Account.* If you have multiple email accounts on the phone, you must enable Default Account for one of them. When composing a new email message, Email uses the default account automatically as the sending account—although you're always free to choose a different account before sending. (When replying to or forwarding a message, Email uses the *current* account instead of the default account.)

15. Tap More Settings to review or change the important account settings explained in steps 16–23.

16. *Account Name.* To change the name used to label the account in Email's account list, tap Account Name, make the necessary changes, and tap OK.

17. *Your Name.* To change the name used to identify you to recipients of your email, tap Your Name, make the desired changes, and tap OK.

< ☺ More settings

Common settings

Account name
Home Email ⊙ —⑯

Your name
Chris Smith ⊙ —⑰

Always Cc/Bcc myself
Include my email address in Cc/Bcc line ⊙ —⑱

Forward with attachments ☑ —⑲

18. *Always Cc/Bcc Myself.* Specify whether outgoing messages automatically include this account in the *CC* (carbon copy) or *BCC* (blind carbon copy) recipient list. The purpose is to ensure that a backup copy of each outgoing message from this account is also delivered to the account's Inbox. If your email account automatically keeps a copy of each outgoing message in a folder called Sent (or a similar name), choose None for this setting.

19. *Forward with Attachments.* Check this option if you want to forward received email with any attachments that the original message contained; otherwise, only the message body is forwarded.

20. *Show Images.* Check this option to automatically display all linked images that are present in messages. As explained later in "Show Images Judiciously," it's best to leave this option unchecked.

21. *Number of Emails to Load.* Tap to set the number of recent messages to be shown at one time. You can specify from 25 to Total (all).

22. *Auto Download Attachments.* Check this option to instruct Email to automatically download attachments when your phone is connected to a Wi-Fi network (in other words, not over your cellular connection). This is usually a good choice unless you receive many massive attachments, in which case you may prefer to download them manually as needed.

23. *Auto Resend Times.* Tap this option to specify the number of times Email tries to resend a message on encountering an error.

24. *Security Options.* If you need to encrypt the messages you send, sign them with a digital signature, or both, tap Security Options. You are more likely to need these options for corporate email than for personal email.

25. In the Server Settings section at the bottom of the More Settings screen, tap Incoming Settings or Outgoing Settings to modify the settings for the incoming or outgoing mail server (described in "Adding Email Accounts," earlier in this chapter).

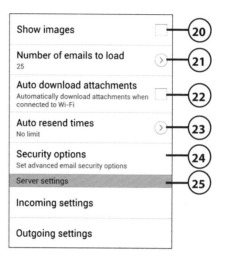

SHOW IMAGES JUDICIOUSLY

>>>Go Further

If you shop on the Internet, you probably receive sales fliers from sites such as Amazon.com, Newegg, and JC Penny. To make these messages smaller, they frequently contain *links to images on the web* rather than the actual images. To automatically see the images, you must enable Show Images in step 20.

Unfortunately, spammers also include linked images in their emails. If you display them in a spam message, the image is retrieved by Email—simultaneously verifying to the spammer that your email address is a real, active one. *Loads* of spam is liable to follow. The safest approach is to disable Show Images. To view linked images in a trusted, *safe* message, tap the Show Images button that appears directly under the message header. Another option for trusted messages—if the message provides it—is to click a link to view the message in your phone's browser (Internet or Chrome).

Download and display linked images

Deleting an Account

You can delete any email account that you no longer want on your phone. Deleting an account simultaneously removes the account's messages and other data from your phone. (Note that deleting an account merely removes it from the phone; it doesn't *cancel* the account.)

1. Within Email, press the Menu key and tap Settings.

2. The Settings screen appears and displays your list of email accounts. Tap the trash icon at the top of the screen.

3. Tap the check box of each account that you want to remove from the phone, and then tap the Delete button.

4. Tap the OK button in the Delete confirmation dialog box.

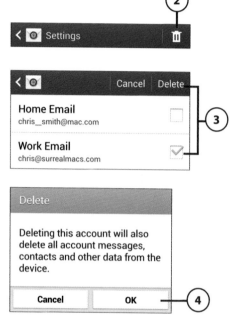

Retrieving Mail

Email can be delivered to your phone in two ways. First, the Email app performs a check for new mail automatically for each account according to the account's Sync Schedule settings—every 15 minutes or once per hour, for example. For information on setting a retrieval schedule for an account, see step 7 of "Editing Account Settings." Second, you can manually check for new mail whenever you like—regardless of an account's schedule—by tapping the Refresh icon.

1. Launch Email by tapping its Home screen icon or by tapping Apps, followed by Email.

2. If you need to switch to a different Inbox or folder, tap the menu icon to display the accounts list.

3. Tap the Inbox or folder you want to view. Tap Combined Inbox if you want to check all your accounts at once.

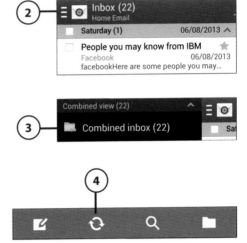

Interpreting the Accounts Information

If present, the number to the right of an account in the list indicates the number of unread messages it contains. By scanning the list, you can quickly determine which accounts have new messages.

4. To check for new messages, tap the Refresh icon at the bottom of the screen.

Reading Mail

When new mail arrives or you want to review older messages, you can read the email on your phone. You can read messages in portrait mode or—by rotating the phone—in land-scape mode.

1. Launch Email by tapping its Home screen icon or by tapping Apps and then Email.

Number of unread messages

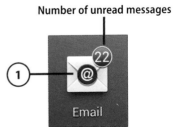

Other Ways to Launch Email

You can also open Email by responding to a received mail notification or tapping a message header in the Email widget:

- Open the Notification panel by dragging downward. Tap the Email notification.

- If you've installed the Email widget on a Home screen page, tap a message header to open that message in Email.

Email notification

2. *Optional:* To change the Inbox or folder displayed, tap the menu icon and make a new selection. Select Combined View to simultaneously view all accounts' Inboxes, select a specific account to view only its Inbox, or select Show All Folders to view a different folder within the current account or selection.

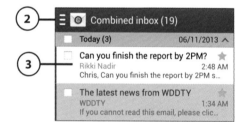

3. In the current message list, tap the header of the message that you want to read. Headers with light backgrounds are unread messages; headers with gray backgrounds are previously read messages.

4. The message appears. You can change the magnification by pinching your fingers together or spreading them apart. Drag to see parts of the message that are off-screen. Alternatively, you can rotate your phone to view the message in landscape mode.

5. To read another message in the current list, do either of the following:

   - Tap the Back icon or press the Back key to return to the message list. Tap the header of the next message that you want to read.

   - Swipe the screen to the left or right to view the next or previous consecutive message in the list, respectively.

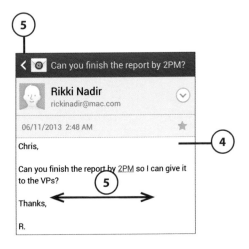

Viewing and Saving Attachments

Some email messages contain *attachments* (accompanying files), such as photos and documents. If you want, you can download the attachments and—if you have compatible app(s)—view the files on your phone.

1. In the Email message list, files that contain attachments are denoted by a paper clip icon. Tap the message header to open the message.

2. Tap the Attachments tab to view the list of attached files.

3. To preview an attachment, tap its Preview button. Your phone downloads the file and, if a compatible app is installed, displays or plays the file's contents.

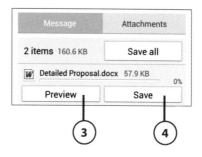

4. *Optional*: To save a copy of the file on your phone, tap its Save button. To save all the attachments, tap the Save All button. The file or files are stored in the Download folder of the phone's built-in memory.

Revisiting a Downloaded Attachment

To later view a downloaded attachment, launch My Files, open the Download folder, and tap the filename. If it's an image file, you can also open it by launching Gallery, opening the Download folder, and tapping the file's thumbnail. You can also open attachments by launching the Downloads app.

Folder location (path)

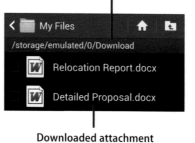

Downloaded attachment

>>>Go Further

STANDARD VS. CONVERSATION VIEW

To more easily find messages, you can configure the message list in either of two views: standard or conversation. To select a view, press the Menu key and tap View Mode. In standard view, each message, reply, and forwarded message is shown with a separate message header, and the messages are organized in groups, such as Date or Sender. You can collapse or expand the headers for any group by tapping the icon to the right of the group designator. In addition, you can sort standard view in several other ways, such as by sender or read/unread status. Press the Menu key and tap Sort By to set a new sort order.

In conversation view, messages are grouped by conversation, according to their Subject. For example, suppose that you and a co-worker exchange several messages with the subject Budget Proposal. In the Inbox, all received messages with the subject Budget Proposal and RE: Budget Proposal are grouped under a single expandable message header.

Although helpful, conversation view falls short when compared to its implementation in Microsoft Outlook and other email clients. Although conversation view groups together messages *from* the same person (in the Inbox) or *to* the same person (in Sent), you can see only one side of a conversation. To view the entire conversation, you have to switch back and forth between the account's Inbox and Sent folders.

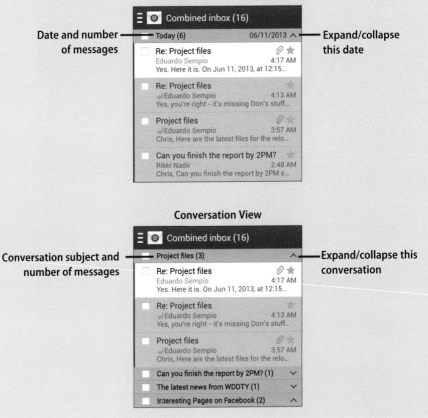

Standard View (grouped by date)

Date and number of messages — Expand/collapse this date

Conversation View

Conversation subject and number of messages — Expand/collapse this conversation

Composing and Sending Mail

Within Email, you can create new messages, as well as reply to or forward received messages.

Creating a New Email Message

1. In Email, display the message list for Combined Inbox or a specific account, and then tap the Create Message icon at the bottom of the screen.

2. A new message screen appears, addressed from the current account. (If you're viewing the Combined Inbox message list, your default email account is proposed instead.)

3. *Optional:* To send the message from a different account, tap the account name in the From box. In the Select Email Address dialog box, select the account from which the message will be sent.

4. *Optional:* Tap the Cc/Bcc area to display separate *Cc* (carbon copy) and *Bcc* (blind carbon copy) boxes.

5. Tap the To, Cc, or Bcc box, and add one or more recipients by doing the following:

   - To select recipients from Contacts, tap the Contacts icon to the right of the To, Cc, or Bcc box. Select each person that you want to add and then tap Done. (If there are multiple email addresses for a person and you haven't specified a

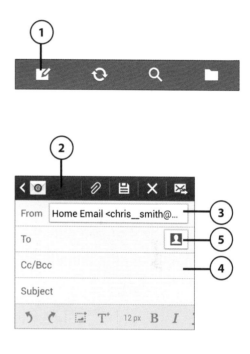

default address for her, a dialog box appears in which you can choose the appropriate address.)

Filter the Contacts

In addition to selecting people from the normal Contacts list, you can select people from any of the other lists (Groups, Favorites, or Logs) by tapping the appropriate tab at the top of the screen.

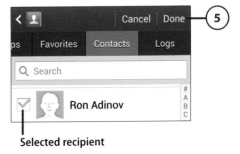

Selected recipient

- Select the To, Cc, or Bcc box, and begin typing part of the recipient's name, email address, or other identifying information stored in the person or company's contact record. Select the recipient from the match list that appears.

6. Enter the message subject in the Subject box.

7. Type or use voice input to enter the message body.

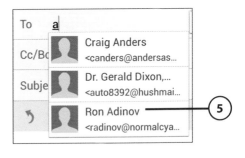

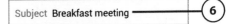

Be Gone Plain Text!

While composing the message, you can tap icons in the toolbar to format selected text, insert material, and assist in editing or making corrections. The icons' functions are similar to those in a typical word-processing application. You can use Undo and Redo to correct errors and typos, insert boilerplate text and other material into the message body, and format currently selected text by changing its size, color, highlighting, or style. Read "Entering Text" and "Editing Text" in Chapter 2 for additional helpful information.

8. Tap the Send icon to transmit the message.

Attachments and Inserts

An email message can optionally include embedded material or be accompanied by attached files. For instructions, see "Adding Attachments and Inserts," later in this section.

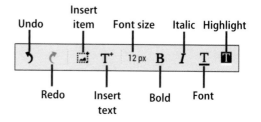

Undo   Insert item   Font size   Italic   Highlight   Redo   Insert text   Bold   Font

Replying to Mail

1. With the email message open for reading, tap the Reply icon.

2. A message appears, formatted as a reply to the original sender. The text insertion mark is positioned for your reply. The original message text displays at the bottom of the window.

3. Enter your reply text in the top section of the message window.

4. If desired, you can edit the original message text, or you can delete it by clearing the check box in the Original Message bar.

5. Tap the Send icon to send the message.

From   Home Email <chris_smith@...

To   Rikki Nadir

Cc/Bcc

Subject   RE: Can you finish the report by

Yes, I'll get it to you by then.

Original message

Chris,

Can you finish the report by 2PM so I can give it to the VPs?

Forwarding Mail

1. With the email message open for reading, tap the Forward icon.

2. A message formatted for forwarding appears. Specify recipients in the To, Cc, and/or Bcc boxes, as described in "Creating a New Email Message."

3. You can optionally add your own text to a forwarded message. Enter it in the top section of the message window. (You can trim or edit the original message text in the bottom section of the window, if desired, or remove it by clearing the check box in the Original Message bar.)

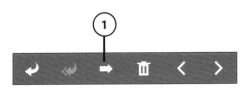

Original Message Attachments

Whether attachments received in the original message are also forwarded depends on the Forward with Attachments setting. If you notice that the original attachments aren't automatically added to forwarded messages, see step 19 in "Editing Account Settings."

4. Tap the Send icon to send the message.

Adding Attachments and Inserts

Any message sent from Email—whether a new message, reply, or forward—can optionally include one or more file attachments, such as photos and Office documents. The
recipient uses a compatible program or app to open and view the attachments. (The
maximum size for a message and attachments created in Email is 50MB. Note, however,
that the recipient's email account may have a size limit for incoming messages that is
smaller than this.)

In addition to sending file attachments with a message, you can insert any of the following directly into the body of a message: an image file from Gallery, selected text from a
Contacts record, a location, or a Calendar event.

Adding Attachments

1. Create a new message, a reply, or
   a forward, as described earlier in
   this section.

2. At any point during the message-
   creation process, tap the Attach
   icon.

3. Choose the type of item that you
   want to attach. (Choose My Files
   to select any file that's stored on
   your phone or choose a specific
   item type.)

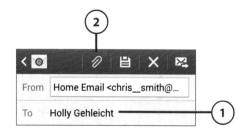

**Create an Attachment
On-the-Fly**
You can choose Take Picture,
Record Video, or Record Audio to
use the phone to create a photo,
video, or audio recording to send
as an attachment.

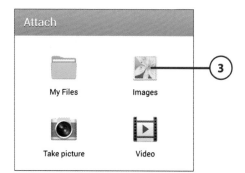

4. Select the particular file that you want to attach to the message, and respond to any dialog boxes or menus that appear. When sending a picture, for example, you can specify a resizing percentage.

5. To add other attachments, repeat steps 2–4. To remove an attachment, expand the attachments list and tap the red minus (–) sign to the right of the item.

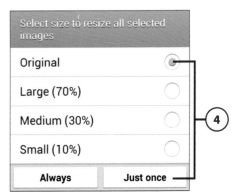

Expand/collapse attachment list

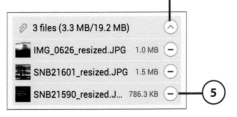

Adding Inserts

1. In the message you're composing, position the text insertion mark at the spot in the message body where you want to insert the item.

2. Tap the Insert icon in the toolbar.

3. Choose an item type to insert. Options include an image from Gallery, an S Memo, Calendar events, selected elements of a Contacts record (such as an email address), and a physical location/address.

4. The image or text appears in the message body at the text insertion mark.

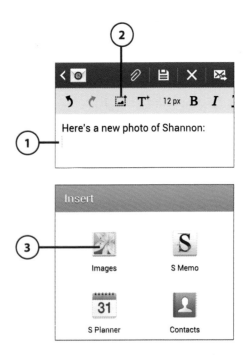

Resizing Inserted Images

You can change the size of an inserted photo by tapping it and then dragging one or more of the handles that appear around its edges. To resize proportionately, drag any corner handle.

Here's a new photo of Shannon:

4

Resize proportionately

Managing the Mail

Although the Email app has fewer message-management options than a typical PC or Mac email client, you can manage message list clutter by deleting unwanted messages, moving messages to different folders, changing the status of messages from read to unread (and vice versa), and flagging important messages.

Deleting Messages

You can delete messages while you're viewing a message list or reading a particular message:

- While reading a message, tap the Delete icon at the bottom of the screen, and then tap Delete in the confirmation dialog box.

Delete icon

- You can simultaneously delete multiple messages while viewing a message list. Tap the check box to the left of each message that you

want to delete, tap the Delete icon at the bottom of the screen, and then tap Delete in the confirmation dialog box.

Selected messages

Delete icon

Delete a Message Group or Conversation

In *standard view*, you can select an entire group of messages for deletion (such as all messages for a particular day or from a particular sender) by selecting the check box at the left end of the blue group header above the messages. In *conversation view*, you can select all messages in a conversation for deletion by selecting the check box in the conversation header.

To delete the selected messages, tap the Delete icon and then tap Delete in the confirmation dialog box.

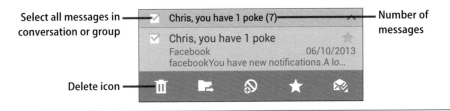

Select all messages in conversation or group

Number of messages

Delete icon

- While viewing a message list, you can simultaneously delete all messages in the current folder (an account's Inbox or Junk folder, for example). Press the Menu key, tap Delete All, and then tap the Delete button in the confirmation dialog box that appears. (Not all carriers support the Delete All command.)

Delete all messages in the current view

Moving Messages

You can move an email message to a different folder in the current account, as well as to a folder in another account. For example, you may be able to move a message from the Trash back into the Inbox or a project-related message into a project folder. You can move messages while you're viewing a message list or reading the message.

While Reading a Message

1. Press the Menu key and tap Move.

2. In the Move To dialog box, select a destination folder in the current account or a different account.

While Viewing a Message List

1. Select each message that you want to move to a particular destination folder. (Each selected message is preceded by a green check mark.)

2. Tap the Move icon below the message list. (Note that the position of the icon varies.)

3. In the Move To dialog box, select a destination folder in the current account or a different account (as described in step 2 of the preceding task).

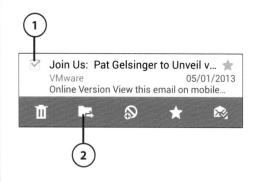

Creating Account Subfolders

Although custom account folders are typically created in your Mac/PC email application or, for web-based clients such as Hotmail, using your browser, you can also create them in Email. Tap the menu icon at the upper-left corner of a message list to display the list of accounts and folders, and then tap Show All Folders for the account in which you want to create the folder. (Don't tap Show All Folders in the Combined View section—you can't create folders from there.) Tap the plus (+) icon at the top of the screen, select a *parent folder* in which to create the new folder, name the folder, and tap OK.

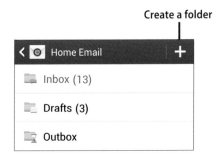

Create a folder

Changing the Message Read Status

Sometimes it's useful to change a previously read message's status to unread or a new message to read. For example, if you've fallen behind in reading incoming messages from an account, you can mark the unimportant ones as already read.

- While reading a message, you can mark it as unread by pressing the Menu key and tapping Mark as Unread in the pop-up menu that appears. The message list immediately reappears, and the message shows that it hasn't been read.

- While viewing the message list, you can toggle the read status of multiple messages by tapping the check box of each message of the same kind (read or unread), and then tapping the Mark as Read or Mark as Unread icon at the bottom of the window.

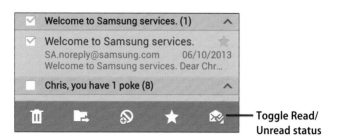

Toggle Read/
Unread status

Marking Important Messages

If you'd like to mark certain messages as important, you can designate them as *favorites* (POP3 and IMAP accounts) or *flag* them (Exchange Server/ ActiveSync accounts).

- *Favorite messages.* In a message list or while reading the message, tap the star icon to the right of the message subject. To remove the star from a previously marked favorite, tap the star icon again.

Favorite

Marking Multiple Messages as Favorites

While viewing the message list, you can simultaneously mark *multiple* messages as favorites. Tap the check box in each message header that you want to mark as a favorite. Then tap the star icon at the bottom of the screen. You can remove stars in the same fashion—select several starred headers and tap the hollow star icon at the bottom of the screen.

Selected
message

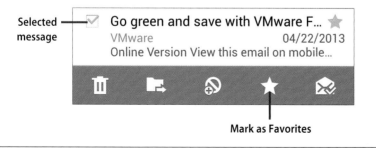

Mark as Favorites

- *Flagged messages.* In an Exchange ActiveSync message list or when viewing one of its messages, tap the flag icon to the right of the message header. The icon works as a toggle. Tap it to cycle between flagged (red flag), completed (blue check mark), and cleared (blank). When viewing a message list, you can simultaneously change the flag status of multiple messages by selecting each header, tapping the Flag icon at the bottom of the screen, and choosing Flag, Unflag, or Mark as Complete from the menu that appears.

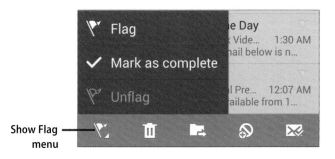

Show Flag menu

Using the Gmail App

In addition to the Email app, your phone includes a dedicated Gmail app—designed to access Google's Gmail service only. The Gmail app shares many similarities with Email, but also has some key differences. (For the sake of convenience, however, you might prefer to simply add your Gmail account to the Email app.)

When you first set up your phone, the setup wizard walks you through the process of adding your Gmail account—so the Gmail app is ready to run. To launch Gmail, go to the Home screen, tap Apps, and then Gmail. Following are some general and account-specific settings that you'll want to review when configuring and using the app:

- *Add another Gmail account.* If you have multiple Gmail accounts, you can add the others, specify the default account, and switch among them as needed. To add an account, press the Menu key, tap Settings, and then tap Add Account.

Configure General Settings — General settings

Add another Gmail account — ADD ACCOUNT

Gmail account — chrissmth013@gmail.com

- *Configure general settings for your accounts.* Gmail works well with the default settings, but you can get better results by spending a few minutes choosing settings that suit your needs. Press the Menu key, tap Settings, and then tap General Settings.

Opt to delete messages, archive messages, or both — Archive & delete actions

Clear this check box — Reply all

Require confirmation for message deletions — Confirm before deleting

- *Configure account-specific settings.* After tapping Settings, select an account name. You can configure sound and vibration notifications, specify a signature, and set the number of days of mail to sync.

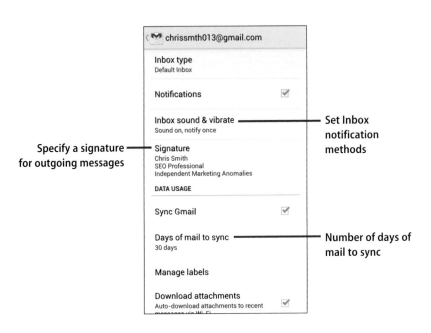

Specify a signature for outgoing messages — Signature

Set Inbox notification methods

Number of days of mail to sync

- *Organize your messages with labels.* Whereas most email services use folders to store messages, Gmail uses a system of *labels*—tags you can apply to messages to categorize them. To apply a label to an open message, tap the Menu key, tab Change labels, select the label(s) you want to apply, and tap OK.

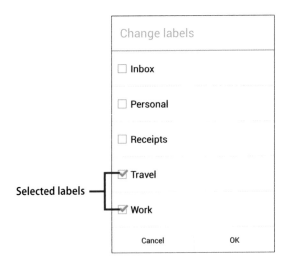

Selected labels

- *View your messages by labels.* In the Inbox message list, tap the upper-left icon to display the list of Inboxes and labels—or carefully swipe the list in from the left edge of the screen. Then tap the label whose messages you want to view.

Display the list of ——— Inboxes and labels

Tap a label to ——— display its messages

✉ Inbox	
chrissmth013@gmail.com	
INBOX	Jun 8
Inbox	20
Priority Inbox	2	Jun 8
ALL LABELS	Jun 5
Starred	3
Important	6	May 29
Chats	
Sent	May 22
Outbox	May 19
Drafts	2
All mail	20	May 6
Spam	May 1

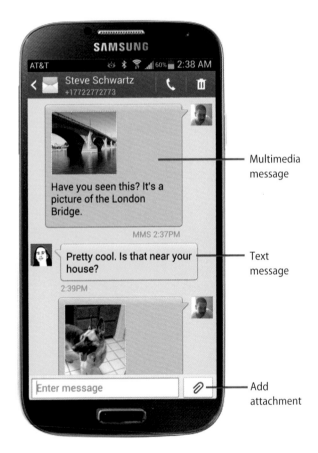

Multimedia
message

Text
message

Add
attachment

In this chapter, you explore the fine points of texting with the Messaging app, using Flipboard to stay current with your favorite social networking sites, and participating in chat sessions. Topics include the following:

→ Sending and receiving text and multimedia messages, managing conversations, and configuring Messaging
→ Using Flipboard to keep up with news, entertainment, and social networking friends and colleagues
→ Using imo and ChatON to participate in chat sessions

Messaging, Chatting, and Socializing

After mastering the calling features of the Galaxy S 4, many users want to explore the world of *texting*—the exchange of short text and multimedia messages. Compared to a phone call, texting is equally immediate but considerably briefer and less intrusive. This chapter also introduces you to Flipboard, so you can stay up to date with what's happening in your favorite social networking sites, and—if you're so inclined—to connect with friends on popular chat services.

Text and Multimedia Messaging

Phone calls can be time-consuming and, depending on the caller's timing, intrusive. To get a quick message to a friend or colleague, you can *text* that person by sending a text or multimedia message. A message exchange between you and another person is called a *conversation* or *thread*. The messaging process is similar to what you're probably familiar with from Yahoo! Messenger, Microsoft Messenger, iChat, or Google Talk online chats. Either party can start a conversation. After the conversation is initiated, it can progress in a back-and-forth manner with each person's contributions shown in colored balloons.

Two types of messages can be exchanged: *Short Message Service* (*SMS*) text messages and *Multimedia Messaging Service* (*MMS*) messages to which you've attached a photo, video or audio clip, or similar item. Although text messages are normally exchanged between mobile phones, your service may also allow you to text to an email account or landline.

Texting is strikingly similar to emailing. You specify recipients, compose the message text, and—optionally—add attachments. The main differences are that texting generally occurs between mobile phones, the messages must be short (160 characters or less), and a subject is optional rather than the norm.

You can use the Messaging app to create both text (SMS) and multimedia (MMS) messages. When creating a message, what distinguishes a text message from a multimedia message is that the latter contains an attachment, such as a photo or video clip.

Some Differences Among Carriers

Different carriers have slightly different messaging features, determined by their implementation of text and multimedia messaging. For instance, although Sprint can receive attached contact info from AT&T users, the reverse isn't true. Similarly, Settings options depend on your carrier, too. As a result, not all the information in this section will apply to all users, and you may find that a few options and procedures available to you aren't discussed.

Composing a Text Message (SMS)

A text message can contain only text and is limited to 160 characters. If a message is longer, it is transmitted as multiple messages but recombined on the recipient's screen.

1. Tap the Messaging icon at the bottom of the Home screen. (If you've removed the Messaging shortcut, tap Apps and then tap Messaging.)

2. A screen showing all ongoing conversations appears. Tap the Compose Message icon.

3. A message can have one or multiple recipients. To choose recipients from your stored contacts, tap the Contacts icon. (If you know that the recipient doesn't have a Contacts record, type the person's mobile phone number in the Enter Recipient box and skip to step 7.)

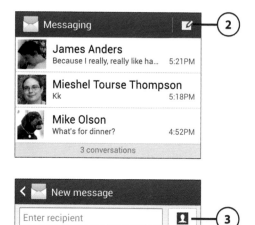

Adding Recipients by Typing

Another method of adding recipients is to type part of the person's contact record (such as a name, number, or email address) in the Enter Recipient box and select the correct entry from the match list.

Finding Recipients in Contacts

To find someone in Contacts, you can scroll through the list by flicking up or down, go directly to an alphabetical section of the list by tapping its index letter, or drag down or up in the index letters and release your finger when the first letter of the person's name displays.

You can also filter the list to show only certain people. To view people with whom you've recently spoken or messaged, tap the Logs tab. Tap the Favorites tab to restrict the list to contacts you've marked as *favorites*. To search for a person, type part of the name, email address, or phone number in the Search box; press the Back key to view the results; and tap the person's check box.

4. Select a recipient from the list by tapping the person's check box.

5. If the selected contact has only one phone number or you've set a default number for him, that phone number is automatically used. Otherwise, a screen appears that lists the person's numbers and email addresses. Tap the number to which you want to send the message. The contact list reappears and the person's name is checked as a recipient.

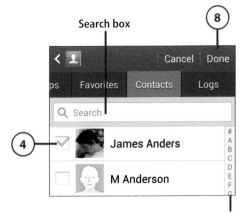

Search box

Index letters

Limited or Default Contact Info

If the selected record has only one piece of usable contact information (a single phone number or an email address) or you've set a default number for the person, Messaging assumes that's where you want to send the message. In that case, no selection screen appears and the person's record is automatically checked. Before sending the message, you may want to open the Contacts app and ensure that the person's record contains a mobile phone number.

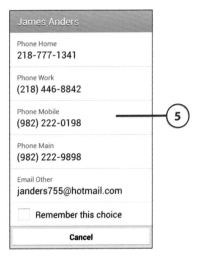

6. To add other recipients, select them from the contact list as you did in steps 4 and 5.

7. *Optional:* To remove a recipient, tap the Enter Recipient box to show all current recipients. Tap the recipient that you want to remove, and then tap Remove. Similarly, you can modify the person's phone number or email address by tapping Edit.

8. When you finish, tap Done to create the recipient list. The message screen reappears.

9. Enter your message in the large text box. You can type the message or tap the microphone key to dictate your message. (If the microphone isn't shown on the key, press and hold the key, and *then* select the microphone.) As you type or dictate, the number of remaining characters is shown above the Send button.

Adding a Subject

Unlike email messages, text messages generally don't have a Subject. If you'd like to add one, ensure that the Enter Message box is active, press the Menu key, and tap Add Subject.

Inserting Smileys

If you like to insert a *smiley* (also called an *emoticon*) into a message you're creating, press the Menu key, tap Insert Smiley, and select the smiley that you want to insert. The smiley appears at the text insertion mark.

10. *Optional:* To insert a location, contact record, memo, calendar item, or a stock phrase into the message, press the Menu key, tap Add Text, and select an option.

11. Tap the Send button to transmit the message.

Saving a Message as a Draft

If you aren't ready to send the message, you can save it as a draft by pressing the Back key. To later open the message, select it in the conversation list. You can then edit, send, or delete it.

Recipient(s)

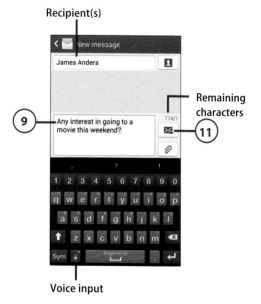

Remaining characters

Voice input

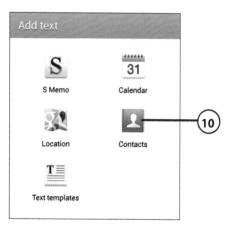

Draft

>>>Go Further

LAZY MESSAGING

All messages aren't creative, novel thoughts. If you text frequently, many of your messages are short, simple phrases that you use regularly, such as "When will you be home?", "Where are you?", or "Can't talk now. I'm in a meeting." Rather than laboriously type such messages whenever one's needed, you can pick it from a list. Press the Menu key, tap Add Text, tap Text Templates, and select the phrase you want to send from the scrolling list.

Note that many phrases aren't complete; they're the *beginnings* of messages that you must complete, such as "Don't forget to…", "Meet me at…", and "I'll be there at…" In addition, these phrases don't have to be the sole message content. When you select a phrase, it's inserted at the text insertion mark—so it can be added to the beginning, middle, or end of a message.

To modify the Text Templates phrases, go to the main Messaging screen, press the Menu key, tap Settings, and tap Text Templates. You can do any of the following:

- To delete unwanted phrases, tap the Trash icon, select the phrases that you want to delete, and tap Done.

- To add a new phrase, tap the + (plus) icon, enter the phrase, and tap Save.

- To edit or delete a phrase, press and hold the phrase, and tap Edit or Delete in the menu that appears. Tap Save when you finish editing or tap OK to confirm the deletion, respectively.

Text templates

Text templates
Can't talk right now. Send…
Call me.
Where are you?

Add **Delete**

‹ ✉ Text templates	+	🗑
Can't talk right now. Send me a m…
Call me.

Selected phrase

Tag, you're it!
Edit
Delete

>>>Go Further

MORE WAYS TO START A CONVERSATION

Choosing a contact record is only one of the ways to start a texting conversation. Others include these:

- Immediately after completing a call, you can begin a conversation with the person by tapping the envelope icon.

- To text someone to whom you've recently spoken, open the call log by tapping Phone on the Home screen and then tapping the Logs tab. Find the person in the log and then swipe the entry to the left. You can use this swipe technique in Contacts and Favorites, too. (You can also swipe to the right to initiate a phone call to the person.)

- Open Contacts, select the person's record, and then tap the envelope icon to the right of the mobile phone number.

- You can also send a message to a *group* you've defined (see "Working with Contact Groups" in Chapter 5). Launch Contacts, tap the Groups tab, press and hold the group name, and tap Send Message. Select the group members that you want to message and tap Done.

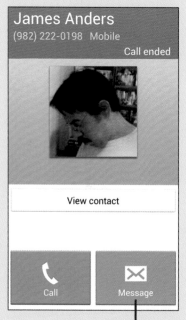

Send message

MORE MESSAGE-COMPOSITION OPTIONS

>>>Go Further

Although somewhat unusual, the following composition options can sometimes be very useful:

- *Embedded links in messages.* If a message contains a web address, email address, or phone number displayed as underlined text, the recipient can tap the text and choose Open URL, Send Email, or Call to visit the page using the phone's browser, address a new email message to the person, or dial the phone number, respectively.

- *Texting to email or a landline.* If a recipient doesn't have a mobile phone, you can send text messages to an email address. Some carriers, such as Sprint, even allow you to send texts to a landline phone. Create the message as you normally would, but specify an email address or landline number in the Enter Recipient box. As appropriate, the text message is emailed, or the service calls the landline and a computer voice reads the text when the phone is answered. (Emoticons are read, too!)

- *Schedule a message.* Rather than send a message immediately, you can set a date and time at which it will be delivered. (The scheduled time must be at least 6 minutes in advance.) Prior to tapping the Send button, press the Menu key, and tap Scheduled Message. Set a date and time for delivery, tap OK, and tap the Send button. A copy of the message (in gray) with the scheduled delivery time appears in the conversation. When sent, the message color changes to match that of your normal outgoing messages.

Scheduled message

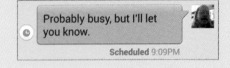

Composing a Multimedia Message (MMS)

A *multimedia message (MMS)* is any message that has one or more attachments—regardless of the attachment type(s).

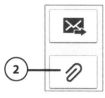

1. Perform steps 1 through 10 of the "Composing a Text Message (SMS)" task.

2. At any time during the message-creation process, tap the paper clip button.

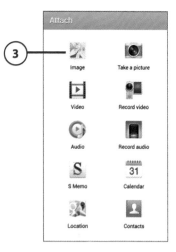

3. Select the item type that you want to attach to the message. If you're attaching a file that's already on your phone, continue with step 4. If you want to create a *new* file or insert a map location, skip to step 5.

4. *Attach an existing file.* Select the item(s) to attach, opening enclosing folders if necessary. For most attachment types, you complete the selection process by tapping Done. Go to step 6.

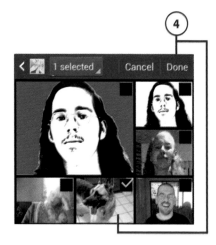

Size Matters

Existing video clips and audio recordings such as songs are often too large to transmit as part of an MMS message. Messaging rejects such items as attachments. Photos, on the other hand, are automatically compressed to meet MMS size limits.

5. *Create an attachment.* Take a new picture or capture a video, and tap Save to add it to the message or Discard to try again. When you finish recording an audio clip, tap the Stop button to save it, listen to the clip, and then tap the Attach button.

6. A thumbnail representing the media is inserted into the message or the item is shown as a named file attachment. As you add items, the total size of the message and attachments updates.

7. If you want to view/play, replace, or remove a multimedia item, press its thumbnail and select the appropriate option. (If you remove *all* attachments from a message, it reverts to a text message.)

Another Removal Option

You can also remove a multimedia item by selecting it and tapping the Delete key.

8. When the message is complete, tap Send.

Recording an audio clip

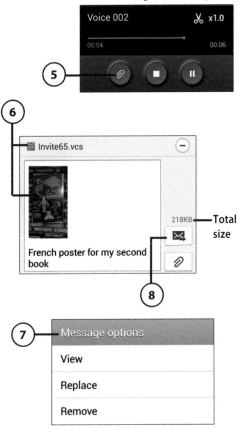

It's Not All Good

YOUR MILEAGE MAY VARY

When it works, nothing is cooler than having a photo, video, or other MMS attachment appear on your screen during a texting session. Unfortunately, MMS transmissions aren't 100% reliable. Each message must pass through multiple servers and conversions. As a result, multimedia messages sometimes arrive late, vanish altogether, or are dramatically compressed. The moral? MMS messages are more appropriate for fun than for mission-critical transmissions. When sending important data—especially when it needs to be delivered quickly and uncompressed, stick to computer-to-computer email. For lengthy back-and-forth text conversations, you might also consider trying one of the many chat apps—such as the ones discussed at the end of this chapter.

Managing Conversations

There's more to participating in a conversation than just creating new messages. The following tasks explain how to respond to new message notifications; continue, review, and delete conversations; and search for messages.

Responding to a New Message Notification

If you're in Messaging and a message for the current conversation arrives, it simply appears onscreen as a new balloon. If you're doing something else with the phone, the phone is resting quietly on your desk, or you're viewing a different conversation, a new message notification appears.

Number of new messages

Depending on your Messaging settings (see "Configuring Messaging Settings," later in this chapter) and what you're doing with the phone, you may be notified of a new message in one of several ways.

Messaging

- The message text appears briefly in the status bar and is replaced by an envelope icon. The Messaging icon on the Home screen shows the number of new messages.

- You can also view the new message by opening the Notification panel and tapping the new message notification.

Notification panel

New message

- Finally, you can launch Messaging (if it isn't currently running) and open the conversation that contains the new message.

New message indicator

Lock Screen Notification

If your screen is dark when a message arrives, press the Power button to display your lock screen. To view the announced message in Messaging, tap the new message indicator. You can also launch Messaging from this screen—whether a new message is waiting or not—by swiping the Messaging icon at the bottom of the screen upward (if it's present).

Lock screen

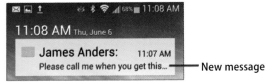

New message

Continuing a Conversation

The default length for a conversation on your phone is 200 text or 20 multimedia messages—whichever occurs first. As long as the length limit hasn't been exceeded, a conversation can be continued immediately or whenever either participant desires—days, weeks, or even months after it was begun.

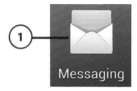

1. If Messaging isn't running, launch it by tapping the Messaging icon on the Home screen.

2. On Messaging's main screen, select the conversation that you want to continue. The conversation appears.

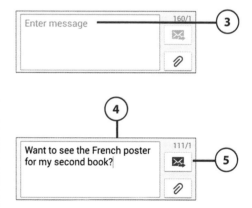

3. Tap in the Enter Message box.

4. Create a text or multimedia message as described in "Composing a Text Message (SMS)" or "Composing a Multimedia Message (MMS)," earlier in this chapter.

5. Tap the Send button to transmit the message. It is appended to the end of the conversation.

Reviewing a Conversation

As long as you haven't deleted a conversation, you can reread it whenever you like. This is especially useful when a conversation contains important information, such as the time of an upcoming meeting, a phone number, a web address (URL), or driving directions. To review a conversation, select it on the Messaging screen (as described in the previous task) and scroll through the messages by flicking or dragging up and down.

Reviewing a conversation

Deleting Conversations

For the sake of privacy, saving storage space, or eliminating clutter in the conversation list on the Messaging main screen, you can delete entire conversations (*threads*).

1. Launch Messaging by tapping its icon on the Home screen. (If you're currently in a conversation, press the Back key until the conversation list appears.)

2. Press the Menu key and tap Delete Threads.

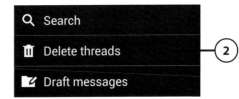

Deleting a Single Conversation

To delete a *single* conversation, press and hold the conversation, and tap Delete Thread in the dialog box that appears.

3. Select the conversations that you want to delete, or tap Select all to select all conversations.

4. Tap the Delete button.

5. Confirm the conversation deletion(s) by tapping OK.

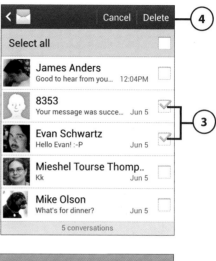

Deleting Messages

In addition to deleting entire conversations, you can selectively delete messages from a conversation.

1. In Messaging, open the conversation from which you want to delete messages.

2. Press the Menu key and tap Delete Messages.

3. Scroll through the conversation, and select each message that you want to delete.

4. Tap the Delete button.

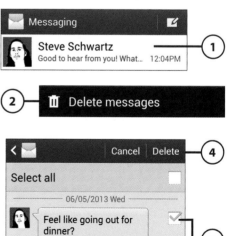

5. Tap OK to confirm the deletions.

Deleting a Single Message

To delete a *single* message in a conversation, you can press and hold the message, and then tap Delete Message in the Message Options dialog box that appears.

> **Delete**
>
> Selected messages will be deleted
>
> | Cancel | OK — **5** |

Other Options for Individual Messages

In addition to deleting individual messages, you can copy message text to the Clipboard (for pasting elsewhere), lock a message (to prevent it from being deleted), save the multimedia elements in an MMS message to an SD card, forward a message to others, or view a message's properties.

1. Within a conversation, press and hold a message for which you want to display options. The Message Options dialog box appears. SMS and MMS messages offer slightly different options—as explained in step 2.

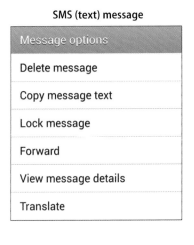

SMS (text) message

Message options
Delete message
Copy message text
Lock message
Forward
View message details
Translate

MMS (multimedia) message

Message options
Delete message
View slideshow
Copy message text
Lock message
Save attachment
Forward
View message details
Translate

2. Tap a menu option to perform one of the following actions on the message:

- *Delete Message*. Delete the current message.
- *View slideshow (MMS messages only)*. Displays message text and certain types of attachments (such as photos) as a slideshow.
- *Copy Message Text*. Copy the message text to the Clipboard, making it eligible for pasting into another message or app, such as an email message.
- *Lock Message*. Prevent an important message from being inadvertently deleted—even if you delete the conversation that contains the message. After a message has been locked, the Lock Message command is replaced by Unlock Message. You can optionally override the lock while attempting to delete the message or delete its conversation.
- *Save Attachment (MMS messages only)*. Save an attached item, such as a picture or video, to the Download folder.
- *Forward*. Send the message to another recipient—passing along a picture, phone number, address, or driving directions, for example.
- *View Message Details*. Examine the message properties, such as who sent it and when, the date and time it was received, and its total size including attachments.
- *Translate*. Translate the message text from its current language to another one.

Searching for Messages

You can search all conversations for specific text.

1. If Messaging isn't currently running, tap its Home screen icon.

2. On the Messaging main screen (the conversation list), press the Menu key and tap Search. A Search Messages text box appears.

3. Enter the search text; matches appear as you type. Continue typing until the desired message is shown, and then tap to select it.

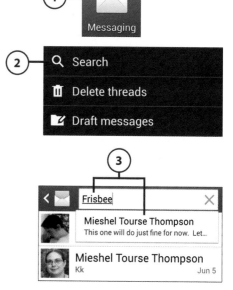

4. The conversation appears and displays the selected message. The matching text is shown in blue. (Note that there may be other matches in the conversation.)

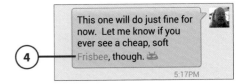

Configuring Messaging Settings

You can customize the way Messaging works by changing its settings. All changes take effect immediately. Note that Settings options differ among carriers, depending on the features that each supports. The most common settings are discussed here.

1. Launch Messaging. If you're already in or viewing a conversation, press the Back key until the conversation list appears.

2. Press the Menu key and tap Settings. The Settings screen appears. Scroll as necessary to view the entire menu. The following steps explain the most important settings (organized by category) and list the carriers that support each setting. When no carrier is listed for a setting, *all* carriers support it.

3. **General Settings.** You can modify these settings to free up space on the phone.

- Enable Delete Old Messages to automatically delete the oldest messages in any conversation that exceed either the text or multimedia message limit (see the next bullet). When disabled, the maximum text and multimedia messages per conversation are ignored.

- Tap Text Message Limit or Multimedia Message Limit to change the maximum number of messages of that type that are allowed in a conversation.

- A *text template* is boilerplate text that you can use to quickly create messages or responses to incoming calls. Examples include "What's up?" and "Please call me." Tap Text Templates to modify the current list of templates, as described in "Lazy

Messaging," earlier in this chapter. (T-Mobile users can find this command in the normal menu rather than in Settings.)

- *Verizon:* Enable Restore Messages to restore saved messages.

Settings (Sprint)

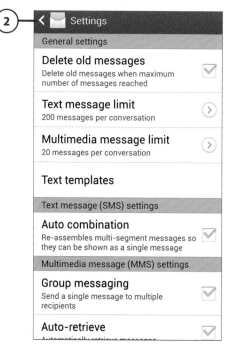

4. **Text Message (SMS) Settings.** These settings govern the creation and handling of text messages.

- *Sprint, U.S. Cellular:* When Auto Combination is enabled, text messages that exceed the maximum length limit are automatically combined into single messages. In general, enabled is the preferred setting.

- *T-Mobile, Verizon, U.S. Cellular:* When Delivery Reports is enabled, you're notified when messages are successfully delivered.

5. **Multimedia Message (MMS) Settings.** These settings govern the creation and handling of multimedia messages.

- When Auto-retrieve is enabled, the entire content of each multimedia message is automatically retrieved—the message header, body, and attachments. Otherwise, only the message header is retrieved. (If you're on a limited data plan and have friends who constantly attach material to their messages or you find that Auto-retrieve uses too much of your battery charge, you might want to disable this setting.)

- Enable MMS Alert if you want to be notified that the message you're creating is a multimedia message rather than a text message. If messaging or data charges are a concern for you, enabling this setting can be useful.

- *AT&T, Sprint, U.S. Cellular, Verizon:* When Group Messaging is enabled, you can create a single message for delivery to multiple recipients. When disabled, the carrier sends a separate copy of the message for each specified recipient.

- *T-Mobile, U.S. Cellular, Verizon:* When Delivery Reports is enabled, you're notified when messages are successfully delivered.

- *T-Mobile:* When Read Reports is enabled, a request to be notified when the message has been read is also sent.

- *Sprint, T-Mobile, U.S. Cellular, Verizon:* When Roaming Auto-Retrieve is enabled, MMS messages and their contents are automatically downloaded even when you're roaming.

- *AT&T, T-Mobile:* Setting a Creation Mode enables you to specify the type of multimedia (MMS) messages that you can create. The intent is to avoid creating messages for which your plan assesses special charges. Contact your carrier for the proper setting: Restricted, Warning, or Free.

6. **Display Settings.** The following settings (supported by all carriers) determine the appearance of conversations.

  - Bubble Style enables you to vary the color and/or style of the message bubbles. The selected top bubble is used to display your messages, and the bottom one is used for messages received from others. (The top and bottom sets scroll horizontally—and independently—to show additional colors and styles.) Select a top and a bottom bubble style, and then tap Save.

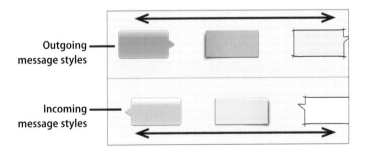

Outgoing message styles

Incoming message styles

  - Background Style enables you to specify a different color background or a photo on which to display the conversations. The style thumbnails scroll horizontally. Select a style and tap Save. (Select the first thumbnail to use an existing image or take a photo to use as the background.)

  - When enabled, Use the Volume Key lets you use the hardware volume control on the left side of the phone to increase or decrease the size of message text.

7. **Push Message Settings (AT&T, T-Mobile).** When Push Messages is enabled (default setting) and new messages are received by the network, they are *pushed* to your phone. That is, you don't have to perform an action to receive the messages—they are simply transmitted to you.

8. **Cell Broadcast (CB) Settings (AT&T).** When CB Activation is enabled, your phone can receive messages that are designated for many users within a specified area; that is, *broadcast messages*. Normal SMS and MMS messages are intended for one-to-one or one-to-few transmission. You can modify the Channel Configuration setting (specifying the channel on which you'll receive CB messages) only when CB Activation is enabled.

9. **Notification Settings.** The following settings (supported by all carriers) determine whether you receive notifications of newly received messages, as well as the manner in which the notifications are presented.

   • Enable Notifications if you want to receive one or more notifications when a new message is received. To specify the types of notification methods to use, you must first enable this setting.

   • Tap Select Ringtone to pick a ringtone to announce new messages. Select a ringtone, and then tap OK.

Ringtone Options

When you tap a ringtone on the Ringtone screen, its sound plays—enabling you to sample many ringtones before committing to one. If you'd rather *not* hear a ringtone when a message arrives, select Silent.

   • With Vibrate enabled, the phone vibrates whenever a new message is received.

   • Tap Message Alert Repetition to specify how frequently you will be notified of the receipt of new messages.

   • When Preview message is enabled, notifications also appear in the status bar and on the lock screen.

Want to Know More?

For more information about message notifications, see "Responding to a New Message Notification," earlier in this chapter.

10. **Emergency Message Settings.** These settings are used to specify the types of emergency alert messages that you want to receive and special notification options that will be applied.

- Tap Emergency Alerts to enable/disable different types of alerts. By default, all alert types are enabled. You can disable any type of alert other than Presidential.

Emergency alert types

- Tap Alert Reminder to specify how frequently you want to be reminded of an active alert.

11. **Signature Settings.** This pair of settings (supported by all carriers) enables you to append a text signature to each outgoing message—in the same fashion as you can with email messages. Add Signature must be enabled to create or edit the Signature Text.

12. **Spam Message Settings.** These settings (supported by all carriers except Verizon) enable you to reduce or avoid unwanted (*spam*) messages. Spam Settings is the master control—that is, it must be enabled to use any of the spam options.

- Tap Add to Spam Numbers to manually add numbers of people and companies whose messages you want automatically blocked.

Add a Spam Number Without Typing

When you receive a spam message, press and hold the entry in the conversation list, and tap Add to Spam Numbers in the dialog box that appears.

James Anders

View contact

Delete thread

Block messages ———— Add to spam numbers
from this number

- Similar to creating a junk mail rule in an email program, you can specify a key phrase or words (such as Viagra, credit, or mortgage) that are frequently found in spam messages that you receive. Tap Add to Spam Phrases and enter phrases which—if found in an incoming message—will result in blocking the message's delivery.

- Enable Block Unknown Senders to block messages from people and companies who have no Contacts record.

13. When you finish reviewing and changing settings, press the Back key. Changes take effect immediately.

Restore the Default Settings

You can revert to the default Messaging settings by pressing the Menu key and tapping Restore Default Settings.

MESSAGING CONSIDERATIONS

>>>Go Further

Here are a few practical and etiquette considerations for texting:

- *Know your service plan.* Although your Galaxy S 4 can create and receive text and multimedia messages, your plan determines how you're charged—whether messages are unlimited, you're limited to a certain number per month, or there is a per-message charge. Received messages generally count, too—including unsolicited ones. Review your plan before you leap into texting.

- *Check with the recipient before texting.* Whether you *should* text someone depends on many factors, such as the recipient's phone (not all phones can display multimedia messages and many older phones can't even accept text messages) and the recipient's data plan. Unless someone has texted you first, it's a good idea to ask before initiating a conversation.

- *You can refuse all incoming messages.* If your plan doesn't allow for texting or it's expensive and you have no interest in receiving messages, contact your plan provider to see if there's a way to block incoming messages. Incoming messages typically cost the same as those you initiate, so you may prefer to refuse them.

Social Networking with Flipboard

In addition to making phone calls, playing games, and listening to your favorite tunes, you can use your Galaxy S 4 for social or business networking, while keeping up with the news of the day. As an example, you can use Flipboard to read articles, watch videos, and follow feeds posted by your Facebook, Twitter, and LinkedIn friends and business colleagues. If you're looking for a more interactive experience, you can use your phone to participate in text chats with friends—as explained in "Chatting On Your Galaxy S 4," at the end of this chapter.

Dedicated Apps

Rather than use Flipboard for a full-blown—and potentially overwhelming—social networking *experience*, you may prefer to install dedicated apps for the social networking sites that you consider most important. The major sites, such as Facebook, Twitter, and LinkedIn, all have dedicated official Android apps that you can download from Google Play/Play Store.

Adding Social Networking Accounts

One of the first steps in using Flipboard is to link your social networking service (*SNS*) accounts that you want to track. If you aren't currently a member of a social network, visit its website and sign up first. Flipboard currently supports Facebook, Twitter, LinkedIn, Google+, Google Reader, Instagram, Flickr, Tumblr, 500px, Sina Weibo, Renren, SoundCloud, YouTube, New York Times, and Financial Times.

1. From the Home screen, launch Flipboard by tapping Apps and then Flipboard.

2. To link an account to Flipboard, tap the menu icon (three stacked bars) and then tap Accounts on the screen that appears.

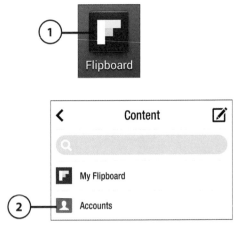

3. Scroll to the Add an Account section, and tap the name of the account that you want to track with Flipboard. Only accounts that you haven't already linked are listed.

4. Sign into your account by entering your username (or email address) and account password. Then tap the Sign In button.

Lost Passwords

If you can't *remember* your account username, email address, or password, use your browser to visit the social networking site. There's usually a conspicuous link you can click to request the forgotten info.

5. Review the SNS's permissions statement and tap Accept. If you don't approve of the permission requirements, tap Cancel or No Thanks.

6. The site's current feed appears. When you're ready to return to the main Flipboard screen, tap the Back icon or press the Back key.

Removing an SNS Account

Although you can't remove an SNS account from within Flipboard, there is a way to do it. From the Home screen, press the Menu key, tap Settings, select the Accounts tab, and tap the account that you want to remove. Tap the Remove Account button at the bottom of the screen and confirm the removal in the Remove Account dialog box.

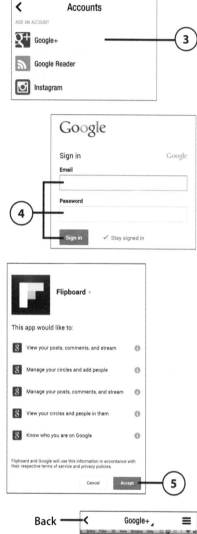

Adding Content Feeds

In addition to SNS feeds, you can add content (such as news, music, and movies) from a variety of sources.

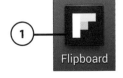

Flipboard

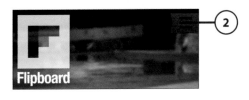

Flipboard

About the Main Pages

Flipboard's main pages serve as a visual table of contents. The number of pages expands and contracts as you add or remove content categories and subcategories. Within these pages, every content category and subcategory has its own thumbnail that takes you directly to its content.

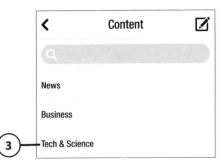

1. From the Home screen, launch Flipboard by tapping Apps and then Flipboard.

2. Tap the menu icon in the upper-right corner of the main page. (On other pages, the menu icon is white.)

3. In the scrolling list, tap a content area that you want to configure, such as News or Tech & Science.

4. A vertically scrolling content list appears. To view a sample of a content source, tap its name. To add the source to your Flipboard feed, tap the box to the right of its name. Repeat this step for other content sources that you want to add. When you finish, tap the Back icon or press the Back key.

5. The selected content feeds are added and now available to you from Flipboard's main pages.

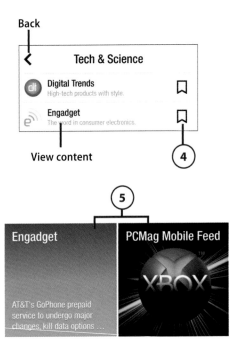

Viewing and Interacting with Content and Feeds

You can use Flipboard to view content and status updates, as well as post your own updates.

1. Launch Flipboard or, if it's already running, tap the Back icon or press the Back key until the main pages appear.

2. To locate the content that you want to view, navigate through the main pages by flicking up and down. When you see the desired category or subcategory, tap its thumbnail.

3. To navigate within a category or subcategory, flick up and down as you do in the main pages. When you see an item that you want to read or view, tap anywhere within its content to view the complete item.

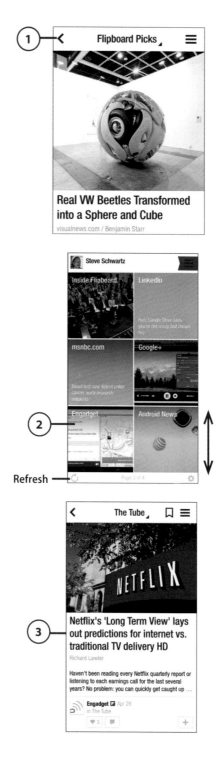

Refresh

4. When reading a lengthy article, flick up and down to scroll the material. To interact with an item, you can tap icons on the page, such as Like, Comment, or Share. Different content sources and feeds have different icons and options. When you finish, tap the Back icon or press the Back key to return to the content pages.

5. To post a status update, tap the menu icon on any page, tap the Compose icon on the Content page, tap your name, select the account to which the update will post, tap the Back icon, compose the update, and tap Send.

Add a Photo

To attach a photo to a status update, press the Menu key, and tap Take Photo or Choose from Library.

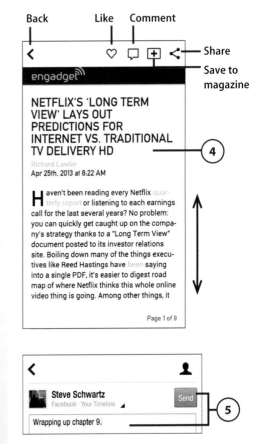

OTHER WAYS TO KEEP CURRENT WITH SOCIAL NETWORKING

Although Flipboard feeds are in a convenient format, you may prefer another option for checking recent Facebook, Twitter, LinkedIn, or other SNS activity. First, you can use the Internet or Chrome app to go directly to the SNS website, just as you would with your computer. Second, each service offers a free, dedicated app that you can download from Google Play. Tap the Play Store icon and search for Facebook, Twitter, or LinkedIn, for example.

Chatting on Your Galaxy S 4

Before texting became popular, people relied on dedicated chat programs to conduct online conversations. Many of those same programs are now available as Android apps. Unlike texting, chat messages carry no per-message surcharge, and there's no limit to the number of messages that can be exchanged in a billing cycle.

As an example of a general chat program with a wide audience, you should consider imo, a free app from Play Store/Google Play. (Downloading apps from Google Play is explained in Chapter 10.) Most chat programs only let you chat with other users of that program. If you have chat friends who use many different chat programs, you have only a few options:

- Install a dedicated app for each chat program and hop among them as you attempt to find friends who are online and available to chat.

- Convince your friends to switch to a specific chat service such as ChatON (discussed later) to chat with you.

imo, however, offers a simpler solution. It links to 10 popular chat services—including Yahoo! Messenger, AIM/ICQ, Google Talk, Jabber, Steam, and Facebook—enabling you to chat with friends on many services while using a single app. To learn more about imo's features and how to use it, visit https://imo.im/android.html.

Another Chat Option: ChatON

ChatON, Samsung's dedicated chat service, is preinstalled on many Galaxy S 4's. If it isn't on yours or you have a friend with a different Android phone, ChatON can be downloaded from Play Store/Google Play. Unlike imo, ChatON can be used only to chat with other ChatON users. ChatON has a clean, text message–style chat interface and includes many interesting features, such as group chats, animated emoticons, support for file attachments, and voice/video calling. All you have to do is convince your friends that they need yet another dedicated chat service/app if they want to chat with you.

Search   Share

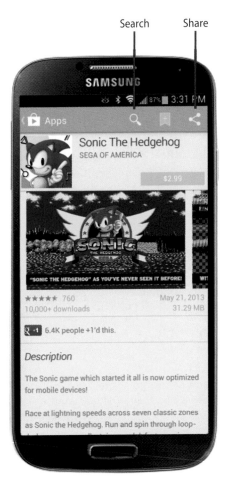

This chapter covers the essentials of downloading, installing, running, and maintaining applications on your phone. Topics include the following:

→ Running an application
→ Downloading and installing applications from Google Play (Android Market)
→ Enabling application downloads from other sources
→ Downloading applications from the Amazon.com Appstore
→ Adding Home screen shortcuts to your favorite applications
→ Uninstalling unwanted applications
→ Installing application updates

Installing and Using Applications

Applications (or *apps*, as they're called when referring to smartphone software) are programs that run on your phone. They add new functionality to the phone, such as enabling you to stream video, manipulate databases, play video games, and do almost anything else you can imagine.

The Galaxy S 4 comes with dozens of apps preinstalled, ready for you to use. In addition, you can download and install other apps from Google Play, the Amazon Appstore, Samsung Apps, and developers' websites.

Running an App

In this section, you learn the fundamentals of running apps: launching an app, using the hardware keys (Menu, Home, and Back) with apps, switching among running apps, and exiting from an app. The information covered here applies to any app you encounter.

Launching an App

As with programs on a computer, you can launch phone apps directly or indirectly (by performing an action that requires the app to be running).

Directly Launching an App

To launch a particular app, you can do any of the following:

App icons

Apps icon

- On any Home screen page, tap the app's icon. (In addition to the app icons that are preinstalled on the Home screen pages, you may have added shortcuts to some of your favorite apps to make them more readily accessible.)

- Tap Apps at the bottom of any Home screen page. Ensure that the Apps tab is selected, and then tap the icon of the app that you want to run.

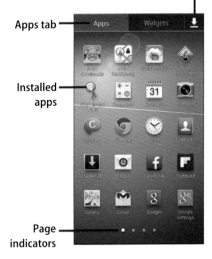

Downloaded apps

Apps tab

Installed apps

Page indicators

Navigation

Because you probably have several pages of apps, you can move from page to page by swiping the screen to the right or left or by tapping a navigation dot below the app icons.

To display only the apps that you've downloaded, tap the icon in the upper-right corner of the screen, or press the Menu key and tap Downloaded Applications.

- On almost any screen, you can press and hold the Home key to display a list of recently run apps, as well as ones that are currently running. Scroll vertically until you see the app that you want to launch or to which you want to switch, and then tap its thumbnail.

Indirectly Launching an App

In addition to tapping an app's icon, many actions that you perform on the phone can cause an app to launch. Consider these common examples:

Recent and running apps

- In any program or widget, tapping a link to material stored on the web, to an *HTML* (web) file stored on the phone, or to a particular web page or site causes the Internet or Chrome app to launch to display the page. App help files are sometimes handled this way.

- Tapping a *mailto:* (email address) link on a web page or in an app causes Email to launch to create a new message to that address.

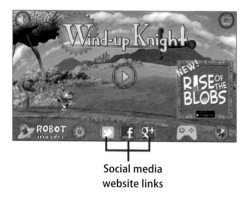

Social media website links

Not Just Links

In addition to tapping links, if you tap a phone number or email address on a web page, the number is entered into Phone in preparation for dialing or you can create a new Email/Gmail message to the address, respectively.

contact us at affiliates@new.com

mailto: link

- Tapping a file icon (such as a music, video, or photo file) in My Files, in Downloads, on the Home screen, or in a folder you created causes an appropriate app to launch and present the file's material. Tapping a document icon, such as a PDF or Microsoft Office document, may also cause an app to launch and display the file's contents. Either case depends on having an app installed that is capable of reading and displaying the file, such as Polaris Office.

- Performing certain actions in an app can cause a related app to launch. For example, clicking the Contacts icon to select message recipients in Email or Messaging launches Contacts.

- Tapping certain entries in the Notification panel, such as a new email notification, causes the appropriate app to launch.

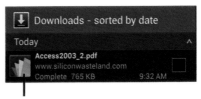

PDF file

Contacts icon

Using the Hardware Keys

The three hardware keys at the bottom of the phone (Menu, Home, and Back) can be useful—and occasionally *essential*—when running apps.

Light 'em Up!

When the keys aren't in use, only the Home key—a physical button—is visible. Until you tap one of the three keys or the touchscreen, the Menu and Back keys are hidden. Whether you can *see* the keys, however, is irrelevant. If you tap the currently hidden Menu or Back key, the key still performs its function.

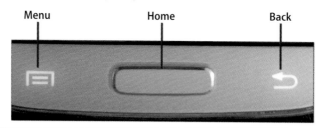

Accessing Menus

In apps that contain menus, you can press the Menu key on various screens to see the available options. Setting app-specific preferences is usually handled in this manner, for example. Note that menus are often context-sensitive—that is, they change depending on what you're currently doing.

Menu options (Email app)

Other Menus

In addition to menus that are tied to the Menu key, apps may contain other menus. Some automatically appear onscreen (such as the Select menu in Gallery), whereas others are contextual menus that pop up when you press and hold an item (such as a contact record in Contacts).

Contacts ———— James Anders
contextual menu

Edit

Delete

Join contact

Share contact via message

Returning to the Home Screen

To immediately exit the current app, press the Home key. The most recently accessed page of the Home screen appears.

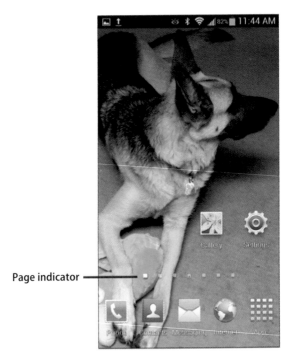

Page indicator

Navigating Within an App

Within most apps, forward navigation options are obvious. You tap entries, icons, thumbnails, or buttons to go to the next screen or to perform an action. However, the method of *returning* to the previous section or screen isn't always as obvious. When it doesn't happen automatically, you can usually press the Back key. (Some apps also have a Back icon in the upper-left corner of the screen that you can tap.)

In addition to moving you back through sections or screens (when using Internet or Chrome to view web pages or when modifying Call Settings in Phone, for example), you can also press the Back key to avoid making a selection in a dialog box or menu, leave the Notification panel, or dismiss the onscreen keyboard.

It's Not All Good

ONE TOO MANY PRESSES

Using the Back key has a major drawback. If you press it one too many times, you'll find that you've inadvertently exited the current program and are now staring at the Home screen. When this happens, simply relaunch the app.

Switching Among Running Apps

Although many apps automatically quit when you leave them (see "Exiting an App"), you can use the Task Manager to switch among those that are running.

1. On almost any screen, press and hold the Home button until the list of recent and active applications appears.

2. Tap the Task Manager button.

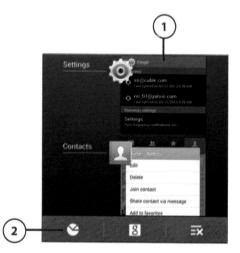

3. Ensure that the Active Applications tab is selected. To switch to any running app, tap its name.

Using Multi Window to Run Two Apps

With the new Multi Window feature enabled, you can split the screen to run two apps at the same time. Note that only certain apps can currently operate in Multi Window, such as Email, Gallery, Internet, and Messaging.

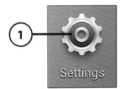

Enabling/Disabling Multi Window

1. On the Home screen, tap Apps, followed by Settings.

2. Select the My Device tab and tap Display.

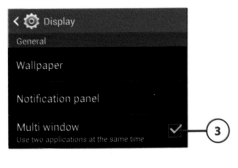

3. Tap Multi Window to toggle its state between enabled and disabled.

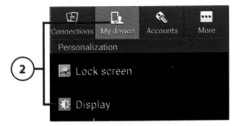

Enabled but Hidden

If you only occasionally use Multi Window or find its ever-present tab annoying, you don't have to repeatedly open Settings to enable and disable it. Just press and hold the Back key to instantly hide or reveal the Multi Window tab.

Working with Multi Window

1. Open the vertically scrolling Multi Window bar by tapping its exposed tab.

2. To launch a Multi Window app, do any of the following:

   - Tap an app's icon on the bar to launch the app in full-screen mode.

   - To launch a second app in split-screen mode, press and hold the app's icon and drag it into the top or bottom half of the screen.

   - To replace an app running in split-screen mode, press and hold an icon, and then drag it into the top or bottom half of the screen.

3. To modify the display when you're in split-screen mode, you can do either of the following:

   - Resize the two sections of the screen by dragging the bar that divides them.

   - Tap the dividing bar to reveal a three-icon menu. In order, tap the first icon to swap the apps' onscreen positions, tap the second icon to expand the app to full screen, or tap the third icon to close the app. (The latter commands affect the app that's on their side of the divider. To select the app you want to change, tap the top or bottom half of the screen prior to tapping the expand or close icon.)

Gallery app

Multi Window tab

Divider

YouTube app

Multi Window Notes

Note the following when using Multi Window:

- If you launch an app that is incompatible with Multi Window, active Multi Window apps are cleared from the screen.
- If you launch a series of Multi Window apps (each one replacing another), you can frequently step backward through them by pressing the Back key.
- Opening Settings doesn't interfere with Multi Window. When you're done making changes in Settings, press the Back key to resume using the open Multi Window app(s).

Customizing the Multi Window Display

You can do any of the following to customize the Multi Window display:

- *Change the tab position.* With only the tab exposed, press and hold the tab, and then drag up or down to a new position on the Multi Window bar.
- *Change the location of the Multi Window bar.* The Multi Window bar can be on the left or right side of the screen (in both standard and landscape rotation). With Multi Window open, press and hold the tab until Multi Window undocks, and then drag it to the opposite side of the screen.
- *Edit the Multi Window icons.* With Multi Window open, tap the Edit button. You can drag icons off the bar (into the open window), drag them from the window onto the bar, or rearrange them. (Press and hold an icon, and then drag it to a new position on the bar.) When you finish editing the icons, tap Done.

Exiting an App

If you're new to smartphones, you've probably noticed a major difference between phone apps and computer programs: *Most apps have no Quit or Exit command.* The few that do have such a command are typically those that, if left running, would run up data-related charges or rapidly drain the battery.

Whenever you perform an action that leaves the current app, such as powering off the phone, pressing the Back key, or pressing the Home key, the Android operating system decides whether to quit or suspend the app. Similarly, if app activities are causing the phone to run low on memory, Android performs these same functions as needed. However, if you want to quit an app *manually* to ensure that it's no longer running, draining the battery, using memory, or running up data charges, you can use the Task Manager.

1. As described in "Switching Among Running Apps," launch the Task Manager and tap the Active Applications tab (if it isn't currently selected).

2. To quit a specific app, tap its End button. To simultaneously quit all listed apps, tap the End All button.

Downloading and Installing Apps from Google Play

Formerly known as Android Market, Google Play is the most common place for you to find Android apps for your phone. In addition to apps, you can download ebooks, movies, and music from Google Play.

1. Launch Google Play by tapping its Home screen icon (Play Store) or by tapping Apps and then Play Store.

2. Tap Apps, Music, or another link on the main screen to indicate the type of material that you're seeking or want to browse.

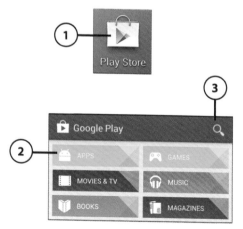

3. Do one of the following:

   - To browse for apps, continue tapping links to focus your search.

   - If you know the name or type of app for which you're searching, tap the search icon at the top of the screen and begin typing. A drop-down list of potential matches appears as you type. Tap one or continue typing to further narrow the search.

4. To view a listed app, tap its name.

5. Review the description and user ratings for the app. You can also do the following:

   - Tap the sample screen shots or videos. If multiple screen shots are available, you can view them by swiping left and right.

   - To learn more about the app, read the What's New and Description sections. You can also tap the link to the developer's website (if provided).

6. If you want the app, tap the green icon. If the app is free, the icon will read Install; otherwise, it will contain the price.

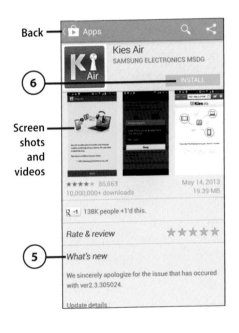

Charge It!

If the app isn't free, you can charge it to a credit or debit card that you've registered with Google Play or—in some cases—add the charge to your monthly carrier bill. Specify a payment method or add a new one, and follow the instructions to complete the purchase.

Adding a credit or debit card creates a Google Wallet account for you. To learn about Google Wallet and where it's accepted, visit www.google.com/wallet/.

Add a payment method

7. Before starting the download, the App Permissions screen appears, detailing how the app interacts with the operating system and uses your personal information. If the permissions are acceptable to you, tap the Accept button. The app is downloaded, installed on your phone, and its icon is added to the Apps pages.

Go Back

To step backward through Google Play to revisit previously viewed screens, press the Back key or tap the location information in the upper-left corner.

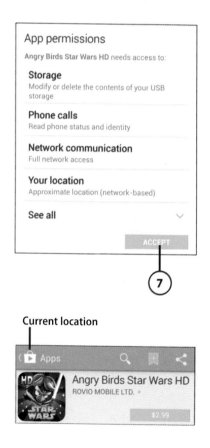

Current location

REQUESTING A REFUND

Whenever you purchase an app from Google Play, you have 15 minutes to try it and decide whether you want to keep it. If not, do the following:

1. Launch Google Play, press the Menu key, and tap My Apps.

2. The My Apps list of Google Play–installed apps appears. Tap the app that you just purchased and want to return.

3. If you're within the 15-minute window, you'll see a Refund button in the app's description window. Tap it to proceed.

4. The Refund button changes to Uninstall. Tap it to remove the app from your phone and initiate the refund to your account.

Customizing Google Play

Google Play has its own Settings screen that enables you to customize the way app updates are handled and provides an option to create a PIN that you can use to authenticate purchases.

1. In Google Play, press the Menu key and tap Settings.

2. The Settings screen appears. Following are the options you can change.

3. *Notifications.* When checked, an item appears in the Notification panel when updates are available for apps that you've downloaded from Google Play. You can download and install the updates by tapping the notification.

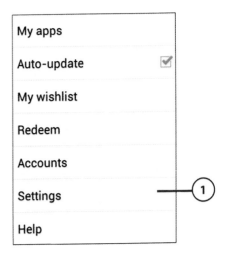

Check for Updates

To manually check for updates, launch Google Play, press the Menu key, and tap My Apps to display the list of your downloaded apps. All apps for which updates are available are listed in the Updates section. Tap Update All to update all of the listed apps; tap the Update text for an app to update only that app.

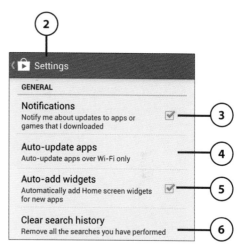

4. *Auto-update Apps*. This setting determines whether updates for apps are automatically down-loaded and installed from Google Play as they become available. To specify how and when automatic updates occur, tap the Auto-update Apps text.

5. *Auto-add Widgets*. When this option is checked and you down-load a new app, a shortcut to the app is automatically added to your Home screen.

6. *Clear Search History*. Tap this option to delete all previous searches that you've performed in Google Play.

Update all apps in Updates section

Update this app only

7. *Content Filtering*. To prevent certain types of apps from being downloaded, tap Content Filtering, enter or remove check marks on the Allow Apps Rated For screen, and tap OK.

8. *Password*. When checked, Google Play requests your Google/Gmail password whenever you purchase an app, movie, song, ebook, or other content.

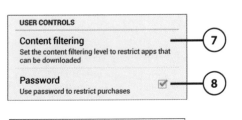

USER CONTROLS
Content filtering — ⑦
Set the content filtering level to restrict apps that can be downloaded
Password ☑ — ⑧
Use password to restrict purchases

Allow apps rated for

Everyone	☑
Low maturity	☑
Medium maturity	☑
High maturity	☑
Show all apps	☑

Set the content filtering level to restrict apps that can be downloaded to this device. More about content filtering.

| Cancel | OK — ⑦ |

USING THE GOOGLE PLAY WEBSITE

>>>Go Further

In addition to using the Play Store app to choose apps and content for your phone, you can use your computer to access the Google Play website. The larger screen and convenient keyboard can be helpful when searching for apps and other material. Go to https://play.google.com/, sign in to your Google/Gmail account (if required), and hunt to your heart's content. Any paid for or free app that you select will download to your phone. (Click the My Android Apps tab at the top of the screen to see a list of all apps that you've downloaded from Google Play.)

Enabling App Downloads from Other Sources

Google Play is the *official* source of Android apps. However, if you'd like to download and install apps from unofficial sources, such as developer websites or the Amazon Appstore, you must change one of your phone's settings.

1. On the Home screen, tap Apps, followed by Settings.

2. Select the More tab, and tap Security.

3. In the Device Administration section, enable Unknown Sources. When checked, you can download apps from any source that you choose.

4. Confirm by tapping OK in the dialog box that appears.

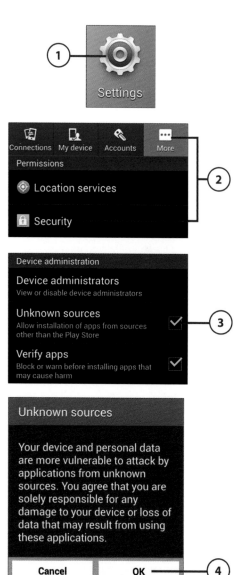

Using the Amazon Appstore for Android

The popular online retailer Amazon.com is another major source of free and paid Android apps. If you already have an Amazon account, you can use it to purchase apps for your phone, too. (If you haven't already done so, you must allow downloading of apps from Unknown Sources, as explained in "Enabling App Downloads from Other Sources.")

Installing the Amazon Appstore App

1. From the Home screen, tap Apps, followed by Internet or Chrome.

2. Enter http://www.amazon.com/ getappstore in the address box or select it from the suggestion list as you type.

3. Tap the Download the Amazon Appstore button.

4. When the download completes, open the Notification panel and tap the AmazonApps-release.apk entry.

5. Review the Privacy and Device Access information for the app and tap Install. Tap Open on the following screen.

6. The Welcome screen appears. To associate this account with your Amazon.com account, enter your email address and Amazon password, and then tap Sign In. (If you don't currently have an Amazon account, you can create one by tapping the Create an Account button.)

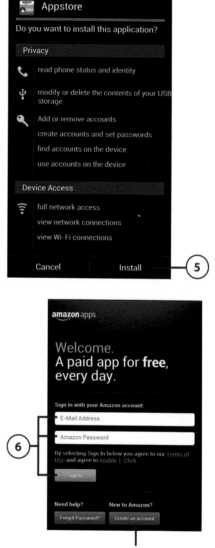

Create account

Downloading Apps from the Amazon Appstore

1. On the Home screen, tap Apps and then tap Appstore.

2. The Appstore opening screen appears.

3. *Browsing.* The main screen presents general categories you can use to begin your browsing. Apps within a category scroll left and right. You can tap app thumbnails or, if you don't see something that catches your eye, tap See All to view all apps in that category. After doing so, you'll note that you can further focus the browsing in the larger categories by selecting a subcategory from the Category icon and/or applying a sorting or filtering option from the Refine icon, such as Price or Avg. Customer Review.

Select a category

Paths to Better Browsing

You can quickly filter the apps by choosing a specific software category. Press the Menu key, tap the All Categories icon, and then tap the category in the scrolling menu. On the other hand, if you're at a loss concerning where to start, return to the main screen and examine the Recommended for You list—apps that might interest you, based on your previous downloads.

4. *Searching.* If you know the name or type of app that you want, you can perform a search. Tap in the search box and enter the search text. When sufficient characters have been typed, a list of potential matches appears. Tap to select a suggestion or continue typing to further refine the suggestions.

More Precise Searches

You can search all apps by performing the search on the main screen or search within a category or subcategory by navigating to that category before beginning the search (refer to step 3).

5. When you see an app that interests you, tap its entry and review the product description, screenshots, and reviews. Tap any screenshot to see it at full size.

6. If you decide to download the app, tap its Free or price button.

First Download Only

Until you enable Amazon's 1-Click ordering and specify a preferred payment method, you can't download apps. The first time you attempt to download an item, you'll be stepped through the process of completing your Amazon account setup. To add a payment method to your account, use your computer's browser to visit www.amazon.com, log into your account, and go to Add a Credit or Debit Card.

7. The button's label changes to Get App (for a free app) or Buy App (for a paid app). Tap the button to initiate the download, charging it to your designated credit or debit card if it's not free.

8. The permissions that the app requires are shown. Scroll through the permissions, and tap Install to install the app or Cancel if you've changed your mind.

9. The app is installed on your phone and its icon is added to Apps. If you'd like to run it now, tap Open; otherwise, tap Done. Check your email for a receipt from Amazon.

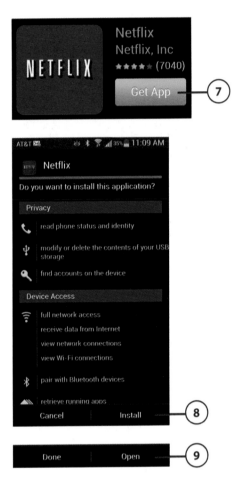

Customizing the Amazon Appstore

1. Press the Menu key and tap Settings.

2. The Settings screen appears, enabling you to change important Appstore options. Altering most settings requires that you supply your Amazon.com user password.

3. *Gift Cards.* If you have an Amazon gift card or a promotional code, tap this option to add it to your account (enabling you to apply the amount to app purchases). Enter the gift card or claim code and then tap Redeem.

4. *Use Wi-Fi When Downloading Apps.* To avoid using your data connection to download large apps, tap this option to specify that apps larger than *X* MB should be downloaded only using Wi-Fi. (Apps smaller than the specified size can be downloaded using 3G/4G, if you don't have Wi-Fi access at that moment.)

5. *Parental Controls.* When this option is enabled and anyone attempts to purchase *in-app material* such as subscriptions or game add-ons, your Amazon.com password or a PIN is requested. Tap Enable Parental Controls to enable the feature.

If Use PIN isn't checked, your Amazon.com password is requested for in-app purchases. If Use PIN is checked, you must enter a numeric PIN instead of the password.

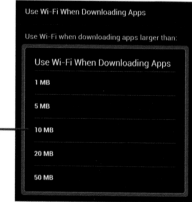

6. *In-App Purchasing.* When this option is enabled, you can buy app add-ons or subscriptions from within any app that offers them. (This option is enabled by default.)

7. *Notifications.* Enable the various Notifications options to allow the Amazon Appstore to transmit notifications to the phone whenever something important occurs. (To enable *any* notification options, you must enable the first one.)

8. *Collect App Usage Data.* When enabled, Amazon collects usage data concerning the frequency and duration that you use the apps you've downloaded from the Appstore.

MORE AMAZON APPSTORE COMMANDS

You might find the following additional Appstore commands helpful:

- Press the Menu key and tap My Apps to get the list of apps that you've downloaded from the Appstore. Tapping a category on the My Apps screen enables you to view installed apps on the current phone (Device), apps you've previous downloaded for this or another device (Cloud), or only those apps for which an update is available (App Updates). Tap a button to open, download, or update a listed app.

My Apps   /

Categories ———   Device   Cloud   App Updates

You have 3 apps installed   Refresh

Adobe Reader
Adobe Systems   Open

Netflix
Netflix, Inc   Open

- When browsing for new apps, note that every app page has Save for Later and Share This App buttons at the bottom of the screen. When viewing an app of interest, tap Save for Later to add the app to a list that you can view by pressing Menu, tapping More, and Saved for Later. Tap the Share button to forward information about the app to a friend via email or text message.

Save for later   ›   —— **Save for later**

Report an issue   ›

Share this app   ›   —— **Share with a friend**

- To return directly to the main screen, tap the Appstore logo at the top of the screen, or press the Menu key and tap Store Home.

Managing Apps

You can manage your installed apps by creating Home screen shortcuts to your favorite ones and uninstalling the apps you no longer want.

Creating Home Screen Shortcuts

To simplify the process of accessing your favorite apps, you can add Home screen shortcuts to them. You can accomplish this by using menus or by manually dragging them from Apps. (To learn more about moving and removing shortcuts, see "Customizing the Home Screen" in Chapter 3.)

1. Navigate to the Home screen page where you want to add the app shortcut, and then tap the Apps icon.

2. Press and hold the icon of the app for which you want to create a shortcut.

3. Drag it into position on the previously selected Home screen page (or to another page, if you like) and release the icon when it's in the desired spot.

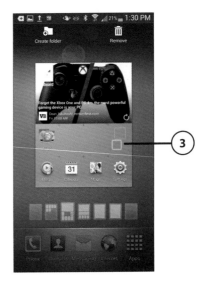

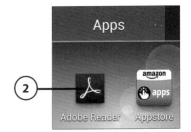

Uninstalling Apps

If you're unhappy with an app or no longer need it, you can *uninstall* it, removing it from your phone and reclaiming the storage space it was using. Note, however, that only apps you've downloaded can be uninstalled; you can't remove the built-in, core apps.

Uninstalling Using the Application Manager

1. On the Home screen, tap Apps, followed by Settings.

2. Select the More tab and tap Application Manager.

3. Select the Downloaded tab, scroll to find the app that you want to uninstall, and tap its entry.

4. Tap the app's Uninstall button. (Only apps that you are permitted to remove have an active Uninstall button.)

5. Tap the OK button on the confirmation screen that appears.

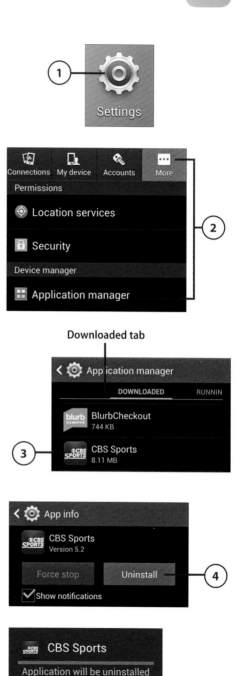

Downloaded tab

Uninstalling Using the Task Manager

1. On almost any screen, press and hold the Home key until the list of recent and active applications appears. Tap the Task Manager button.

2. Tap the Downloaded tab, scroll to find the app that you want to remove, and tap its Uninstall button.

3. Tap the OK button on the confirmation screen that appears.

Downloaded tab

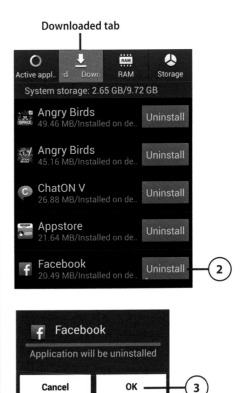

Uninstalling Using Google Play

1. From the Home screen, launch Google Play by tapping Apps and then tapping Play Store. (You may also have a Play Store shortcut on a Home screen page that you can tap.)

2. Press the Menu key and tap My Apps.

3. Select the Installed tab, and tap the app that you want to uninstall.

4. On the app's Google Play page, tap the Uninstall button. (Although this button is available for most apps, it isn't presented for system apps such as Group Play.)

5. In the dialog box that appears, confirm the app's removal by tapping OK.

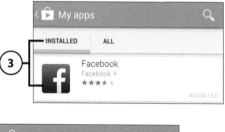

Updating Apps

Developers occasionally release updates of their apps. When an update of an installed app becomes available at Google Play, a notification appears in the Notification panel. The core apps are often updated through GooglePlay, too.

1. Launch Google Play by performing steps 1 and 2 of "Uninstalling Using Google Play." With the Installed tab selected, a list of the apps for which updates are available is displayed.

2. Do either of the following:

   • To update an individual app, tap its Update text, and tap the Update button on the screen that appears.

   • To simultaneously update all listed apps, tap Update All at the top of the list.

   The selected updates download and install.

Another Update or Uninstall Option

You can also update or uninstall an app by going to its page in Google Play and tapping the appropriate button.

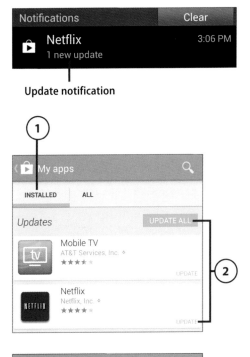

Update notification

Google Play page

MORE ABOUT UPDATES

Here's some additional information about updating that you may find helpful:

- Updating apps from the Amazon Appstore works in much the same way as Google Play. When you tap an update notification, Amazon Appstore launches and takes you to the My Apps section. Select the App Updates tab to view the list of new updates and then install one or all.
- You can manually check for Google Play or Amazon Appstore updates by launching the appropriate app, pressing the Menu key, and tapping My Apps.
- If you've downloaded an app directly from a developer's website, you should periodically revisit the site to check for newer versions.

MOVING APPS TO YOUR MEMORY CARD

In July 2013, carriers delivered a software update for the Galaxy S 4 that made it possible to move some apps from built-in memory to an add-in memory card—enabling users to reclaim the device memory used by large apps.

1. Open Settings, select the More tab, and tap Application Manager.
2. Swipe horizontally to display the On SD Card tab.
3. To move a listed app to your memory card, tap its check box.
4. On the App Info screen for the app, tap Move to SD Card.

If you later want to move an app back to the phone's built-in memory, repeat steps 1–3 for the app and then tap the Move to Device Storage button.

Selected tab

Selected app

Move to memory card

In this chapter, you discover how to use the phone's GPS chip with two of the preinstalled location-based apps. Topics include the following:

→ Enabling and disabling GPS

→ Obtaining directions from the current location to your destination

→ Finding specific addresses and nearby businesses

Using GPS Apps

The Galaxy S 4 has an embedded *Global Positioning System* (*GPS*) chip that enables the network to determine your phone's current location. When the GPS is active, the phone can use E911 emergency location services to transmit your location (see "Emergency Calling" in Chapter 4), as well as run a variety of apps that display maps of your surroundings, provide turn-by-turn driving and walking directions, determine the distance to various locations, and show you where you are in relation to your friends.

Enabling/Disabling GPS

As with Bluetooth and Wi-Fi, you can enable and disable the phone's GPS as needed. Because the regular polling of GPS drains the battery and consumes data, you can disable the feature when you aren't using it.

Use any of the following methods to enable or disable GPS:

Notification panel

Enable/disable GPS

- Pull down the Notification panel and tap the GPS icon to toggle its current state.

- Open Settings (switch to the Home screen and tap Apps, Settings, or use one of the other methods discussed in Chapter 1). Select the More tab and tap Location Services. Tap Use GPS Satellites to toggle its current state.

- If you perform an action in an app that requires GPS (such as requesting navigation instructions) but GPS isn't enabled, you are usually asked to enable it in Location Services. After enabling GPS by tapping the Use GPS Satellites check box, press the Back key to return to the app.

Enable/disable GPS

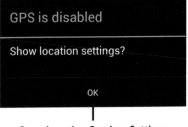

Open Location Services Settings

Getting Directions

The most common use of GPS is to get turn-by-turn driving, bicycling, or walking directions from your current location (determined by the GPS) to a destination. Turn-by-turn directions are provided by Google Navigation. In addition to running this app directly, other apps such as Local and Maps link to Navigation when navigation assistance is requested. Some carriers, such as AT&T, also provide their own navigation app that you can elect to use rather than using Navigation.

Pick One—Any One

Google Navigation, Maps, and Local are interconnected. Essentially, it doesn't matter which one you launch. At any time, you can open the current GPS app's main menu to use the resources of one of the other apps: Navigation, Maps, or Local.

Main menu icon

Using Google Navigation

Navigation is a GPS-based app that provides voice-guided directions between any two points. If you use Maps, Local, or a carrier-provided GPS app, you can usually switch to Navigation for directions by tapping a Navigation button, icon, or menu command.

1. Enable the GPS using one of the methods described in the previous section, "Enabling/Disabling GPS."

2. On the Home screen, tap Apps, followed by Navigation.

3. Specify your mode of travel (Driving, Walking, or Bicycling) by tapping the menu icon, and then indicate your destination by speaking into the microphone, typing, or tapping the Go Home icon (as described in steps 4–6).

Where Am I?

To check your current location, tap the Map icon. You can customize the map by pressing the Menu key, tapping Layers, and selecting the items or views that you want to display. When you finish, tap Destination to return to Navigation's main screen.

4. If the destination is your house, tap the Go Home icon.

Recent Destinations

If you've recently traveled to this destination using the GPS, you may be able to select it from the Recent Destinations list.

5. To set your destination by speaking, tap the Speak Destination icon and say where you want to go. If necessary, choose a location from the ones suggested.

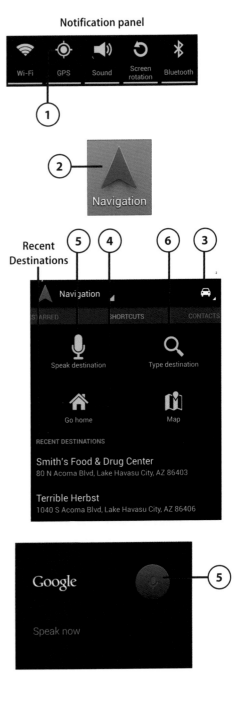

Notification panel

Wi-Fi GPS Sound Screen rotation Bluetooth

Navigation

Recent Destinations

Navigation

STARRED SHORTCUTS CONTACTS

Speak destination Type destination

Go home Map

RECENT DESTINATIONS

Smith's Food & Drug Center
80 N Acoma Blvd, Lake Havasu City, AZ 86403

Terrible Herbst
1040 S Acoma Blvd, Lake Havasu City, AZ 86406

Google

Speak now

6. To set your destination by typing, tap the Type Destination icon, enter the search text, and tap the Search key. If necessary, choose a location from the ones suggested.

Use Navigation or the Provider's App?

As mentioned, some service providers include their own navigation app as an alternative to Navigation. Prior to displaying the map to your destination, a Complete Action Using dialog box appears. Select the navigation app that you want to use for this trip and then tap Always or Just Once.

7. The route appears. As you travel, you receive audible instructions at each change in direction.

Provider's app   Navigation

Menu

8. When you reach the destination,
do one of the following:

- To return to the main screen to
set a new destination, press the
Menu key or tap the menu icon
(in the lower-right corner), tap
More, and tap Set Destination.

- If you're done using Navigation,
press the Menu key and tap
Exit Navigation. (As an alternative, repeatedly press the Back
key until the Exit Navigation?
dialog box appears, and then
tap OK.) You can disable the
GPS, if you're done using it.

>>>Go Further

OTHER NAVIGATION OPTIONS

In addition to using voice instructions to get to where you want to go, here
are some other options to explore while using Navigation:

- To display the buildings and terrain *en route* (as shown in the previous
task), open the menu, tap Layers, and tap Satellite. To reveal nearby
businesses, tap Gas Stations, Restaurants, and so on.

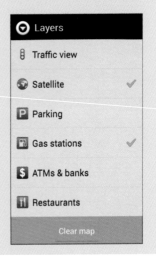

- Tap anywhere to reveal several useful icons. You can tap the + (plus) or − (minus) icon to zoom in or out. Tap the right or left arrow icon to step forward or backward through the route.

- To get a text list of turn-by-turn directions, press the Menu key and tap Directions List.

Previous — Next

Directions List

Zoom controls

- To view alternate routes to your destination, press the Menu key and tap Route and Alternates. Tap the Alternate Routes icon to display alternate route thumbnails. To view an alternate route, tap its thumbnail. After selecting the route you want to take, tap the Navigation icon.

Alternate route thumbnails

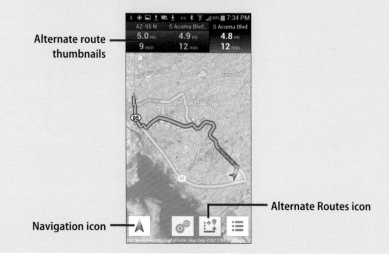

Alternate Routes icon

Navigation icon

Using Google Local

Formerly known as Places, Local helps you find nearby places to eat, drink, or sleep. Each listed business typically includes a description, address, phone number, photos, and user reviews. After selecting a destination, you can get voice or text directions from your current location.

1. Enable the GPS using one of the methods described earlier in "Enabling/Disabling GPS."

2. On the Home screen, tap Apps, followed by Local.

3. The opening screen of Local appears.

4. *Optional:* To start driving from a location other than your present one, tap the location indicator. In the Choose Your Location dialog box, tap Enter an Address. (To start from a location that's close to the one shown at the bottom of the screen, you can tap the At *location* text.)

5. To set your destination, do one of the following:

   • *General Destination.* To see a list of businesses of a given type that are in your area, tap a general icon at the top of the screen or scroll to the In This Area list and tap a more specific text link.

Settings

Location sources

Use GPS satellites
Allows apps to use GPS to pinpoint your location ✓ ①

② Local

④

⑤

◆ ↑ 🖼   ⑤ ✱ 🛜 ⏚41%▄ 5:24 PM

👤 Local ⬩   🔍

📍 Lake Havasu City ⬩

⑤   🍴   ☕   🍸   ⭐
     Restaurants   Cafes   Bars   Attractions

Help friends find your reviews
Publish your existing reviews to Google+ Local to help your friends discover your favorite places.

③   **Publish reviews**

WRITE REVIEWS FOR RECENT PLACES

Java Rush
2231 McCulloch Blvd N, Lake Havasu...   ✕
from search history

Starbucks
55 S Lake Havasu Ave, Lake Havasu...   ✕
from search history

📍 **At Schwartz Steven?**
Check-in, review or view details

⑤

IN THIS AREA	
pizza restaurants	mexican restaur...
chinese restaur...	coffee shops
resorts	motels
steakhouse	burger restaura...
barbecue restau...	happy hour

- *Specific Destination.* If there's a *specific* place you have in mind, tap the Search icon at the top of the screen. Type or speak the destination, tap the Search key on the keyboard, and select your destination from the list that appears.

Try a General Search

In addition to searching for a particular business, you can search for a *class* of business by entering a search phrase, such as *gas station* or *dentist*. After executing the search, you can filter the results by tapping buttons at the top of the screen.

6. Review the information that appears, and do one of the following:

   - To see the place's location on a map, tap the Map icon. After viewing the map, press the Menu key and tap the Directions icon.

   - To go directly to the Directions screen (skipping the map display), tap the Directions icon.

Filters

Clear search

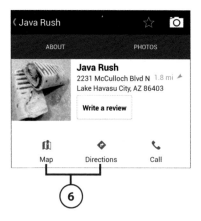

7. The Directions screen shows the starting point and destination. Select a transportation method (driving, public transportation, bike, or walking) by tapping its icon.

8. *Optional:* Tap the Get Directions button to view turn-by-turn instructions on the map. You can step through the route by tapping segments or the next or previous icon. You can scroll the screen by dragging, and zoom in or out by spreading your fingers apart or pinching them together.

Navigate from Get Directions

If you prefer audio instructions, tap the Navigation icon.

9. Tap the Navigation button for turn-by-turn audio directions. If a Complete Action Using dialog box appears, select Navigation or an alternate navigation app.

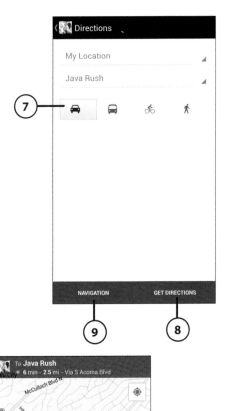

10. The route appears. As you travel, you receive audible instructions at each change in direction.

11. When you reach your destination, tap the menu icon (or press the Menu key) and select Exit Navigation. You can also disable the GPS, if you want.

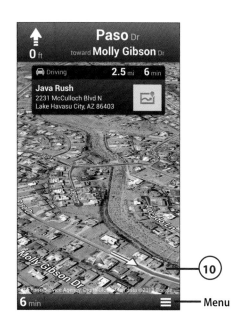

Menu

Music app

In this chapter, you find out how to play your favorite music on the phone. Topics include the following:

→ Using the Music app to play songs stored on the phone
→ Creating, using, and managing song playlists
→ Using Group Play to broadcast songs to multiple phones

Playing and Managing Music

If you're in the mood for musical entertainment, your Galaxy S 4 is up to the task. In this chapter, you find out how to use the built-in Music app to play songs and other tracks stored on your phone. With the new Group Play feature, you can play a song on several phones, creating a stereo effect.

Some Songs Can't Be Played

Most music tracks stored on your PC or Mac will play in Music. Copy-protected songs, such as those encoded with Apple's *AAC (protected)* codec, can be copied to the phone but will refuse to play.

Playing Stored Songs with the Music App

You might have amassed a collection of your favorite tracks in iTunes, Windows Media Player, or another PC or Mac media organizer. By following the techniques described in Chapter 15, you can use USB, Wi-Fi, or Bluetooth to copy those songs to your phone. Using Music, you can play these songs whenever you want.

1. On the Home screen, tap the Music shortcut (if you haven't removed it). Otherwise, tap Apps and then tap Music.

Another Music Player

A second music player app is pre-installed on the Galaxy S 4. Play Music (or Google Play Music) is a general music player that works much like Music. In addition to playing content stored on your phone, Play Music links directly to Google Play, enabling you to easily preview and buy new songs. Be sure to check out its customizable equalizer.

2. To find the first song you'd like to hear, tap Songs, Albums, or Artists to view an alphabetical list of your songs, albums, or artists/groups; alternatively, tap Playlists to view *playlists* (groups of songs) you've created, as well as your favorite, most played, recently played, and recently added tracks. See the "Working with Playlists" section for additional information. For instructions on customizing the tabs, see "More Fun with Music" at the end of this section.

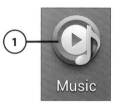

Searching for a Song

You can search for music, too. Press the Menu key and tap Search to search for a song title, album, or artist you want to hear. (In most views, you can also press and hold the Menu key to automatically initiate a search.)

3. If the song you want isn't visible, continue tapping icons to narrow the results. For instance, when viewing the Artists list, tap an artist, tap an album, and then tap the song that you want to play.

Additional Options for the Selected Song

If you press and hold a song title in any view other than Playlists, a pop-up menu appears. You can delete the song from the phone (Delete), set it as a new phone or contact ringtone (Set As), or add it to a playlist (Add to Playlist), for example. If the song is currently playing, press the Menu key to display these options.

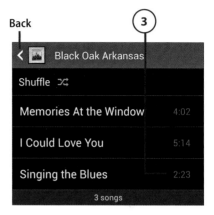

Back

3

Song pop-up menu

4. The song begins to play (top).

5. *Optional:* Switch to a dedicated, full-screen view (bottom) by tapping the album icon or its placeholder. To restore the original view, tap the down arrow icon or press the Back key.

Song Selection Affects Playback

The song you initially select determines what other songs automatically play after the selected song ends, as well as what additional songs are available to you without returning to the main selection screen. For instance, if you select a song from an album, all additional songs from the album will play until the last track is completed.

The order in which the songs play is determined by the state of the Shuffle icon. When there's a slash through it, songs play in listed order. If you tap the icon to remove the slash, the songs in the selection play in random order (shuffled).

6. Tap the Play/Pause button to pause or continue playback. In list view, tapping the name of the active song (shown in blue) has the same effect.

7. *Full-screen view only:* Drag the playback slider or tap a spot on the line to go forward or backward in the song.

8. Tap the Previous or Next button or swipe the screen to the left or right to play the previous or next track in the album or current selection, respectively.

Shuffle icon

9. *Full-screen view only:* Tap the List button to play a different song from the current album or selection. To make a *new* selection (such as choosing a different album), press the Back key until you reach the main Music screen.

10. Press the phone's volume control or tap the onscreen speaker icon (in full-screen view only) to increase or decrease the volume. Adjust the volume by pressing the volume control or adjusting the slider.

11. *Optional:* To change the equalizer setting, tap the *SoundAlive* icon on the volume slider, select a setting in the SoundAlive dialog box, and tap OK. (You can also open the dialog box by pressing the Menu key and tapping Settings, SoundAlive.) Some settings, such as Virtual 7.1 ch, can be selected only when you're using earphones.

Basic Controls Available Outside of Music

If all you want to do is pause, continue play, or switch songs within the current album, playlist, or selection, you can do so from the Notification panel. You can do the same using the Music widget (if it's installed).

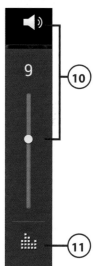

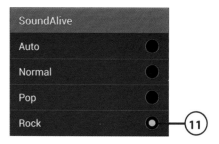

12. If you leave the Music screens (to run another app, for example), you can return to Music by launching it again or tapping the album icon in the Notification panel.

13. *Optional:* Quit Music by pressing the Menu key and tapping End.

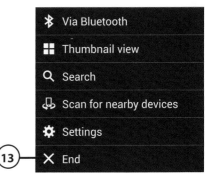

Working with Playlists

Playing a specific song or album isn't always what you want to do. For such times, you can create special song selections called playlists. A *playlist* is any combination of tracks that you want to play together. For instance, you might create a playlist that includes all albums by a favorite group or songs from a genre (such as blues, techno, or classical) performed by many different artists.

Creating a Playlist

You can create a new playlist in several ways, but the simplest—and the one you're most likely to remember—is to start from Playlists view.

1. Within Music, press the Back key as many times as necessary to reach the main screen, and tap the Playlists tab.

2. Press the Menu key, and tap Create Playlist.

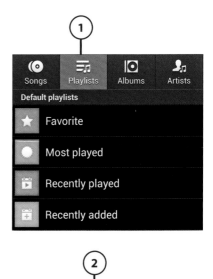

3. Name the new playlist, and tap OK.

4. The new, empty playlist appears.

Adding Songs to a Playlist

Here are some of the ways to add songs to a playlist:

- To select from an alphabetical list of all songs on your phone, open the playlist. Tap Add Music for a newly created playlist, or tap the plus (+) icon for a previously created playlist. Select the songs/tracks, and tap Done.

- To add entire albums or an artist to the playlist, tap a view tab (such as Albums or Artists) to help you find the material that you want to include in the playlist. Press and hold the artist or album name, tap Add to Playlist in the dialog box that appears, and then tap the name of the playlist to which you want to add the material.

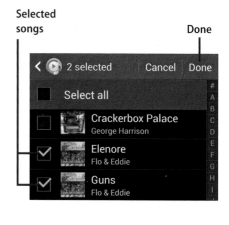

Selected songs

Done

Selected artist

Add all songs

- While browsing songs from an album or by an artist, you can add multiple songs by pressing the Menu key, tapping Add to Playlist, selecting the songs, tapping Done, and then selecting the target playlist.

- While playing a song, you can add it to a playlist by pressing the Menu key, tapping Add to Playlist, and selecting the play-list. (In list view, you can also press and hold the song title to reveal this menu.)

Selected songs   Done

Marked as a favorite

Built-in Playlists

In addition to the custom playlists you create, Music provides several playlists that it automatically maintains: Most Played, Recently Played, and Recently Added. An additional playlist called Favorite contains all songs that you've marked as favorites. To mark a playing song as a favorite, switch to full-screen view and tap the star icon above the playback indicator. To remove a song from the Favorite playlist, tap the star icon again or open the Favorite play-list, press and hold the song title, and tap Remove in the menu that appears.

Playing Songs from a Playlist

To play songs from a playlist, follow these steps.

1. Return to the main Music screen by pressing the Back key as many times as necessary. Tap the Playlists tab to view the defined playlists, and tap the playlist that you want to hear. Your created playlists (My Playlists) appear below the built-in ones (Default Playlists).

2. Tap the song you want to hear first. (If you select the first song, the entire playlist plays.)

3. The selected song (shown in blue) begins to play. When it's done, other songs from the playlist play until Music reaches the last song in the playlist or you halt playback.

4. *Optional*: Tap the album icon (or its placeholder) in the controller to switch to full-screen view.

5. *Optional*: Tap the Shuffle icon to toggle between playing the songs in order (slashed) and playing them in random order (no slash). The Shuffle icon is visible only in full-screen or list view.

Picking a Different Song

If you'd rather hear a different song from the playlist, tap the List button and select the new song.

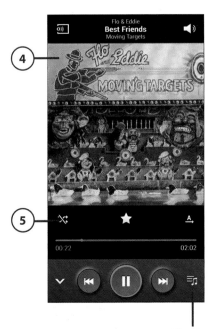

List view

Managing Playlists

Using Menu commands, you can add songs to or remove songs from the current custom playlist, change the playback order, or edit the playlist's title. You can also delete custom playlists that you no longer want.

1. Open the custom playlist that you want to modify. (On the main Music screen, tap Playlists, and then tap the playlist's name in the My Playlists section.)

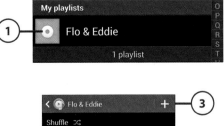

2. Press the Menu key to display the menu.

3. *Add songs.* Tap the plus (+) icon to add songs to the playlist. Select the songs/tracks and tap Done.

4. *Remove songs.* Tap Remove to remove songs from the playlist. On the Remove screen, select each song that you want to remove and tap Remove. (Note that removing a song from a playlist doesn't *delete* it; it just removes the song from the current playlist.)

5. *Edit the playlist title.* Tap Edit Title. In the dialog box that appears, modify the title and tap OK.

6. *Change song order.* Tap Change Order to set a new playback order for the songs in the playlist. To change a song's position, drag it up or down in the list by its dot pattern. When you finish, tap Done.

Deleting a Playlist

You can delete any custom playlist by pressing and holding its name on the Playlists screen. Tap Delete in the dialog box that appears. (*Caution:* The playlist is deleted immediately; no confirmation dialog box appears.)

It's Not All Good

MUSIC/iTUNES SHORTCOMINGS

When copying songs from computer to phone, you'll quickly note two major iTunes-related shortcomings. First, because iTunes supports synchronizing only with Apple hardware, such as the iPhone, iPod, and iPad, there's no painless way to copy tracks from your computer's iTunes library to the S 4. You have two options:

- Manually select songs on your computer and copy them to the phone using any of the methods discussed in Chapter 15. Like most Android apps, Music doesn't care where on your phone your tracks are stored, so you can copy them into any folder (or folders) that you want. To locate the music files on your Mac, check the /Users/*username*/Music/iTunes/ iTunes Music folder. You can find iTunes for Windows music in the \Users\ *username*\Music\iTunes\iTunes Media\Music folder. If you have other songs stored on your PC, you need to know the folders in which they're stored.

- Install a music-management app (such as doubleTwist with Magic Radio or iSyncr) that simplifies the process of downloading and, optionally, syncing music with that of your iTunes-based PC or Mac song library.

Second, although most of your albums have cover art in iTunes, many of those images will be missing in Music. The easiest way to fill in the blanks is to install an Android app that can tap into online music databases. Currently, three of the most popular ones are Cover Art Downloader, Album Art Grabber, and Cover Art Grabber—all free.

MORE FUN WITH MUSIC

>>>Go Further

To get the most from Music, here are two additional tips for you:

- The external speaker in your Galaxy S 4 has similar fidelity to that of the inexpensive transistor radios that were commonplace in the early 1960s. For better sound, place the phone on a solid surface, such as a desk or table. For *much* better sound, connect your earphones. Several SoundAlive equalizer settings are only available when you use earphones.

- Be sure to explore the Settings menu (press the Menu key and tap Settings). For example, Music Menu enables you to control the tabs that appear atop the lists; Music Auto Off ends the music after a time interval (like a sleep timer); and Voice Control enables you to control playback by saying keywords, such as play, pause, next, and volume down.

Sharing Songs with Group Play

Group Play, an app introduced with the Galaxy S 4, creates a Mobile Access Point on your phone, enabling you to share music, photos, or documents with up to 10 nearby Samsung phones and devices that are also running Group Play. Preinstalled on the Galaxy S 4, Group Play is also available on Google Play as a free download for the Galaxy S III, Galaxy Note II and 10.1, and Galaxy Tab 10.1.

Broadcast, Not Transferred

Group Play material is merely displayed or played on the group members' screens—much like streaming music or videos. For information on transferring songs and other files between phones, see Chapter 15.

1. From the Home screen, tap Apps, Group Play to launch the app on the phone that will share the music. Instruct the others to do the same on their phones.

2. Tap the Create Group button. (The Set Group Password check box determines whether others will be requested to enter a PIN to join the group.)

3. Instruct the others to tap the Join Group button. (If there are other nearby groups, they'll be asked to choose the one they want to join.)

4. Tap Share Music.

5. Select the songs/tracks that you want to play. (All eligible songs display in a scrolling list.) Tap OK.

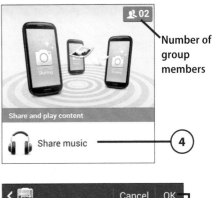

Number of group members

MP3 Files Only

In Group Play, only songs in MP3 format are listed and can be played.

6. The music begins to play on your phone.

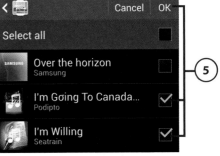

Settings

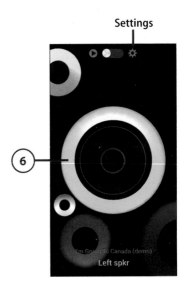

7. Instruct the others to tap Share Music. The music plays on their phones, too.

8. The song(s) selected in step 5 play in a continuous loop. To end the broadcast, press the Back key and tap OK in the confirmation dialog box.

9. The main Group Play screen reappears. You can continue the sharing session by selecting new content (repeating steps 4–7) or exit the program by pressing the Back key and tapping Yes in the confirmation dialog box. The others exit by doing the same.

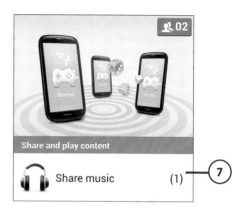

>>>Go Further

EXPLORING GROUP PLAY FOR MUSIC SETTINGS

While the music plays, you can do any of the following:

- To change the speaker style for all participants, press the Menu key, tap Speaker Style, select a style, and tap Apply.
- You can tap icons at the bottom of the screen to control playback, such as pausing the current song or skipping to the next one. You can also drag the slider to a new position in the track.
- Tap the Volume icon to change the volume for your phone, individual phones, or all phones.
- Tap a speaker to assign or reassign phones to that speaker. Numbers in parentheses show the number of phones assigned to each speaker.
- Tap the Member icon to display the group membership.
- Tap the Back icon in the upper-left corner to end music sharing.

When you finish making changes, tap the Play icon to restore the speaker display on your phone.

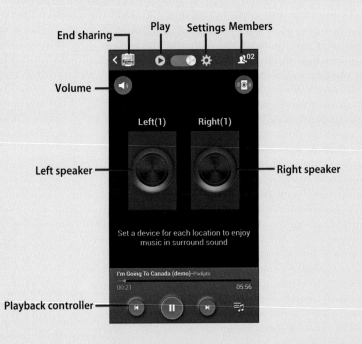

It's Not All Good

IF ONLY...

Although creating a monster stereo from two or more phones is a cool, fun feature, Group Play has some gotchas:

- You can only share music files in MP3 format. Files in other formats that you transfer to the phone won't be listed on the music selection screen. Unfortunately, the default format for songs ripped from CDs to iTunes or Windows Media Player—as well as those purchased from the iTunes Store—is not MP3. (Songs purchased from Google Play or Amazon.com, on the other hand, are MP3s.) If the songs that you want to share are in some other format, you must convert them to MP3s.

- The animated speakers are a big part of the Group Play experience. Unlike when playing videos, however, members' screens still go dark when their Screen Timeout period is exceeded. To avoid this, members can temporarily increase their timeout (Settings, My Device tab, Display, Screen Timeout) or enable Smart Stay and continuously look at the screen (Settings, My Device tab, Smart Screen, Smart Stay).

- Periodically—and often mysteriously—group members can spontaneously disconnect from Group Play. If this happens, they should press the Back key as many times as necessary to reconnect. If that fails, they can usually resolve the problem by exiting from the Group Play app, relaunching it, and repeating the steps to connect to the group and share music.

>>>Go Further

STREAMING MUSIC TO THE PHONE WITH PANDORA

In addition to playing songs that are stored on your phone, other apps can *stream* music to the phone from the Internet or your computer. (Streamed music resides on a server, not on your phone.) With the appropriate Android apps, you can listen to music transmitted over 3G/4G, Wi-Fi, or Bluetooth.

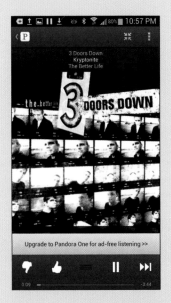

Pandora Internet Radio is one of the most popular Internet-based music streaming services. You define favorite *stations* by selecting from presets (such as Blues or Southern Rock), or you can create more specific stations based on artists, groups, or particular songs. Pandora sets the content for each station according to your specifications, and adds songs and groups that it considers similar. To download Pandora, launch the Play Store app, tap the search icon, and begin by typing **Pandora**. Select the *Pandora Internet Radio* entry.

The free version of Pandora is ad supported. And there are *lots* of ads—so many that it may remind you of using a browser without a pop-up blocker. Aside from the occasional voice advertisement, though, you can listen to several songs in a row without interruption.

In this chapter, you learn to use the phone's cameras to shoot, edit, share, and manage photos of yourself and other subjects. Topics include the following:

→ Using the front and rear cameras to shoot self-portraits and photos of other subjects

→ Viewing, managing, and sharing the current photo

→ Viewing stored photos in Gallery

→ Using Photo Editor to make simple edits to your shots

→ Generating a slideshow from selected folders or photos

Shooting, Editing, and Sharing Photos

If you keep your phone handy, you have no excuse for missing an unexpected photo opportunity. Using the pair of built-in cameras on the Galaxy S 4, you can easily shoot posed and candid high-resolution photos of friends, family, yourself, and anything else that catches your eye.

Setting a Storage Location for Photos and Videos

If you've added a memory card to the phone, be sure to set the Storage setting to Memory Card (as explained in "Using the Settings Dialog Box," later in this chapter).

Shooting Photos

You can shoot photos of subjects in front of you using the 13MP *(megapixel)* rear camera or take self-portraits with the 2MP front camera.

Shooting Self-Portraits with the Front Camera

Use *self-portrait mode* to take pictures of yourself—or yourself and a friend or two. Note that you can't use the flash or zoom in this mode.

1. Tap the Camera shortcut on the Home screen (if you haven't removed it). Otherwise, tap Apps and then tap Camera.

Lock Screen Quick Launch
You can also launch Camera from the lock screen by sliding the Camera icon upward (if it's present). For instructions on configuring the lock screen in this manner, see "Setting Lock Screen Options" in Chapter 17.

Lock screen icon

2. On the viewfinder screen, determine whether the rear or front camera is active. If the rear camera is active, switch to the front camera by tapping the Self Portrait icon.

3. *Optional:* To review or adjust the camera settings that will be used for the shot, tap the Settings icon twice. (The first tap reveals the Quick Settings icons; the second opens the Settings dialog box.) Make any desired changes on the Camera and General tabs of the Settings dialog box, and then dismiss the dialog box by pressing the Back key or tapping elsewhere onscreen. For additional information about Settings, see "Changing the Camera Settings," later in this section.

4. *Optional:* Tap the Mode button to set a shooting mode, such as Beauty Face or Best Photo. The default setting is Auto. The current mode is displayed near the top of the viewfinder screen. To learn more about modes, see "Selecting a Shooting Mode," later in this chapter.

5. *Optional:* Tap the Effects panel icon to open the panel and apply a special effect, such as Vignette. The effect is shown on the viewfinder screen as you frame the shot. To disable the effect on subsequent shots, open the panel, and select No Effect.

6. When you're ready to take the picture, tap the Camera button.

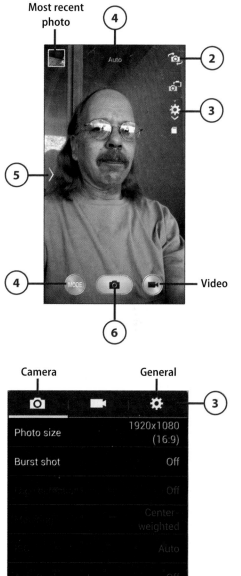

Most recent photo

Video

Camera   General

Where's the Photo?

To review all photos taken with the cameras, launch the Gallery app and open the Camera folder. (If you have an add-in memory card, there may be *two* Camera folders.) To go straight from the Camera app to the most recent photo you've taken, tap its thumbnail in the upper-left corner of the viewfinder screen.

Shooting Photos with the Rear Camera

Of course, most of the photos you'll shoot with your Galaxy S 4 will be of other people and subjects. Shooting photos of others is similar to shooting self-portraits, but it uses the higher-resolution rear camera and has many additional options. Note that virtually every step in the following task is optional, and you can perform steps 2–6 in any order that's convenient for you.

1. Launch the Camera app and determine whether the rear or front camera is active. If the front camera is active, switch to the rear camera by tapping the Self Portrait icon.

2. Whether you use the front or rear camera, you can take any photo in portrait (right-side up) or landscape (sideways) mode. To shoot in landscape mode, turn the phone sideways.

3. *Optional:* Frame your subject by zooming in or out. (The Galaxy S 4 has a 4x digital zoom.) Press the volume up/down button on the side of the phone, or you can touch the viewfinder screen with two fingers and spread them apart to zoom in or pinch them together to zoom out.

4. *Optional:* Review or adjust the camera settings that will be used for the shot. To open the Settings dialog box, tap the Settings

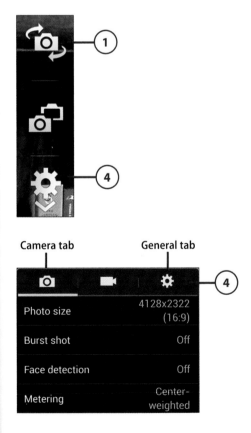

icon twice, or press the Menu
key and tap Settings. Make any
necessary changes on the Camera
and General tabs of the Settings
dialog box, and then dismiss
the dialog box by pressing the
Back key or tapping elsewhere
onscreen. For additional
information about Settings, see
"Changing the Camera Settings,"
later in this section.

5. *Optional:* Tap the Mode button at
   the bottom of the screen to set a
   shooting mode, such as Beauty
   Face or Best Photo. The default
   setting is Auto. The currently
   selected mode is displayed near
   the top of the viewfinder screen.
   To learn more about modes, see
   "Selecting a Shooting Mode," later
   in this chapter.

6. *Optional:* Tap the Effects panel
   icon to open the panel and apply
   a special effect, such as Grey-
   scale, Sepia, or Moody. The effect
   is shown on the viewfinder screen
   as you frame the shot. To disable
   the effect on subsequent shots,
   open the panel and select No
   Effect.

7. *Optional:* To set the focus to a
   particular area, tap that spot on
   the viewfinder screen. The focus
   rectangle turns green when the
   lighting and focus are sufficient to
   snap the photo.

8. When you're ready to take the
   picture, tap the Camera button.

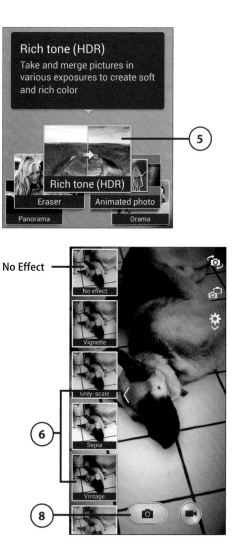

Avoid Odd Angles for Faces

When shooting portraits, you can avoid misshapen faces by holding the camera at the same angle as that of your subject. If your results are subpar, try another shot while ensuring that the phone isn't tilted—even a little.

Changing the Camera Settings

Before taking a photo, you can apply optional settings to enable or disable the flash and adjust the exposure, resolution, ISO, and so on. Note that some settings are available only for the rear-facing camera and others only for self-portraits. Also, certain automated settings can interact with and prevent you from altering manual settings. For example, when Anti-Shake is enabled, you cannot set ISO.

You can change settings in three places: the Quick Settings menu, the Settings dialog box, and by selecting a shooting mode.

Using Quick Settings

The Quick Settings are six icons on the viewfinder screen from which you can make settings adjustments prior to taking a photo or recording a video. To reveal the Quick Settings, tap the Settings icon. The permanent Quick Settings are Settings, Recording Mode, and Share. The other three icons (Flash, Auto Night Detection, and Voice Control) are explained later in "The Settings Dialog Box." You can replace them with icons of your choosing, as described at the end of this section.

Ever-Present Icons

When the Quick Settings are hidden, the current Flash setting is displayed beside or beneath the Settings icon. The current Storage setting (Device or Memory Card) is also shown, specifying where the shot will be saved. This pair of icons is for display purposes only; you can't interact with them.

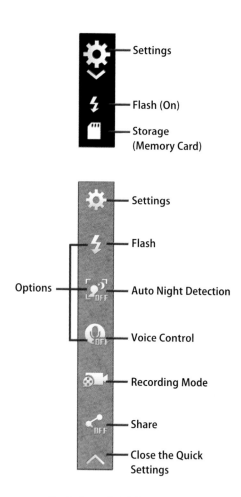

Settings

Flash (On)

Storage
(Memory Card)

Settings

Flash

Options —

Auto Night Detection

Voice Control

Recording Mode

Share

Close the Quick Settings

- *Settings.* Tap the Settings icon to open the Settings dialog box. You can also open it by pressing the Menu key and tapping Settings.

- *Recording Mode.* Applicable only when shooting videos, you can set one of these special recording modes: small movie for inclusion in a multimedia message, slow motion, or fast motion.

- *Share.* When enabled, photos are automatically shared with others using the selected method, such as Buddy Photo Share.

Customize the Quick Settings

You can replace the Flash, Auto Night Detection, and Voice Control icons with other icons of your choosing. Press the Menu key and tap Edit Quick Settings. To replace an icon, select a replacement icon in the large array, press and hold the icon, and then drag it onto an eligible icon in Quick Settings.

Replacing a Quick Settings icon

Using the Settings Dialog Box

To open the Settings dialog box, tap the Settings icon at the top of the screen twice. (You can also press the Menu key and tap Settings.) Settings are organized in three tabs: Camera, Video, and General. Settings that apply to still photos are on the Camera and General tabs.

Camera Settings

- *Photo Size*. To shoot at the camera's highest resolution, select 13M: 4128×3096 (4:3). If you want the photo to match the screen's dimensions, select the next lower resolution of 9.6M: 4128×2322 (16:9). If you're running out of storage space or intend to share the photo on the web or in email, you can select a lower resolution.

Alter the Resolution After the Shot

Using almost any image-editing program (such as Photoshop), you can reduce the resolution *after* shooting the photo.

Camera

Photo size		4128x2322 (16:9)
Burst shot		Off
Face detection		Off
Metering		Center-weighted
ISO		Auto
Anti-Shake		On
Auto night detection		Off
		Rich tone only

Photo size

13M 4128x3096 (4:3)
W9.6M 4128x2322 (16:9)
8M 3264x2448 (4:3)
W6M 3264x1836 (16:9)
W2.4M 2048x1152 (16:9)

Megapixels

- *Burst Shot.* When enabled, you can quickly take up to 20 shots by holding down the Camera button. The Burst Shot photos are stored in Device memory, regardless of your Storage setting.

- *Face Detection.* Enable Face Detection when you want the camera to search for a face in the shot and optimize the focus for the face.

- *Metering.* Specify the method used to perform light metering: Center-Weighted, Matrix, or Spot.

- *ISO.* The ISO setting is for film speed or sensitivity to light. You can use a lower ISO for shots taken on a bright, sunny day and use a higher ISO for dimly lit shots or ones taken in dark settings. Options include Auto (allow the camera to set the ISO), 100, 200, 400, and 800.

- *Anti-shake.* Anti-shake adjusts shots for unintended blur caused by camera movement.

- *Auto Night Detection.* Detects and adjusts for low-light conditions.

- *Save As.* This setting is only enabled when the shooting mode is Rich Tone (HDR).

General Settings

General

- *GPS Tag.* When enabled, the image file's metadata contains information that shows where the shots were taken, based on the GPS.

- *Review.* When enabled and you take a shot, the photo immediately opens in Gallery, so you can examine, delete, or edit it.

- *Volume Key.* This setting dictates what happens when you press the Volume key. Options include Zoom Key (zooms in or out), Camera Key (snaps a photo), or Record Key (starts a video recording).

GPS tag	Off
Review	Off
Volume key	The zoom key
Timer	Off
White balance	Auto
Exposure value	0
Guidelines	Off
Flash	Auto
Voice control	Off
Contextual filename	Off
Save as flipped	Off
Storage	Memory card
Shutter sound	On
Reset	

- *Timer.* To instruct the camera to snap the upcoming picture after a preset delay, select a 2-, 5-, or 10-second delay.

Timer Shots

With a 35mm camera, you'd use its timer to give yourself a few seconds to dash into a photo. With your Galaxy S 4, however, using the timer assumes that you have some way to make the phone stand on its own. You can prop it up or mount it in a tripod designed for smartphones.

Exposure slider

Exposure value

- *White Balance.* To adjust shots for current lighting "temperature" and how white will be displayed, select Auto (allow the camera to determine the best setting), Daylight, Cloudy, Incandescent, or Fluorescent.

- *Exposure Value.* Drag the Exposure value slider to the right to adjust for a dark scene or to the left for an overly bright scene.

- *Guidelines.* When enabled, white guidelines divide the screen into a 3×3 grid to make it easier to center and frame the subject matter.

- *Flash.* Tap Flash repeatedly to cycle through its three states: On, Off, and Auto. When set to Auto, the camera fires the flash when current lighting dictates that it's needed. To avoid blinding you, Flash is automatically disabled when taking self-portraits.

- *Voice Control.* You can optionally use voice commands (*Smile,
Cheese, Capture,* or *Shoot*) to
snap photos. When you set Voice
Control to On, you're taken to the
My Device tab, Voice Control section of Settings. You must enable
both Voice Control and Camera
to use voice commands to take
photos.

- *Contextual Filename.* When
enabled, your current location is
used as the suffix of each shot's
filename. While shooting, you
must also enable GPS Tags and
activate GPS on the phone.

- *Save as Flipped.* This setting is
available only when shooting a
self-portrait with the front-facing
camera. Enable it to automatically
flip each shot horizontally.

- *Storage.* Specify where photos
are stored as they're shot: Device
(internal memory) or Memory
Card (add-in memory card). An
icon for this setting is displayed in
Quick Settings.

- *Shutter Sound.* When enabled,
pressing the Camera button
results in a sound effect like a
shutter snap.

- *Reset.* Select this option and
tap OK to reset all settings in
the Settings dialog box to their
default values. Remove the check
mark if you want to leave previously modified Quick Settings
intact.

Voice Control

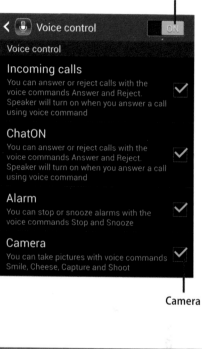

Camera

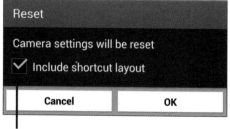

Restore default Quick Settings

Selecting a Shooting Mode

When you're in a rush—but not *that* much of a rush—you can select a shooting mode that automatically specifies a combination of camera settings or enables a special feature for the upcoming shot(s). Tap the Mode button and select one of these options:

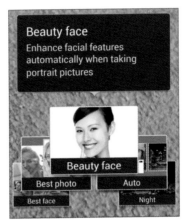

Shooting modes

- *Auto.* The default mode that snaps a single normal photo.

- *Night.* Enables you to shoot at night without using the flash.

- *Sports.* Useful when taking action shots.

- *Panorama.* Takes multiple shots as you pan across a scene and then stitches them together. Tap the Camera button to start the shot, slowly pan the camera, and then tap the button again to conclude the process. Reset the camera to Auto when you finish.

- *Eraser.* Takes five photos approximately 1–2 seconds apart and then creates a composite photo that eliminates any person or thing that wanders into the shot. You can optionally restore the moving items by tapping the running man icon.

Restore erased objects —— Save

- *Rich Tone (HDR).* Takes photos in *High Dynamic Range* (*HDR*) mode, increasing the amount of detail. When selected, the Save As setting on the Camera tab is also enabled.

- *Animated Photo.* Enables you to take a sequence of photos of a moving person, animal, or object; specify which parts of the object remain stationary and which ones move; and generate an animated GIF.

- *Drama.* Combines multiple shots of a moving person or object into a single photo. Press the Camera button once to take the shot. Tap thumbnails of the images you want to include, and tap Save to store the composite photo. Drama works best when the subject moves *through* the shot—from one side of the frame to the other—rather than toward or away from you.

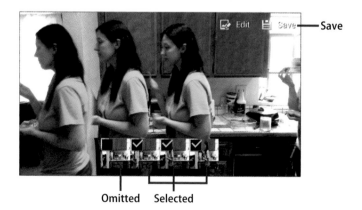

Save

Omitted   Selected

- *Sound & Shot.* Enables you to add up to 9 seconds of recorded audio to the photo you're shooting.

- *Best Face.* Enables you to take multiple shots of a group of people, pick the best expression for each person, and then merge them into a single shot. When framing the shot, the camera identifies each face by surrounding it with a yellow rectangle. Tap the Camera button once to take the series of shots. Then—one person at a time—tap the individual's selection rectangle, review the facial expression thumbnails, and tap the one you like best. Repeat this process for every additional person in the group, and then tap the Save icon.

Save

Select each best face to save

Selected expression

- *Best Photo.* Takes eight shots in quick succession and asks you to pick the ones you want to keep. Hold the camera steady, and tap the Camera button once. The photo judged by Camera to be the best is marked with a thumbs-up. Review the shots, tap thumbnails of the photos you want to save, and then tap the Disk icon.

- *Beauty Face.* Smooths the subject's facial features, reducing simple wrinkles, hiding pores and small blemishes, and so on. (People will accuse you of having these shots professionally retouched.)

Reset the Shooting Mode

The most recent shooting mode is retained. After shooting in any of the special modes, remember to reset the shooting mode to Auto. Other settings may also be retained and should be reset as needed.

Reviewing Photos

After taking a photograph, you can immediately examine and perform various actions on it, such as sharing, deleting, or renaming the shot. Read about additional options when viewing *any* stored photo or video in the "Using Gallery" section, later in this chapter.

Automatic Review

If you find that you typically review each photo before taking the next one, you can automate the switch to Gallery. In Camera, open Settings, select the General tab, and set Review to On.

1. To review the photo in Gallery, tap the photo's thumbnail in the upper-left corner of the viewfinder screen.

2. In Gallery, if tool icons aren't visible across the top of the screen, you can make them appear by tapping anywhere onscreen. In order, tapping icons enables you to do the following:

   - Select a different folder to open.

   - Share the image using a variety of methods, such as sending by Email, enclosing in a multi-media message, or posting it to Facebook.

   - Apply the most recently used sharing method.

   - Edit the photo.

   - Delete the photo.

Use last sharing method

Open a different folder

Sharing options ②

Edit

Delete

3. While examining the photo, you can also do any of the following:

   - Review the photo in portrait or landscape orientation by rotating the phone.

   - Zoom in or out by double-tapping the photo, spreading your fingers apart, or pinching your fingers together.

   - Tap other thumbnails at the bottom of the screen or swipe the screen horizontally to view other recent shots.

   - Press the Menu key and choose commands to perform other operations on the photo, such as rename it, mark it as a favorite, use it as Home screen or Lock screen wallpaper, rotate it, or add a note to the front or back.

4. When you're ready to return to Camera, press the Back key.

Selected thumbnail

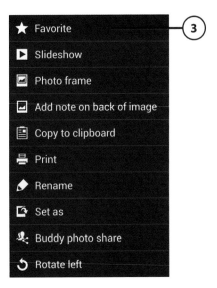

★ Favorite ③

▶ Slideshow

▣ Photo frame

▣ Add note on back of image

▤ Copy to clipboard

🖶 Print

✎ Rename

▣ Set as

👥 Buddy photo share

↺ Rotate left

Using Gallery

All photos and videos that are stored on your phone—regardless of whether you took them with Camera—can be viewed, edited, and managed in the Gallery app.

1. From the Home screen, launch Gallery by tapping the Apps icon, selecting the Apps tab, and tapping the Gallery icon. You can also launch it by tapping a Gallery shortcut on the Home screen.

Gallery

2. On the main Gallery screen, tap the album/folder that holds the pictures you want to view. The Camera folder, for example, contains photos you've taken with the phone's cameras. (Note that *all* folders that contain photos or videos are automatically listed in Gallery, regardless of the files' sources or whether they're in device memory or on an add-in memory card.) The number in parentheses beside each folder shows the number of files in the folder.

Two Views

There are two possible views of the screen: one in which the main album (Camera) is much larger than the other album thumbnails and a second view in which every album thumbnail is the same size. To switch between these views, pinch your fingers together or spread them apart—as you do when zooming. You can use these techniques to change the relative size of thumbnails *within* albums, too.

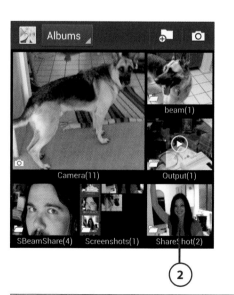

New   Open
Menu   Album   Camera

Number of photos

3. Thumbnails of the photos and videos contained in the folder appear. To view a photo, tap its thumbnail.

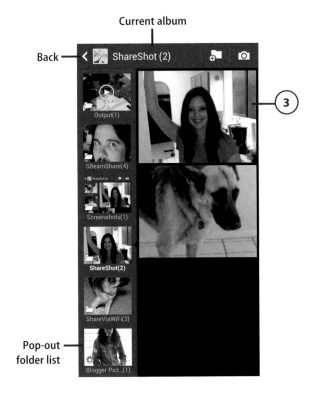

Current album

Back

Pop-out folder list

Pop-Out Folder List

To enable you to quickly switch folders without having to tap the Back icon or press the Back key, a pop-out scrolling list of image folders can optionally be displayed on the left side of the screen. Swipe to the right or left to reveal or hide the folder list.

4. You can view photos in portrait or landscape mode by rotating the phone. (Note that you must have Settings, My Device tab, Display, Auto-Rotate Screen enabled.)

5. You can zoom in or out on the photo by doing any of the following:

- Double-tap the image to double the current magnification. Repeat to shrink it to its previous size in the current orientation (portrait or landscape).

- Touch the screen and pinch your fingers together (zoom out) or spread them apart (zoom in).

- If Zoom (a Motion setting) is enabled, you can zoom in and out by pressing two fingers to the screen and then tilting the phone toward or away from you.

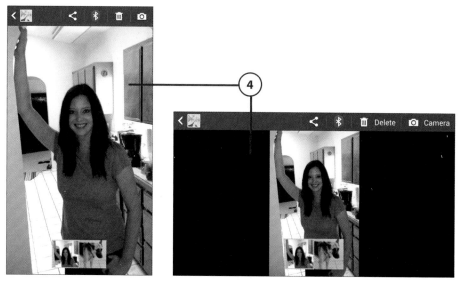

Portrait   Landscape

• If Pan (another Motion setting) is enabled and you've zoomed in on a photo, you can view the parts that are off-screen by pressing one finger to the screen and moving the phone up, down, left, or right.

Opens other folders in Gallery

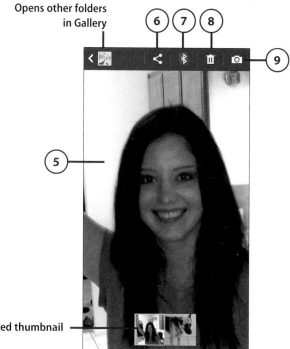

Selected thumbnail

Enabling Zoom

When Zoom is enabled, you can tilt the screen in Gallery to zoom in or out on the current picture. To enable this feature, open Settings, select the My Device tab, tap Motions and Gestures, enable and then tap Motion, and then enable Zoom. If you also want to be able to move around within images by moving the phone, you can enable Pan, too.

Zoom and Pan Motion settings

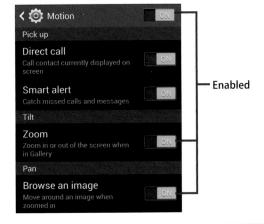

6.   To share the current photo via Email, Messaging, Facebook, or another means, tap the Share Via icon, and then choose a sharing method from the vertically scrolling menu. Options vary according to your installed apps, registered accounts, and carrier, but typically include the following:

- *Email, Gmail.* Send the image file as an email attachment using one of your email accounts or Gmail. See "Emailing Files" in Chapter 15 for instructions.

- *Messaging.* Transmit the photo as part of a multimedia message. See "Composing a Multimedia Message (MMS)" in Chapter 9 for instructions.

- *Bluetooth.* To transmit the photo to a Bluetooth-paired device (such as an iMac or a Bluetooth-equipped laptop), tap the Bluetooth icon and then tap the destination in the list of Bluetooth-paired devices. See "Transferring Files Using Bluetooth" in Chapter 15 for instructions.

- *Wi-Fi Direct.* Send the photo to another cell phone within range of yours that supports Wi-Fi Direct. See "Transferring Files Between Phones" in Chapter 15 for information on using Wi-Fi Direct.

- *Group Play.* Broadcast the photo to up to 10 nearby phones and devices that are running Group Play (see "Sharing Songs with Group Play" in Chapter 12).

Paired Bluetooth device

- *Flipboard*. Post the photo as a status update to your Facebook, Twitter, or similar account using the Flipboard app (see Chapter 9).
- *Google+, Twitter, Facebook*. Post the photo as a status update to your account.
- *Picasa*. Upload the photo to Picasa Web Albums (associated with your Google account). To view the uploaded photo, visit https://picasaweb.google.com.
- *S Memo*. Use the photo as a basis for a new S Memo that you can save and share.
- *ChatON*. Share the photo with ChatON buddies.

7. An icon for the most recently used Share Via method—in this case, Bluetooth—is always displayed, enabling you to quickly repeat the sharing method.

8. To delete the photo, tap the Delete icon. Tap OK in the confirmation dialog box.

9. To launch the Camera app to shoot a photo or video, tap the Camera icon.

10. Press the Menu key to see the following additional options:

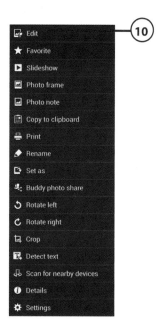

- *Edit.* Open the image for editing in Photo Editor. See "Using Photo Editor," later in this chapter, for instructions.

- *Favorite.* Mark this photo as a favorite. To later view your favorites in Gallery, open the menu and tap Favorites.

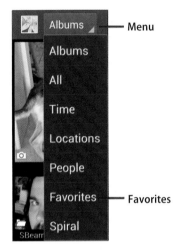

- *Slideshow.* Generate a slideshow from all images in the current folder. See "Running a Slideshow," later in this chapter, for instructions.

- *Photo Frame, Photo Note/Add Note On Back of Image.* Using your finger, you can jot something on the front or back of the photo, respectively. When you finish, tap the check mark icon to save your changes or tap the X icon to discard the note.

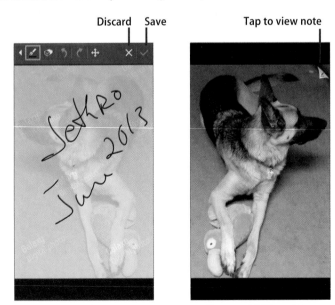

Creating a Photo Note   Picture with Photo Note

- *Copy to Clipboard.* Copy the image so that you can paste it elsewhere, such as into an email message.

- *Print.* Print the photo on a compatible Samsung wireless printer.

- *Rename.* Change the default name assigned to the photo to something meaningful. In the Rename dialog box, enter a new filename and tap OK.

> Rename
>
> 2013-05-12 Jethro & Duck|
>
> Cancel   OK

- *Set As.* Use the photo as a person's image in Contacts, the Home screen wallpaper, the Lock screen wallpaper, or both types of wallpaper.

- *Buddy Photo Share.* Use facial recognition to share the photo with friends who are in the shot.

- *Rotate Left, Rotate Right.* Rotate the image 90 degrees in the specified direction.

- *Crop.* By dragging the selection rectangle and its handles, specify the portion of the image that you want to retain and tap Done. (The cropped image is saved *in addition* to the original image—not as a replacement for it.)

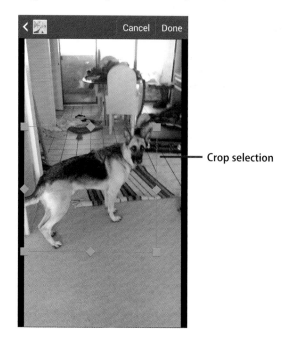

Crop selection

- *Detect Text.* If the photo contains a clear shot of some text, this command attempts to extract the text. Although there's no option to save the extracted text, you can use various sharing methods (such as Email or Gmail) to send the text to yourself or others.

- *Scan for Nearby Devices.* Scan for eligible devices within range with which the media can be shared.

- *Details.* Display the image's title, dimensions, file size, storage location, and other properties.

- *Settings.* Opens Google/Gmail Settings in which you can enable or disable tagging in your photos.

11. To view additional images, do one of the following:

- *Images in the current folder.* Swipe the screen to the left or right. As an alternative, you can tap the thumbnail of the specific image that you want to view. (If the thumbnails aren't visible, tap the current image once to reveal them.)

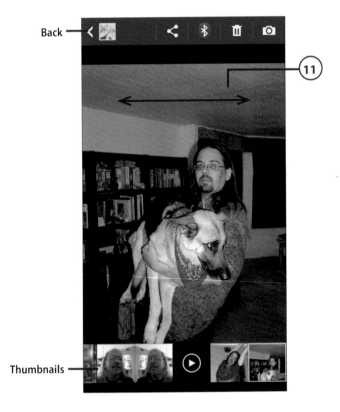

Back

11

Thumbnails

- *Images in a different folder.* Press the Back key or tap the Back icon repeatedly until the main Gallery screen appears; then go to step 2.

FOLDER AND IMAGE SELECTION

In addition to operating on one folder or photo at a time, some commands can be applied to multiple selected folders or images.

- *Folder-selection (main) screen*. You can delete an entire folder or transmit all of its files with a single command. Firmly press the folder and release; a green check mark appears on the folder to show it's selected. Then tap the Share Via or Delete icon. If you want to transmit or delete multiple folders, tap to select the additional folders before tapping a command icon. (To simultaneously select all folders, tap the Selection menu and choose Select All.) The Share Via or Delete command is performed on all selected folders. You can also press the Menu key and tap Slideshow to create a slideshow based on only images in the selected folders.

Folder-selection screen

- *Image-selection screen*. Similarly, after opening a folder, you can select one or more files on which to perform a command. Firmly press and release an image thumbnail to select it; a green check mark appears on the image to show it's selected. To select additional images, tap their thumbnails or choose Select All from the Selection menu. Then tap the Share Via or Delete icon.

Different Options for Different Image Sources

Not all actions can be performed on every folder. For example, you can share and transmit Picasa folders via Bluetooth, but you can't delete them. And you can't perform either action on your Facebook folders or images.

Using Photo Editor

If you don't need the feature set of a dedicated Mac or PC image-editing program, you can use Samsung's built-in Photo Editor app to perform basic edits on any image that's stored on the phone.

1. To edit the photo you're currently viewing in Gallery, press the Menu key and tap Edit.

2. Tool icons are displayed above and below the photo and are explained in the following steps. Tools on the bottom scroll horizontally.

Using Undo, Redo, Discard, and Save

Note the following important tidbits while using Photo Editor:

- You can reverse the most recent edit by tapping Undo or tap it repeatedly to step backward through multiple edits. To reverse an Undo, tap Redo.

- You can complete any edit by tapping the original icon again, tapping the Back icon, or pressing the Back key. Any edits made that you haven't reversed by tapping Undo or Discard are automatically saved. Saves are made to a separate file—not to the original, which remains unaltered. Whether you deliberately save your edits by tapping the Save icon or simply exit Photo Editor, the edited file is saved and named with today's date.

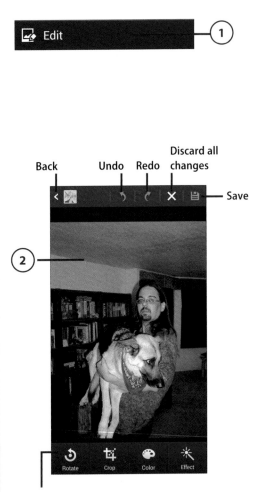

Editing tools, effects, and decorations

- If you tap Discard while applying an edit, all changes made with the current editing tool are simultaneously removed.
- If you tap Discard on the main Photo Editor screen, all edits are discarded.

---

3. *Rotate.* Tap Rotate to rotate or flip the image. Rotate Left and Right rotate the image in 90-degree increments with each tap. Flip Horizontal and Flip Vertical reverse the image horizontally (left-to-right) or vertically (top-to-bottom). Tap the Rotate icon again when you're satisfied with the changes.

Return

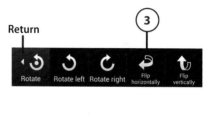

4. *Crop.* Use the Crop tool to retain only a selected portion of the image, while discarding the rest. Tap one of these selection tools in the scrolling list:

Rotation handle

- Select Free if you don't want any restrictions on the cropping dimensions. To constrain the dimensions to a ratio, select 1:1, 4:3, or 16:9. To set the cropping area, drag the rectangle's edge and corner handles to change the size of the selection, drag the rotation handle in the upper-right corner to change the selection rectangle's angle, and/or drag the center of the rectangle to reposition it.

- To create an irregular selection, choose the Lasso tool and use your fingertip to trace around the area you want to crop.

Return ④

When you've selected the part of the image that you want to retain, tap the Crop icon again.

Return ⑤

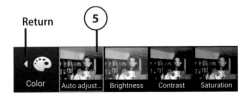

5. *Color.* Use Color to adjust the contrast, brightness, saturation, and other attributes of the entire image. Tap Color and then tap an attribute icon in the horizontally scrolling list. Most icons require that you manipulate one or more sliders—to increase or decrease contrast, for example. Tap Color again when you finish making adjustments.

Effect Undo

6. *Effect.* Tap the Effect icon and select a special effect to apply from the horizontally scrolling list. To compare the image with and without the current effect, press the Effect Undo icon. Note that effects aren't cumulative; each one you apply replaces the current effect. Tap Effect again when you finish.

7. *Portrait.* Tap the Portrait icon to apply facial corrections, such as Red-eye Fix or Beauty Face. Portrait adjustments work best when modifying a headshot. Tap Portrait again when you finish.

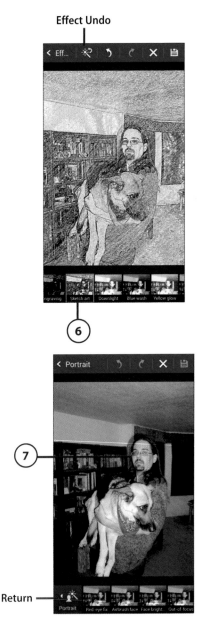

Return

8. *Sticker, Drawing, or Frame.* Tap these icons to apply decorative embellishments to the photo—adding a sticker, freehand drawing, or frame. (Note that stickers can be resized, moved, and rotated.) When you finish, tap Sticker, Drawing, or Frame again.

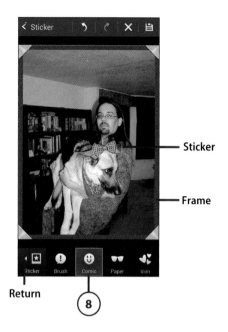

Sticker

Frame

Drawing with the Pen and Eraser

Use the Pen and Eraser tools together to do freehand drawing or write on the image. If you want to correct part of the Pen's drawing, you can remove it using the Eraser.

Return

8

9. When you finish editing, you can save your work as a new image file by tapping the Save icon. The edited image is saved in the current folder using today's date as part of the filename. To rename the image, open it in Gallery, press the Menu key, and tap Rename.

9

10. *Optional:* To edit another image, press the Menu key and tap Select Image. Respond to the Save dialog box by tapping Yes (save edits made to the current image), No (ignore edits made to the current image), or Cancel (continue editing the current image).

Save —————————————— 10

Save changes before opening new photo?

| Cancel | No | Yes |

Running a Slideshow

You can create a slideshow with transition effects and music using all or selected images from one or more folders. The show plays in portrait or landscape mode, depending on the phone's orientation.

1. In Gallery, select the folders, folder, or images that you want to include in the slideshow. (If you're reviewing a photo that you just took with Camera and request a slideshow, the Camera folder is automatically used as the basis for the show.) You can use any of the following selection techniques:

    • On the main screen, select nothing to include all stored photos in the show, or select one or more folders to include all of their photos.

    • If a folder is open, make no selection to use all its photos or select the particular photos that you want to use.

2. Press the Menu key and tap Slideshow.

3. Review or set options for the show in the dialog box that appears:

    • On the Effect tab, select an effect to use when transitioning between slides.

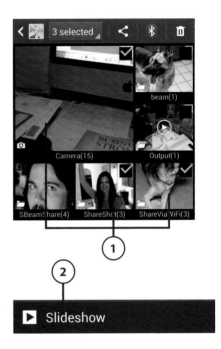

- On the Music tab, select the music track that will accompany the show. To change the current track, tap its name. To select a track other than the ones listed in the Slideshow Music dialog box, tap Add, pick a song, and tap OK. To run the show without music, set the track selection slider to Off; otherwise, ensure that the slider is On.

- On the More tab, specify the speed (number of seconds per slide) and a sort order for the images.

4. Tap the Start button to begin the show.

5. To end the show, tap any slide or press the Back key.

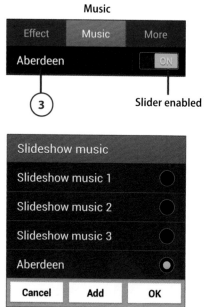

Music

Slider enabled

Slide speed and sort order

Self-Portrait   Settings   Jethro   Video

In this chapter, you find out how to use your phone for viewing videos from a variety of sources, as well as for shooting, trimming, and sharing your own videos. Topics include the following:

→ Streaming video over the Internet to your phone

→ Using the Video app to play videos

→ Converting DVD videos for playback on your phone

→ Recording videos with the rear and front cameras

→ Using dedicated video chat apps

Watching and Creating Videos

With the pair of cameras on the Galaxy S 4, you can record videos of yourself, others, or anything that moves. The phone's high-resolution screen makes it ideal for viewing those videos, as well as movies and TV shows that you've extracted from DVDs, rented or purchased online, or streamed to special video apps.

Streaming Video to the Phone

Streaming video is sent to your phone as a stream of data that plays as it's transmitted. Unlike material that you download, streaming requires an active Internet connection and doesn't result in a file that's permanently stored on your phone. If you want to watch the same video again, you need to stream it again. You can access streaming video through dedicated apps such as YouTube or by clicking web page links.

Streaming with a Dedicated App

The two most common classes of streaming video apps are subscription-based and free. Examples of subscription-based apps include Netflix, HBO Go, and Max Go (for Cinemax). To access Netflix movies, you must be a Netflix streaming subscriber. To access HBO or Cinemax, you must currently receive HBO or Cinemax through a supported satellite or cable TV provider.

After installing and launching one of these apps, you sign in with the username and password that you use to log on to www.netflix.com, www.hbogo.com, or www.maxgo.com. (In the case of subscription TV services, your username and password are generally the ones you use for your cable or satellite provider's website.) The apps are designed to remember this login information, so future launches won't require you to reenter it.

Many other apps for streaming video don't require a subscription for basic access. Examples include YouTube, MTV News, and Adult Swim.

Login

Adult Swim app

Depending on how the streaming app was designed, when you select a video to view, it plays in a dedicated player or in Video, an app that's preinstalled on the Galaxy S 4. The controls most players provide are similar to the ones in Video. In the Adult Swim player, for example, you can tap the screen at any time to display the playback controller and then do any of the following:

Adult Swim player

Pause/Play · Previous segment · Next segment · Share · Position marker · Information

- To start/restart or pause playback, tap the Pause/Play button.

- To jump forward or backward within the current video, drag the position marker to the approximate spot.

- If the current video is split into multiple segments, you can go to the next or previous segment by tapping a segment button.

- To review information about the video you're watching, tap the Information button.

- To share the video with others, tap the Share button and choose a sharing option from the pop-up menu.

- To adjust the playback volume, press the volume control on the left side of the phone.

- To exit the current video, press the Back key.

- Press the Menu key at any time to assist in your search for videos, clips, games, and scheduling information.

Streaming from Web Pages

Video clips are embedded in many web pages. When viewed in the Internet or Chrome app, these clips play in a similar manner to what you'd see in a computer browser—although the controls might be different. For example, some embedded clips display only a progress bar. However, if you search carefully, you might find a Full Screen icon or similarly worded link that enlarges the video and adds normal playback controls.

Full Screen

IT'S GONE!

> > > Go Further

The advantages of streaming are that the videos can be viewed on virtually any popular device (computer, tablet, phone, or iPod touch) that has Internet access. However, there's a downside to streaming. What happens if you want to watch a particular video or clip, but you don't have Internet access, don't want to rack up connection charges with your cellular service, or—if the unthinkable happens—the video is removed from the website or streaming provider's servers? The solution is to get a video capture application that can record a streamed video and convert it to a format that can be played on your computer, phone, or other device. You can start your search with Jaksta Media Recorder—available for both Mac and Windows from www.jaksta.com.

Playing Videos with the Video App

Regardless of whether a video was downloaded, bundled with or converted from a DVD, sent by a friend, or rented or purchased online, all compatible videos stored on your phone play using the Video app.

Technically Speaking

The Video app is not the app that actually plays your videos; it's Video Player—a linked app, *but one that has no shortcut in Apps*. When you want to return from the Home screen or another app to continue viewing a paused video, hold down the Home key to see the list of active and recently run apps. You'll see that both Video and Video Player are listed. If you tap Video Player, playback resumes. Tapping Video takes you to the Video app launch screen rather than to your video.

---

1. From the Home screen, tap Apps, followed by Video.

2. To play a video that's stored on your phone, select the video by tapping its title or thumbnail. (You can find videos that you've created or manually added to the phone by selecting the Personal tab. Select the Download tab to see videos that you've rented or purchased online.)

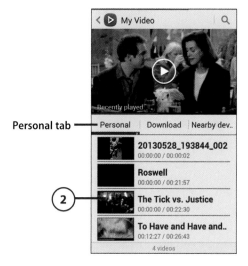

Video Selection Assistance

To make it easier to find the video that you want to watch, your video collection can be displayed as live thumbnails, as a list, or organized by the folders in which videos are stored. Press the Menu key, tap View As, and select an option. If you have many videos, you can specify a different sort order for the thumbnails or list by pressing the Menu key and tapping Sort By.

Personal tab ——

You can also select a video in Gallery, My Files, or another app. Doing this launches Video Player, skipping steps 1 and 2. Tap the Play icon to play the selected movie or clip.

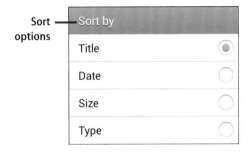

Sort options — Sort by

Title
Date
Size
Type

3. The controller appears and the video begins to play. Rotate the screen to the desired orientation: landscape or portrait.

4. While playing the video, you can tap the screen to display the controller and then do any of the following:

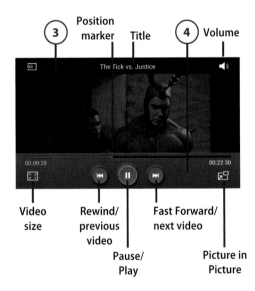

- To start/restart or pause playback, tap the Pause/Play button.

- Tap the Video Size icon to change the way the video is sized to fit the screen. Depending on how the video was encoded and the display type for which it was intended, some sizes may stretch the image in one direction, and others may clip the image horizontally or vertically to fit. Tap the icon repeatedly to see all display options.

- To jump forward or backward in the current video, drag the position marker to the approximate spot.

- Tap the Rewind button to jump to the beginning of the current video or, if you're at the beginning, to the previous video in the list. Press and hold the Rewind button to scroll backward through the current video; the longer you hold the button, the faster it scrolls.

- Tap the Fast Forward button to jump to the next video. Press and hold the Fast Forward button to scroll forward through the current video; the longer you hold the button, the faster it scrolls.

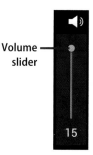

Volume slider

- To adjust playback volume, tap the Volume icon and drag the slider that appears. (You can also change the volume by pressing the Volume control on the left side of the phone.)

- To leave the current video, press the Back key twice. To exit Video, press the Home key.

Smart Pause

If Smart Pause (a new Smart Screen system setting) is enabled, you can pause the current video by turning your eyes away from the screen. When you're ready to resume, face the screen again.

Smart Pause enabled

Smart pause
Video will pause when the device detects that you are facing away from the screen

To enable or disable Smart Pause, open Settings, select the My Device tab, tap Smart Screen, and tap the Smart Pause check box. Smart Pause and the other Smart Screen features work by detecting the presence of your eyes. If you wear glasses, you may have better luck with the Smart Screen features if you remove your glasses.

>>>Go Further

PICTURE IN PICTURE (POP-UP PLAY)

If you want to continue viewing a video while doing other things on your phone (reading email, for instance), tap the Picture in Picture icon. A miniature, movable version of the playing video appears on your Home screen. Use your fingertip to move the video to any part of the screen. If you switch to a different Home screen page or launch an app, the Picture in Picture video moves, too. (Note that this feature is only available for unprotected videos.)

To pause playback, tap the Picture in Picture video. Tap it again to continue, or tap the X icon to end playback. To resume playback in Video, double-tap the Picture in Picture video.

Picture in Picture —

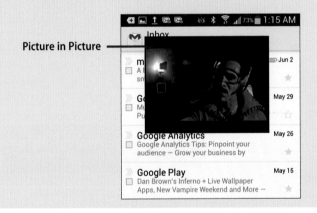

It's Not All Good

THE SAMSUNG HUB CONNECTION

If you generally don't rent or purchase videos using your phone, the connection between Video and Samsung Hub—and the way it's implemented—can be more of a nuisance and a source of confusion than a welcome new feature. The My Video screen that appears when you launch Video is merely one of many screens within the Videos section of Samsung Hub. To go to Samsung Hub from Video, tap the back button at the top of the My Videos screen or swipe the screen to the right. To return from Samsung Hub, go to its Videos section and swipe the screen to the left until Personal Videos reappears.

Using the Video Menu

On Video's main screen, you can press the Menu key to choose from these commands:

Video menu

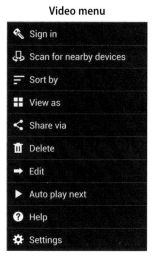

- *Scan for Nearby Devices*. Scan for eligible devices within range with which media can be shared.

- *Sort By, View As*. See "Video Selection Assistance," earlier in this section.

- *Share Via*. Transmit the video to others (Messaging, Email, and Gmail) or another device (Bluetooth and Wi-Fi Direct), or post it on a social networking or chat site (YouTube, ChatON, Google+, and Facebook). Note that many videos are too large to be shared via text messaging, email, or Gmail.

- *Delete*. Delete unwanted videos that are stored on the phone. Tap the check box of each video that you want to delete, tap Done, and tap OK in the confirmation dialog box that appears. (To delete an individual video, you can press and hold the video's thumbnail or name, tap Delete, and then tap OK in the confirmation dialog box.)

- *Edit*. Launch Video Editor to create a video by combining photos and videos. You can add themes, music, voiceovers, and special effects. (If Video Editor isn't installed, choosing this command launches Samsung Apps so you can download and install the app.)

- *Auto Play Next.* When enabled, this option causes Video to automatically play the next video in sequence when the current one finishes.

- *Help.* Review instructions for using Samsung Hub.

- *Settings.* Change settings for accessing and using Samsung Hub.

If you press the Menu key while watching a video, the following additional commands appear:

- *Chapter Preview.* Displays thumbnails representing breakpoints in the video. When you tap a thumbnail, the video resumes at that point.

- *Via Bluetooth.* Transmit the audio to a paired Bluetooth headset.

- *Video Auto Off.* Like the sleep timer on a TV, choose this command to automatically end video playback after a specified period of time or when the current video ends.

- *Details.* Display information about the video, such as its file format, resolution, and size.

Converting DVD Videos for Playback on the Phone

You can use many programs to extract video content from DVDs for playback on the Galaxy S 4 and other devices. The following task shows how to extract video using DVDFab/DVD Ripper, a DVD-to-mobile conversion utility for Windows and Mac OS X from www.dvdfab.com. Each extracted movie or TV show results in a single MPEG-4 (.mp4) file that you can view with the Video app.

Which Version Should I Use?

Currently, there are two versions of the DVDFab line of products: the older DVDFab 8 QT and the new DVDFab 9. Both are available as free 30-day trials. If you decide to purchase a license for DVDFab, you are entitled to use both versions. As an example of converting DVD videos for playback on your phone, the following task employs DVDFab 9.

1. Launch DVDFab on your computer. If the program doesn't go directly to its main screen, click the Ripper icon on the splash screen.

2. Select the Ripper tab. Ensure that the selected profile that will be used to convert the video is correct. If so, go to step 4.

3. To change profiles, click the current profile name. In the dialog box that appears, select the Device tab, select Samsung in the scrolling list, select the Galaxy S4 profile, and click OK.

4. Insert the DVD that contains the material you want to extract. Wait for the program to scan and analyze the DVD's file structure.

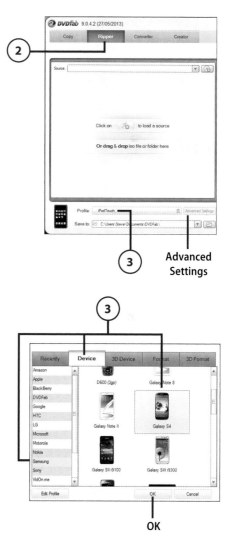

Advanced Settings

OK

5. Select the material that you want to convert to videos for the phone by doing one of the following:

   - If this is a movie DVD, the movie is automatically selected. (Generally, the movie will have the longest Play Time of the items on the DVD.)

   - If this is an *episodic* DVD (containing multiple episodes of a television show, for example), click the check box of each episode that you want to convert. The application analyzes each checked episode; each results in a separate video.

Movie

Title	Play Time	Chapter	Audio ▼	Subtitle ▼
▶ 1	01:38:14	28	EN AC-3/5.1	EN
3	00:00:15	2	EN AC-3/5.1	
5	00:00:09	1	AC-3/1	
6	00:00:19	3	AC-3/1	
7	00:00:11	2	AC-3/1	
8	00:00:01	1	AC-3/1	

Source: E:\ [THE_PRINCESS_BRIDE_DISC1]

TV episodes

Title	Play Time	Chapter	Audio ▼	Subtitle ▼
1	00:53:46	7	EN AC-3/1	EN
2	00:53:46	7	EN AC-3/1	EN
3	00:51:20	7	EN AC-3/1	EN
4	00:51:20	7	EN AC-3/1	EN
5	00:00:12	1	EN AC-3/1	EN
6	00:48:12	1 ▼ - 7 ▼	English AC-3/2 ▼	English ▼
7	00:48:12	7	EN AC-3/2	EN
8	00:02:15	1	EN AC-3/2	
9	00:00:12	1	AC-3/1	
10	00:00:22	4	AC-3/1	

Source: E:\ [KUNG_FU_SEASON_3]

Using the Preview Window

Regardless of a DVD's contents, you can preview each movie, episode, and other material (such as bloopers and deleted scenes) in the Preview window. Previewing can ensure that you've selected the correct video(s) and appropriate audio. Select a video to preview by clicking to the left of its number in the Title column, select the Preview tab, and click Play.

Preview tab

Position marker   Play/Pause

6. For each checked item, select an audio option. Normally, the recommended option will be correct. You can preview the material in the Preview window to ensure that you've chosen normal dialogue rather than the director's commentary.

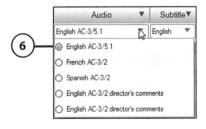

Audio ▼	Subtitle ▼
English AC-3/5.1	English ▼
◉ English AC-3/5.1	
○ French AC-3/2	
○ Spanish AC-3/2	
○ English AC-3/2 director's comments	
○ English AC-3/2 director's comments	

7. For each checked item, you can enable or disable subtitles (if the disk includes them). Select a subtitle language, and do one of the following:

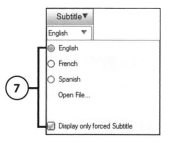

- To disable normal subtitles, ensure that Display Only Forced Subtitle is checked. Subtitles appear only when an actor is momentarily speaking in a foreign language.

- To display subtitles throughout the video, remove the check mark from Display Only Forced Subtitle.

8. *Optional:* You can review or change the settings for resolution and other options for each movie, episode, and clip that you're extracting. Click the Advanced Settings button (to the right of the profile) to review the current settings in the Video, Audio, Subtitle, and Information tabs of the window that appears. Otherwise, if you want to use the default settings, skip to step 14.

Episode Settings

If you're converting multiple TV episodes or several items from a movie DVD, each can have different settings—although, you'll generally want them all to be the same. To change settings for an episode or movie item, select it by clicking to the left of its Title number, and then make the changes. To ensure consistency, be sure to apply these same settings to every episode or selected item.

9. *Video.* You can change Encoding Method and/or Video Quality to improve the visual quality of the video or reduce the size of the video output file.

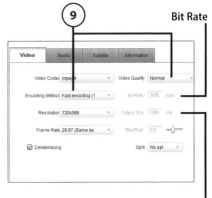

Bit Rate

Output Size

- Encoding Method can be 1- or 2-pass. The latter improves the quality but increases the time required to perform the encoding because it makes two passes through the source video.

- Changes in Video Quality (Small Size, Normal, and High Quality) are reflected in Bit Rate and Output Size. The higher the Video Quality setting, the higher the bit rate (quality) and the larger the file size.

Can You Tell the Difference?

As an experiment, you might try encoding the same movie at the three Video Quality settings and see if you can detect the difference. If you can't or you're willing to accept a small sacrifice in quality, smaller is better because you can fit more videos on your S 4. For example, when encoding the movie shown in this example, the High Quality file size is almost twice that of the Small Size file.

10. *Audio.* Set audio quality/clarity by choosing a Sample Rate and Bit Rate. Higher numbers yield higher-quality audio. (Available Bit Rate options are profile-dependent.) After conversion, if you notice that the playback audio is unusually loud or quiet, you can repeat the conversion with an appropriate change in the Volume setting.

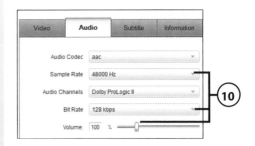

11. *Subtitle*. Direct Render to Video embeds any subtitle text into the video. Because most video players can't toggle subtitles on and off (as DVD players can), rendering them as part of the video is a logical solution. If you disabled subtitles in step 7, this setting is irrelevant.

12. *Information*. You can edit the File Name and/or Title.

- The filename doesn't need to be in capital letters or end in .Title#, and it can contain spaces. Avoid using special characters, such as slashes and colons.

- The Title is the text that identifies the movie or video when it's listed in Video and other players. Edit it to something more descriptive. In this example, I changed both the filename and title to the actual title: *The Princess Bride*.

13. When you finish reviewing settings, click OK to close the Advanced Settings window.

14. The Save To box at the bottom of the window shows the *path* (disk\folder) where the resulting video file will be saved on your computer. To pick a different location, click the down arrow to the right to specify a location you've previously used or click the folder icon to browse for a new location.

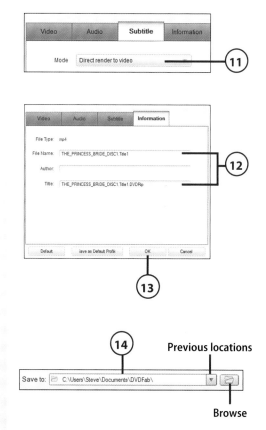

15. Convert the selected video(s) by clicking the Start button.

When you finish extracting videos, transfer them to your phone using any of the file-transfer techniques described in Chapter 15. The new files will appear in the Video file list.

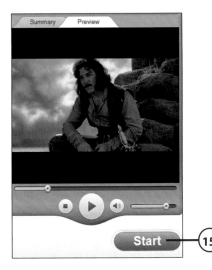

MAKING YOUR OWN PROFILE

The profile specifies default output settings that are compatible with the target device and proportional in size to the video source. The profile used in this demonstration (Galaxy S4) is a user-contributed one. If you think you can create a better profile (using DVDFab's included Profile Editor), keep the following S 4 limitations in mind when choosing settings:

- The primary supported video formats are MPEG-4 and AVI.
- The resolution should be no higher than 1920 × 1080.

As an alternative to using the Galaxy S4 profile, you'll also discover that *many* profiles create results that look fine on the phone. For instance, you might consider using an iPhone profile or a generic MPEG-4/h.264 profile. The key is selecting or specifying a bit rate that's a reasonable compromise between quality (the higher the bit rate, the better the quality) and file size (the lower the bit rate, the smaller the video file).

>>>Go Further

MORE VIDEO SOURCES

In addition to extracting videos from your personal DVD collection, there are other sources of ready-to-play videos for your Galaxy S 4. You can rent or purchase videos by running the Play Store, Play Movies and TV, Samsung Hub, Amazon Appstore, and carrier-provided online store apps; some recent DVDs include a version for phones and other multimedia devices; and you can install software that can convert streaming video to MPEG-4 videos that you can play on the phone.

Recording Videos with the Phone

Using your phone's cameras, you can create movies that are suitable for posting on websites, emailing to friends, and playing on your phone or a flat-screen TV.

1. Launch Camera by doing one of the following:

   • Tap a Camera shortcut on the Home screen.

   • On the Home screen, tap Apps and then Camera.

   • On the lock screen, slide the Camera icon up (if present).

2. Decide whether to shoot the video in portrait or landscape. Rotate the phone to the proper orientation.

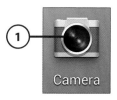

3. *Optional:* To switch between the rear-facing and front-facing cameras, tap the Self Portrait icon.

When You're in a Rush

You won't always have time to leisurely set options before you begin recording. If you're in a hurry to capture something that's happening right now, you can often make do by simply launching Camera, rotating the phone to the appropriate orientation, and pressing the Video button.

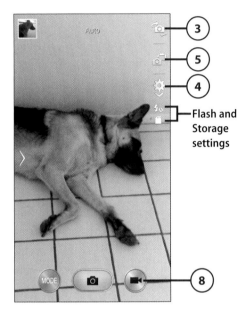

Flash and Storage settings

4. Check the current video settings. Note that most are for photos and have no effect when shooting a video. However, you should pay attention to these settings:

- *Recording Mode.* Tap the Settings icon to reveal the Quick Settings, tap the Recording Mode icon, and select a setting from the menu that appears. Use Normal for a standard recording and Limit for MMS for a video that you want to attach to a multimedia (MMS) message. For a description of the other settings, tap the i (Information) button.

- *Video Size and Video Stabilization.* To set these options, tap the Settings icon twice, and select the Video tab.

  Enable Video Stabilization to reduce the effect of camera shake during recording.

Quick Settings

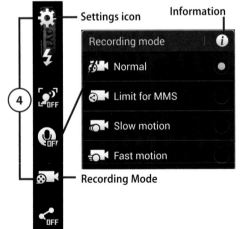

Settings icon

Information

Recording mode

Normal

Limit for MMS

Slow motion

Fast motion

Recording Mode

Select a Video Size that's appropriate for the device on which the video will be played. Each setting specifies the horizontal by vertical dimensions (in pixels). For playback on a flat-screen TV in letterbox format (16:9), select 1920×1080 (16:9) or 1280×720 (16:9), depending on whether the set is capable of displaying 1080 or only 720. Select 1440×1080 (4:3) for television show playback on a 1080-capable flat-screen TV. Select 320×240 (4:3) for playback on the web or for video that you intend to email. Note that the Galaxy S 4 can play videos at any of these resolutions.

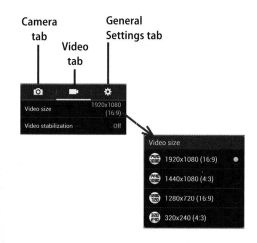

- *Storage*. The video can be stored in the phone's internal memory (Device) or on a memory card, if one's installed. To change this setting, tap the Settings icon twice, select the General Settings tab, and tap Storage.

When you finish making changes, dismiss the menu by tapping anywhere else onscreen or by pressing the Back key.

Dimly Lit Scenes

Although the quality is mediocre, you can shoot in extremely dim or even totally dark settings if you enable Flash in Quick Settings. Flash has three modes: Off, On, and Auto. Repeatedly tap the Flash icon until you see the unadorned lightning bolt (On).

5. *Optional*: To insert yourself into the recording (using the front-facing camera), tap the Front Camera icon. You can drag the self-recording window to any location. To change the window's size, tap it and drag the selection handles that appear around the frame.

6. Set the zoom level by pressing the phone's Volume key, or by placing two fingers on the screen and spreading them apart or squeezing them together. Note that you can vary the zoom level as you record.

7. Set the focal point for the recording by tapping the screen or by dragging the focus rectangle.

8. Tap the Video button to begin recording.

9. During recording, you can temporarily pause by tapping the Pause button. To resume recording, tap the button again. When you finish recording, tap the Stop button. The MPEG-4 video is automatically stored in the DCIM/Camera folder in the phone's built-in memory or on the memory card, depending on the Storage setting in step 4.

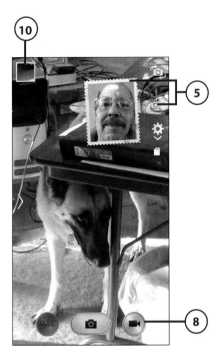

Take a Quick Snapshot

While recording, you can also take photos by tapping the Camera button.

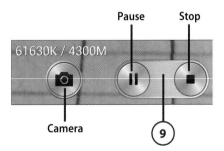

10. If you want to view the resulting video immediately, tap the thumbnail icon in the upper-left corner of the screen. Refer to Chapter 15 for options for sharing your video masterpieces.

Participating in Video Chats

A final video-related use for your front (and, occasionally, rear) camera is participating in *video chats*—Internet-based conversations that combine voice and video. Not only can you hear each other, but you can also *see* the other person's expressions as he/she talks, as well as what's happening nearby. Because of the large amount of data exchanged during video chats, they're best conducted over Wi-Fi or between users who have steady, high-speed connections and unlimited data plans.

To get started with one-on-one or group video chats, launch Google Play (Play Store) and search for *video chat*. As you read the app descriptions, you'll note that most require you and your friends to use the same app and be on the same platform: that is, Android, not Apple's iOS. Some apps also let you connect to desktop or tablet versions of the app. Regardless, to test any of the apps (other than those that permit uninvited chat requests from strangers), you need someone willing to download and try them with you.

Video chat apps in Play Store

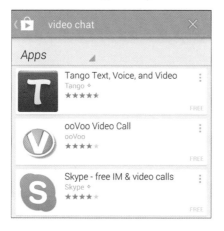

This chapter explains how to transfer selected files between your phone, a computer, and other phones. Topics include the following:

→ Using Samsung Kies to wirelessly transfer files
→ Manually transferring files over a USB cable
→ Transferring files using Bluetooth
→ Emailing files to yourself
→ Using Wi-Fi Direct, S Beam, and Share Shot to transfer files between phones

Transferring and Sharing Files

Although certain types of data, such as Calendar items and Contact records, can be automatically synchronized between the phone and a computer, most other file types—such as photos, videos, music, and various documents—must be manually copied from one device to another or must rely on software that isn't included with the phone. Using the techniques and tools discussed in this chapter, you'll discover many of the ways that you can transfer files between your phone and your computer, as well as between a pair of phones.

You can find instructions for synchronizing Calendar and Contacts data in Chapter 16.

Using Samsung Kies to Transfer Files over Wi-Fi

If you have a wireless router or modem, you can copy files between your phone and computer—or any computer on your network. In this section, you'll see how to accomplish this by running Samsung Kies, a computer application that's used with the phone's Kies via Wi-Fi setting. You can also use Samsung Kies to transfer data over a USB cable, as explained in "Performing USB Transfers with Samsung Kies," later in this chapter.

Setup and Basic Operation

1. *First use only.* Download and install the Windows or Mac version of Samsung Kies from http://www.samsung.com/us/kies/.

2. Launch Samsung Kies on your computer. The control panel on the left edge shows there are no connected devices.

3. On the phone's Home screen, tap Apps, followed by Settings.

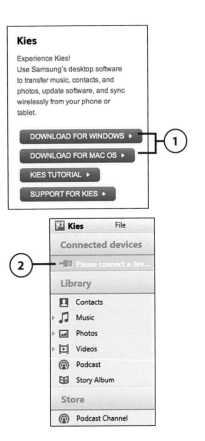

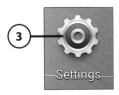

4. Select the Connections tab, scroll to the bottom of the screen, and tap Kies via Wi-Fi.

5. Read the Attention dialog box and tap OK.

6. Tap the name of the computer to which you want to connect. If it isn't displayed, tap the Scan Devices button at the bottom of the screen.

7. *First run only.* A Kies via Wi-Fi dialog box appears on the phone. Enter the displayed passkey in the Wi-Fi Connection Request dialog box that appears on the computer, and then tap OK.

8. After the connection is established, the Kies default view appears and phone content is backed up to the computer. You can restore this default view at any time by clicking the name of your phone in the control panel. As explained in the following task, you can use Samsung Kies to copy files from computer to phone or from phone to computer.

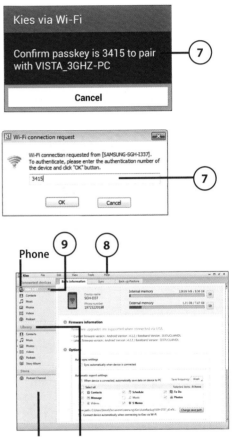

About the Control Panel

The control panel has two main sections. The top one (showing your phone's model number) lists the various content categories that are on the phone. The second section (Library) lists content that's stored on your computer. If you expand either section and select a category such as Music or Photos, a list of these items appears in the window's main area.

9. When you finish using Samsung Kies, tap the Disconnect button on the phone or click the **x** beside the phone's name in the Samsung Kies control panel. Then quit the computer program by choosing File, Exit.

Copying Files

1. In the control panel, expand the phone and Library sections. Select the source and category of material to copy. (To copy from phone to computer, select a category in the phone's section. To copy from computer to phone, select a category in the Library section.)

2. Select the files to copy by clicking their check boxes (in List view) or thumbnails (in Thumbnail view).

Working in Thumbnail View

To select multiple thumbnails, you can Shift-click, Ctrl-click (Windows) or Command-click (Mac) the items.

3. Do one of the following:

   • *Copying from phone to computer.* Click the Save button above the list. In the Select Folder dialog box that appears on the computer, select the computer folder into which the files will be copied, and then click the Select Folder button.

   • *Copying from computer to phone.* Click the Transfer to Device button. (If a memory card is installed, you must choose Internal Memory or External Memory. The latter represents the memory card.)

4. The selected material is copied to the computer or phone.

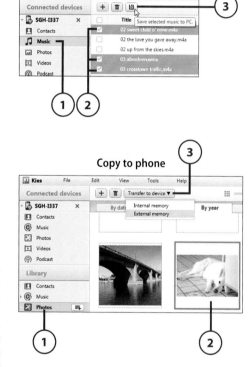

Copy to computer

Copy to phone

MORE OPTIONS

This light introduction merely scratches the surface of what you can do with Samsung Kies. Here are some additional options for you to check out:

- You can double-click most items. When you do, songs and videos play; photos open.

- When you double-click a photo that's on the phone in order to view it, you can immediately save it to your computer by clicking the Save button that appears.

Save

- Photos can be viewed in List or Thumbnail view by clicking the appropriate icon at the top of the window. Select Thumbnail view and the By Folder tab when you want to quickly copy an entire folder (such as Camera) to the computer.

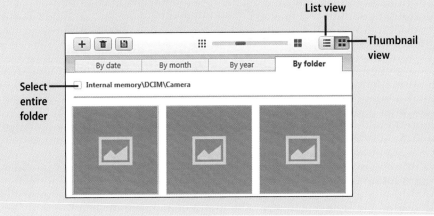

List view

Thumbnail view

Select entire folder

WHAT ABOUT KIES AIR?

>>>Go Further

In addition to the Samsung Kies computer application, Samsung offers Kies Air, a free Android app for performing wireless transfers between your phone and computer. Rather than requiring a separate computer application, Kies Air is a Java applet that runs in your computer's browser. Although Kies Air is included on the Galaxy S III, you must download it from the Play Store if you want to use it on the Galaxy S 4. (On the Home screen, tap Apps, followed by Play Store. Search for *Kies Air*, and install it on the phone.)

To run Kies Air, launch its app, tap the Start button, and then enter the displayed web address and confirmation code in your browser. Note that file transfers from phone to computer are called *downloads* and transfers from computer to phone are *uploads*.

Kies Air

Save the URL

To avoid manually entering the numeric URL each time you use Kies Air, save it as a browser favorite or bookmark. Although the URL may change in later sessions, editing the URL is faster than entering it from scratch each time.

Transferring Files over USB

Using the USB cable provided with your phone, you can connect the phone to a PC or Mac and freely copy files in either direction. The following task temporarily turns your phone into the equivalent of a flash drive. (Note that if you're a Mac user, you must first download and install a free Mac application from www.android.com/filetransfer.)

Windows USB Drivers

To use any USB file transfer method with a Windows PC, you must first install the Samsung USB drivers, as explained in "Tethering the Phone and a PC" in Chapter 18.

Manual USB Transfers to and from a Mac

1. Using the phone's USB cable, connect the phone and the Mac.

2. Open the Notification panel on the phone. In the Ongoing section, it should say Connected as a Media Device. If it says Connected as a Camera, tap the entry and select Media Device (MTP) in the screen that appears.

3. *First run only.* Open the Applications folder on the Dock and select Android File Transfer. (The program should launch automatically in subsequent sessions.)

4. A window appears that lists all files on your phone. Transfer copies of files from the phone by dragging them onto the Mac's Desktop or into a folder. Transfer copies of files from the Mac by dragging them into an appropriate folder in the window.

Built-in memory   Memory card   Phone name

④

Phone or Card?

If you've installed a memory card in the phone, you can access both the built-in memory and the add-in memory card by selecting Phone or Card, respectively.

5. When you finish, disconnect the USB cable from the phone and the Mac. Android File Transfer should quit automatically.

Other Quit Options

If necessary, you can manually quit by pressing Command+Q or by choosing Android File Transfer, Quit Android File Transfer. If that fails, right-click the Android File Transfer icon in the Dock and choose Force Quit.

Manual USB Transfers to and from a PC

1. If you haven't already done so, visit the Support section of Samsung's website (http://www.samsung.com/us/support/) and download the Windows USB driver for your carrier's phone. See "Tethering the Phone and a PC" in Chapter 18 for instructions. You can find your model number by launching Settings, selecting the More tab, and tapping About Device. Note that installing this driver is a one-time process.

2. Using the phone's USB cable, connect the phone and the PC. After the PC recognizes the connected phone and installs the driver software (if necessary), an AutoPlay dialog box appears. Click the option to Open Device to View Files.

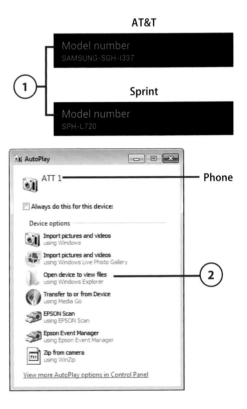

Connect as a Media Device or as a Camera?

Samsung recommends connecting the phone as a Media Device when transferring most types of files and as a Camera to transfer photos from phone to PC. However, my experience with Windows 7 is that it doesn't make a difference. Both AutoPlay dialog boxes offer the option to Open Device to View Files, for example.

3. A file window opens, displaying Phone and Card (if you've installed a memory card) as "drives" or only Phone (if there's no installed memory card). Open Phone to view the folders and files in the phone's internal memory, or open Card to see the folders and files on the memory card. Transfer files from the phone by dragging them onto the Desktop or into a folder. Transfer files from the PC by dragging them into an appropriate folder on the phone or its memory card.

Phone

Where Are My Files?

The hardest part of performing manual USB file transfers from a computer to a phone is that you're expected to know where those files are stored on your computer. If you have no idea, check the Documents folder and its subfolders first. You may find it helpful to explore your hard drive beforehand, making a note of the names and locations of music, photo, and video folders.

When transferring photos from iPhoto (Mac) to the phone, you may find it easier if you first launch iPhoto and drag the image thumbnails onto the Desktop. Transfer *those* images to the phone, and then delete the Desktop copies when you finish.

---

4. When you finish, disconnect the USB cable from the phone and the PC.

It's Not All Good

FILE HANDLING

To perform these USB transfers, you have to understand the Android filing system; that is, you need to learn where the photos, songs, and movies are stored on your phone. If you find this task unpleasant, you might prefer to use a dedicated file-transfer program that can handle the file- and folder-management chores for you.

In addition to the options discussed in this chapter, you should investigate doubleTwist, a free application available from http://doubletwist.com/ that enables you to selectively transfer or synchronize files between your Galaxy S 4 and a PC or Mac.

>>Go Further

PERFORMING USB TRANSFERS WITH SAMSUNG KIES

In addition to supporting wireless transfers, you can use Samsung Kies in USB mode. For trouble-free transfers, follow these simple launch, connect, and disconnect steps:

1. Launch Samsung Kies on your PC or Mac.

2. Use the USB cable supplied with your phone to connect the phone to your computer. (If Kies doesn't recognize your connected phone, open the Notification panel. There should be an entry in the Ongoing section that states "Connected as a media device." If it states "Connected as camera," tap the entry and select Media Device in the screen that appears.)

3. Perform file transfers as described in "Using Samsung Kies to Transfer Files over Wi-Fi," earlier in the chapter.

4. In the Kies control panel, click the **x** beside the phone's name to disconnect it from the computer.

5. Disconnect the USB cable from the phone and computer.

Transferring Files Using Bluetooth

The Samsung Galaxy S 4 is a Bluetooth device and can use Bluetooth to wirelessly exchange data with any Bluetooth-equipped computer, such as an iMac or some current laptops.

Pairing the Phone with the Computer

To use Bluetooth for data transfers, the phone and computer must first be linked (known as *pairing*). The following steps show how to accomplish this one-time procedure on an iMac with its built-in Bluetooth support. If you have a different computer, refer to its Help for instructions on Bluetooth pairing.

1. On the Home screen, tap Apps, followed by Settings.

2. Select the Connections tab, ensure that the Bluetooth slider is On, and tap Bluetooth.

3. Ensure that your phone is checked, making it visible to other devices such as your iMac or laptop.

4. On the iMac's Dock, click the System Preferences icon.

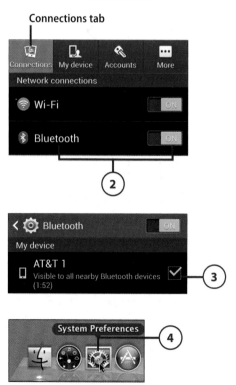

5. In the Internet & Wireless section of System Preferences, click the Bluetooth icon.

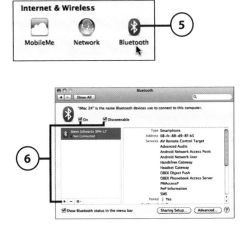

6. Ensure that On and Discoverable are checked, and then click the plus (+) button to add a new Bluetooth device—your Galaxy S 4.

7. The Bluetooth Setup Assistant launches. The phone should be listed as a visible Bluetooth device. Select it in the Devices list and click Continue.

8. The Bluetooth Setup Assistant attempts to pair the phone with the iMac. In the Bluetooth Pairing Request that appears on your phone, tap OK if the number matches the one on the iMac's screen.

9. Click Continue in the Bluetooth Setup Assistant.

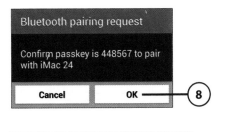

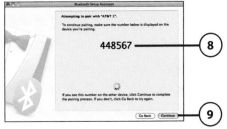

10. Click Quit to exit the Bluetooth Setup Assistant. Close the Bluetooth preferences dialog box.

11. A phone-specific hierarchical menu is added to the iMac's Bluetooth menu.

12. An entry also appears on the phone's Bluetooth settings screen showing that the phone is paired to the iMac. Whenever you perform a Bluetooth operation on the phone, you'll see this pairing information.

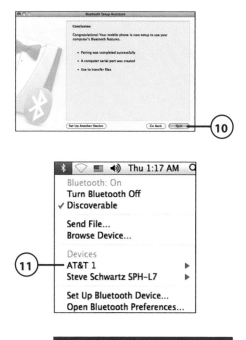

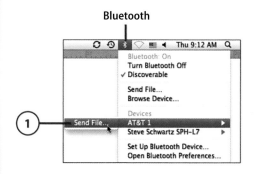

Sending Files from Computer to Phone

When the phone is paired with the computer, you can easily transmit selected files in either direction. The following tasks show how to transfer files over Bluetooth from or to an iMac.

1. From the iMac's Bluetooth menu, choose Send File from the *phone name* submenu.

Bluetooth

2. Select a file in the Select File to Send dialog box. (To select more than one file, hold down the Command key as you click filenames.) Click the Send button.

3. The phone receives a File Transfer request. Tap Accept to receive the file(s) on your phone.

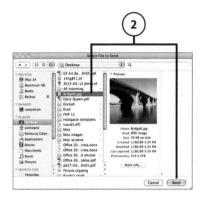

Filing the Files

All files transmitted to the phone via Bluetooth are copied to the Bluetooth folder. To see the files, go to the Home screen, tap the Apps icon, tap My Files, and then open the Bluetooth folder.

It isn't necessary to move these files from the Bluetooth folder into their normal folders. Music, Gallery, and other apps can find new files without any heroic measures on your part—regardless of where they're stored.

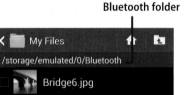

Bluetooth folder

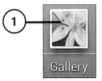

Received file

Sending Files from Phone to Computer

Similarly, you can transmit files from your phone to a paired Bluetooth-equipped computer. For example, photos created with the phone's camera are convenient to send using Bluetooth. The following task shows how to send photo files to an iMac.

1. On the Home screen, tap Apps, followed by Gallery or tap a Gallery shortcut.

2. Open the folder that contains the pictures that you want to send to the computer. (All image folders are shown, regardless of where on the phone they're stored. The number following each folder name is the number of pictures in the folder.)

3. Thumbnails for the folder's images appear. To transmit a single photo, tap its thumbnail to view the image. If you want to transmit *multiple* photos, firmly press one of the thumbnails to select it (indicated by a green check mark) and tap the thumbnails of other photos that you also want to transmit.

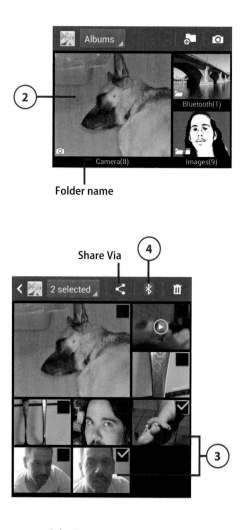

Folder name

Share Via

Using Select All

If a folder contains many images and you want to transmit all or most of them, select any thumbnail, open the Selection menu, and tap Select All. Then tap the thumbnails of the photos that you do *not* want to send, removing their check marks.

Another way to select an entire folder of images is to press and hold its thumbnail on the opening Gallery screen (resulting in a green check mark on the folder).

4. Tap the Bluetooth icon in the toolbar. (If the toolbar isn't visible, tap the image once to make the toolbar appear.)

Selection menu

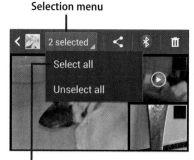

Select all images

No Bluetooth Icon

The toolbar icon shown represents the sharing method you most recently used. If it's not the Bluetooth icon, tap the Share Via icon and select Bluetooth.

In other apps, the Bluetooth transfer command may be worded differently or found somewhere other than on a toolbar. You may have to open a menu or press and hold the item to reveal a pop-up menu.

5. On the Select Device screen, tap the name of your paired computer. That device will receive the transmitted files.

6. An Incoming File Transfer dialog box appears on the iMac.

7. If only one file is being transmitted, click the Accept button. If multiple files are being transmitted, click the Accept All check box and then click Accept. The file(s) are transmitted to the iMac and stored in the default folder.

8. When the transmission(s) finishes, close the Incoming File Transfer dialog box by clicking the red button.

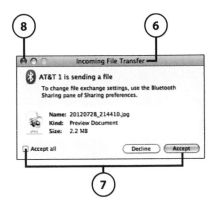

PICK YOUR OWN DESTINATION FOLDER AND ACTION

When files are sent via Bluetooth to a Mac, the folder where they're stored on the Mac is specified in Bluetooth preferences. The default folder is Documents. If you'd rather use a different folder, click the System Preferences icon in the Dock, and then click the Bluetooth icon. In Bluetooth preferences, click the Sharing Setup button. Select Bluetooth Sharing in the Service list, and choose Other from the Folder for Accepted Items drop-down menu. Select a new destination folder, and click the Open button. I created a folder on the Desktop called Bluetooth Files for this purpose.

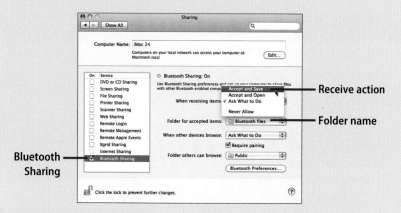

In addition, if you get tired of responding to the Incoming File Transfer dialog box, you can specify that all incoming files are *automatically* transferred. From the When Receiving Items menu, choose Accept and Save or Accept and Open.

Emailing Files

You can also use email to move files from your phone to your computer. As long as the final size of the attachment(s) doesn't exceed the maximum allowable message size for your or the recipient's email account, your phone and most email systems will allow the message to be transmitted. This means that if you restrict yourself to sending photos taken with the phone's camera or songs purchased on the phone, you can deliver them to your computer by emailing them to yourself. Of course, you can also use these techniques to email your photos to friends and relatives.

Emailing Photos from Gallery

The most direct way to email one or more photos from your phone is to use the Gallery app. The images can be sent from any email account that you've added to the Email app.

Work Directly in Email

You can also send photos by composing a new message in Email, tapping the Attach button (the paper clip), and selecting the photo(s) you want to send.

1. On the Home screen, tap Apps, followed by Gallery or tap a Gallery shortcut.

2. In Gallery, open the folder where the pictures are stored by tapping the folder's thumbnail.

3. Do one of the following:

   • To send a single photo, tap its thumbnail to view the photo—opening it on a new screen.

   • To send multiple photos, press and hold the first photo's thumbnail to select the photo. Then lightly tap each additional thumbnail that you also want to send, marking each with a green check mark.

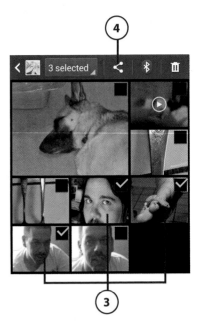

Send the Entire Folder

If you want to select every picture in the current folder, tap the Selection icon on the toolbar and tap Select All. Alternatively, you can press and hold a folder in step 2 to select the entire folder.

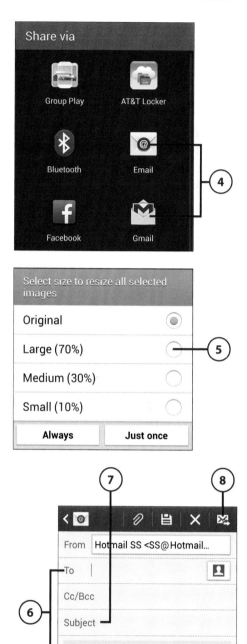

4. Tap the Share Via icon, and then select Email or Gmail. (If the Share Via icon isn't visible, tap the image once to reveal the toolbar.)

5. Images can optionally be resized prior to sending. Select a scaling percentage or Original (*unaltered*). Tap Just Once to apply the specified scaling only for this message, or tap Always to apply the same scaling to future image attachments.

6. The file(s) are added as attachments to a new email message. Specify your own email address in the To box.

7. *Optional:* Add a subject and message text.

8. Tap the Send icon.

9. When your PC or Mac email program receives the message, save the photo files to any convenient location or drag them onto the Desktop.

It's Not All Good

POTENTIAL PROBLEMS

Emailing photos doesn't always go as planned. Emailed photos are occasionally destroyed in the conversion process; others are sometimes delayed for hours or days, and some are never delivered. If emailing a particular photo doesn't pan out, try one of the other phone-to-computer transfer methods described in this chapter.

Emailing Songs from My Files

If you've purchased a song using your phone, you can listen to it on your computer, too. You can email songs as attachments using the Email app or do so directly from My Files, as described here. In either case, you need to know the folder in which the song is stored.

1. On the Home screen, tap Apps, followed by My Files.

2. Navigate to the folder in which the song is stored.

3. Press and hold the song title until a dialog box appears. Tap Share Via.

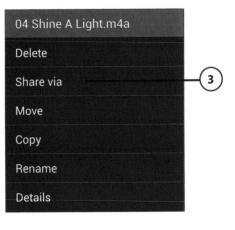

4. Select Email or Gmail as the sharing method.

5. The song file is added as an attachment to a new email message. Finish by performing steps 6–9 of the "Emailing Photos from Gallery" task, earlier in this chapter. Then add or import the song(s) into the music organizer program on your computer, such as iTunes or Windows Media Player.

Some Help, Please

The Android filing system automatically stores files in folders that it creates. For example, as mentioned later in this chapter, folders for files transferred to the phone are often named according to the transfer method used, such as Bluetooth and SBeamShare. For the most part, an app doesn't care where its files are stored. This information is generally invisible—and irrelevant—to you...until, of course, you must know it. To find your song files, start with the Music folder. Then check folders named according to the methods you used to transfer the song files. Finally, if you've added a memory card, be sure to check its folders, too.

Transferring Files Between Phones

By taking advantage of the Galaxy S 4's Wi-Fi Direct support, there are several methods that you can use to exchange files with other Wi-Fi Direct-enabled phones, as well as view material on each other's phones.

Using Wi-Fi Direct

If two phones support Wi-Fi Direct, they can exchange files wirelessly—without the need for a common wireless access point or router. The following task shows how to do it with a pair of Galaxy S 4 phones. The other user should enable Wi-Fi Direct on his or her phone while you're performing these steps.

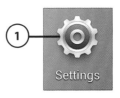

1. On the Home screen, tap Apps, followed by Settings. (Both users should activate Wi-Fi Direct by performing steps 1–7.)

Other Wi-Fi Direct-Capable Phones

Other phones that also support Wi-Fi Direct may have different procedures for enabling the feature.

2. Select the Connections tab, and then tap the Wi-Fi text.

3. If Wi-Fi isn't currently enabled, move its slider to the On position.

A Wi-Fi Direct Shortcut

To go directly to the Wi-Fi screen, open the Notification panel, and press and hold the Wi-Fi icon.

4. Enable Wi-Fi Direct by tapping its button.

5. The Wi-Fi Direct screen appears, and the phone scans for nearby Wi-Fi Direct-enabled devices. When your phone displays the name of the phone to which you want to connect, tap its name. (Only one user needs to do this to establish the two-way connection.)

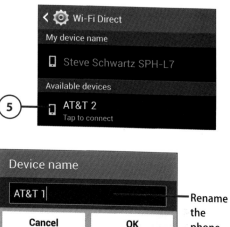

Naming Your Phone

To give your phone a friendlier name, open Settings, select the More tab, tap About Device, and tap Device Name. Enter a new name in the Device Name dialog box, and tap OK.

Rename the phone

6. An Invitation to Connect dialog box appears on the other phone. To allow the connection, the person taps Accept.

7. Each phone lists the other as a connected device, and the Wi-Fi Direct icon appears in the status bar.

8. To send a file such as a photo, song, or video from one phone to the other, select the item(s) in My Files, Gallery, or an appropriate app, and issue a Share or Share Via command, followed by Wi-Fi Direct. (You may have to scroll to see the Wi-Fi Direct command icon.) Select the device to which you want to send the file(s) and tap Done.

9. To finish the Wi-Fi Direct session, either person can return to the Wi-Fi Direct screen, tap the End Connection button, and then tap OK in the End Connection dialog box that appears.

Wi-Fi Direct icon

File Sharing Notes

Consider the following when using Wi-Fi Direct to transmit files between devices:

- The wording of the Share command may vary, depending on the type of selected material and the app you use. It may be Share, Share Via, or Share Music Via, for example.

- Files can be transmitted in either direction between connected devices. They are received in the ShareViaWiFi folder.

- Wi-Fi Direct file transmissions—both successes and failures—are listed in the Notification panel.

Using S Beam

Using a combination of Near Field Communication (*NFC*) and Wi-Fi Direct, S Beam enables you to exchange files and other materials (such as photos, videos, contact records, websites, maps, and YouTube videos) between a pair of Galaxy S 4 phones. NFC must be enabled on both phones; only the sending phone is required to have S Beam enabled.

1. On the Home screen, tap Apps, followed by Settings.

Sending, Receiving, or Both

If both people intend to send files, each must enable S Beam by performing steps 1–7. Otherwise, only the sender must enable S Beam, whereas the recipient must enable NFC (at a minimum).

2. Select the Connections tab. In the Connect and Share section of the screen, drag the S Beam slider to the On position. Doing so simultaneously enables both S Beam and NFC.

3. On the sending phone, launch the app that contains the material you want to transmit, and then display the material. Press the phones back to back, ensuring that neither is displaying the lock screen. Within 10 seconds, a connection is made between the phones, and Touch to Beam appears on the sending phone's screen. Tap the thumbnail to initiate the file transfer. You can separate the two phones while the data transmits.

4. The material is transmitted. When the transmission ends, the material displays on the receiving phone in the appropriate app, such as Gallery or Video. The recipient can find the files in the SBeamShare folder.

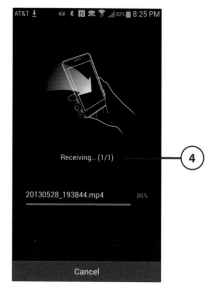

Sending Multiple Gallery Items

You can simultaneously send multiple photos in Gallery. Open the folder that contains the photos, select the thumbnails, and then press the phones together.

5. When you finish transmitting material, the phone(s) can disable S Beam by dragging its slider to the Off position.

5

S Beam
Send files via NFC and Wi-Fi Direct

`OFF`

THE ANDROID BEAM ALTERNATIVE

>>>Go Further

Think of Android Beam as S Beam's smaller sibling. It works like S Beam but is designed to share smaller bits of information (such as the web page you're currently browsing or a map view in Maps) over shorter distances. To enable Android Beam, open Settings, select the Connections tab, enable NFC (if its slider is in the Off position), tap NFC, and then drag the Android Beam slider to the On position. Display the information that you want to transfer, and—ensuring that the lock screen isn't displayed on either phone—touch the phones back to back. Tap the Touch to Beam thumbnail that appears. The material is transmitted and stored in a Beam folder on the recipient's phone. If the file is too large to send using Android Beam, enable S Beam and try the transfer again.

Using Share Shot

Share shot enables you to shoot photos with the Galaxy S 4 camera and—using Wi-Fi Direct—instantly transmit them to as many as five nearby friends. Before you proceed, instruct all participants to enable Wi-Fi Direct by performing steps 1–4 of "Using Wi-Fi Direct," earlier in this chapter.

1. On the Wi-Fi Direct screen, the phone scans for nearby phones and devices that have Wi-Fi Direct enabled. Do one of the following:

   - To share with one other phone or device, tap its name.

   - To share with multiple phones or devices, tap the Multi-Connect button, select the devices, and tap Done.

2. An Invitation to Connect appears on each screen. Each user must tap Accept.

3. On your phone, launch Camera by tapping its Home screen icon, tapping Apps and then Camera, or dragging the lock screen Camera icon upward (if present).

4. In Camera, tap the Settings icon.

5. Tap the Share icon, and then tap Share Shot.

6. Shoot the photos. As each picture is taken, it's stored in your phone's ShareShot folder and transmitted to recipients' RECV folder.

7. When you finish, disable sharing by tapping the Settings icon, followed by the Share Shot icon. Then choose Off in the Share menu.

8. The phone that initiated the connection should tap the End Connection button at the bottom of the Wi-Fi Direct screen. If Wi-Fi is no longer needed, you can disable it, too.

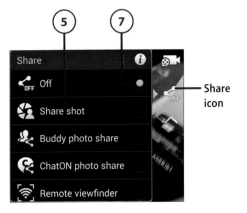

Share icon

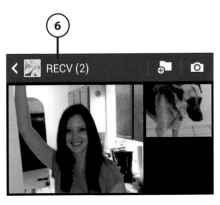

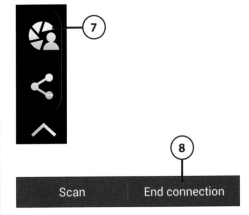

Google/Gmail sync components

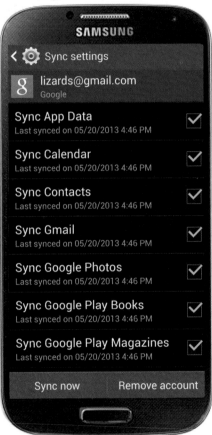

In this chapter, you find out how to synchronize calendar events, contacts, and other data on your phone with data stored elsewhere, such as in your web, computer, and Exchange Server accounts. Topics include the following:

→ Developing a synchronization strategy
→ Configuring the phone for automatic, scheduled syncs
→ Performing manual syncs

Synchronizing Data

When you got your phone, you probably already had important data such as contact records and calendar events stored somewhere else: in one or several computer applications, on websites, or in an Exchange Server account. Instead of keeping that information separate from the data in your phone's apps, you might want to keep all your data sources synchronized. That is, no matter where you edit or create new data, you can synchronize the other data sources automatically or manually to match.

Developing a Sync Strategy

If you want to keep your phone's important data (such as Calendar events and Contacts records) synchronized with data stored on your PC or Mac, on a Microsoft Exchange Server, or in web-based applications, there are currently only two seamless solutions. By *seamless*, I mean that you can accomplish this automatically (or manually with a simple tap) over a 3G/4G or wireless connection.

You don't have to hook up a USB cable or launch a separate application on your Mac or PC to perform a sync.

Although adding software and jumping through hoops are unnecessary, the seamless solutions *do* require that you accept either a Google/Gmail, Samsung, or Exchange Server account as the repository for your contact and calendar data.

Microsoft Exchange Server

If you work for a company or institution that employs Exchange Server to manage email, contacts, calendar, and other business data, your situation is the easiest. If you've added your Exchange email account to the phone, you have instant access on the phone to much of your important data—regardless of whether you create it on the phone or on one of several computers that you use. Each time you edit a contact or create a new calendar event, the server is responsible for synchronizing that data with every computer, phone, and tablet on which your Exchange account is registered.

Unfortunately, most users *don't* have an Exchange Server account. Internet service providers (ISPs) don't provide them. Note, however, that some Exchange hosting services will provide you with an account for a monthly fee. If you need constant access to your contact and calendar data, you might want to check out these services.

An Exception: Hotmail and Live Accounts
All email accounts with the web-based Microsoft Hotmail.com and Live.com are now handled as Microsoft Exchange ActiveSync accounts—not as POP3 accounts, as was the case in the past. If you have one or more of these accounts, you can sync their Calendar, Contacts, Email, and Tasks entries with data on your phone.

Google/Gmail

Because the Galaxy S 4 is an Android-based phone, Android is Google software, and you've probably added a Google/Gmail account to the phone, you can use this account to keep your calendar and contact data in sync. Several approaches facilitate this, but all except the first require concessions:

- If you already use Google and Gmail to manage your contacts and calendar events, you're all set.

- If you're willing to *switch* to Google/Gmail for managing your contacts and calendar events, you probably can export your data from the applications you currently use and import the data into Google Calendar and Contacts.

- Even if you aren't willing to switch to these Google web apps, you can perform the described export/import as a one-time procedure. As long as you're willing to manually maintain the Contacts list on your phone and record all new Calendar events on the phone, you can disable the sync process. Everything important to you will already be on your phone, so there's no reason to sync.

- Finally, if you can live with the notion that chunks of your data will be out of sync much of the time and correct only on your computer, you can use Google/Gmail as an *occasional* data receptacle. Periodically delete your Gmail Contacts data on the web, import your computer's contact data into Gmail Contacts, and then perform a single sync to transfer the up-to-date contact roster to your phone. (For help with importing Microsoft Outlook and Apple Contacts or Address Book contacts into Gmail Contacts, see Chapter 5.)

Using a Samsung, Hotmail, or Live Account

The Samsung account that you created during the phone's initial setup (see "Creating a Samsung Account" in Chapter 1) enables you to use certain apps such as ChatON. Like a Gmail/Google account, you also can use it to sync your calendar and contact data. Similarly, if you've added a Hotmail or Live account to the phone, you can elect to use it to sync the same data.

Samsung account sync components

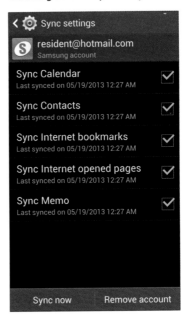

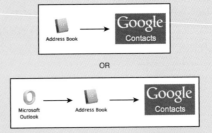

SYNCING ADDRESS BOOK (MAC) OR OUTLOOK 2011 (MAC) CONTACTS WITH GOOGLE CONTACTS

If you're a Mac user and you use its Address Book application to record your contacts, you can sync it with Google Contacts. Or if you use the Contacts component of Microsoft Outlook 2011 for Mac, you can sync it with Address Book—which, in turn, syncs with Google Contacts.

OR

1. *Sync Address Book with Google Contacts.* Launch Address Book on your Mac and choose Address Book, Preferences. Click the Accounts tab, check Synchronize with Google, and click the Configure button. Enter your

Google/Gmail account username and password, and then click OK. (If you don't use Outlook, skip to step 3.)

Accounts

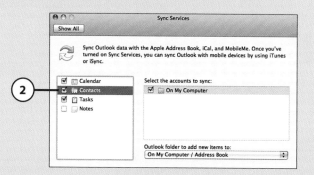

Configure

2. *Sync Outlook 2011 Contacts with the Address Book.* Launch Outlook 2011 on your Mac, choose Outlook, Preferences, and click the Sync Services icon. Ensure that Contacts has a check mark.

3. To perform the initial sync with Google Contacts (whether you're an Address Book or an Outlook 2011 user), choose Sync Now from the Sync menu on the right side of the Mac's menu bar. To perform additional syncs after making changes to Outlook or Address Book contacts, repeat this step.

Sync menu

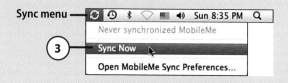

Alternative Software

If you prefer to enter important data on your computer using programs such as Microsoft Outlook (PC or Mac), Address Book (Mac), or iCal (Mac), another option is to search Android Market for an app solution that enables you to continue using those programs. An Android app and a companion application installed on your computer generally manage the sync process.

Missing Sync for Android

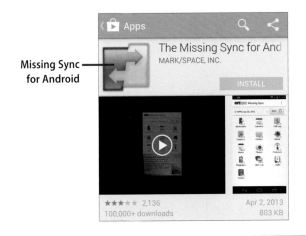

Test with Care

In reading about the Android/computer solutions, you might see a warning from the software company or in user comments concerning potential data loss. Before experimenting with any of these solutions, be sure to back up your data.

The Sneakernet (Manual) Approach

Before the wide acceptance of networking, if a co-worker needed a copy of a Word or Excel document, you'd use *Sneakernet*. That is, you'd copy the file to a floppy disk, walk down the hall, and hand it to whoever needed it. *Moral: Sometimes a manual approach is good enough.*

This also applies to synchronizing data between your phone and computer. If you don't live in Google/Gmail and don't have an Exchange Server account, you might decide to ignore synchronizing. Create new events and contact records on the device you use most, create them on whatever device happens to be handy, or standardize on using your phone or a computer application for adding all the new data. If you decide that a particular record or event is crucial and needs to be in *both* places, re-create the data on the second device when you have time.

Setting Sync Options and Schedules

Data from each account can be synced manually or on a *schedule* (automatically in the background). Most accounts enable you to specify which data types to sync and which ones to ignore. Sync *schedules*, on the other hand, can only be set for email accounts. You can allow any account to sync automatically or disable automatic syncs, syncing manually on selected accounts as needed (whenever your data has significantly changed).

1. On the Home screen, tap Apps, followed by Settings.

2. Select the Accounts tab. The My Accounts section lists your account classes (such as Email or Microsoft Exchange ActiveSync) and specific accounts (such as Facebook or LinkedIn) that can be synchronized.

3. To examine or change the sync settings for an account class or a specific account, tap the account class name or the specific account whose settings you want to examine or change.

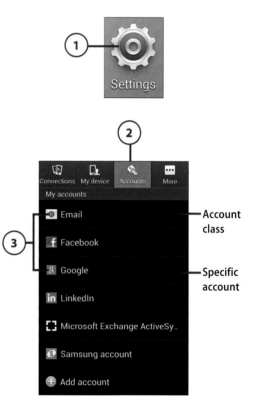

Account class

Specific account

4. *Account classes only:* If you select an account class, such as Email, in step 3, all accounts of that type are shown. Tap the account whose schedule or settings you want to view or change.

5. The Sync Settings screen appears. Synchronization will be performed only for those data elements that are checked. Make any desired changes by tapping check boxes. When you finish, press the Back key or tap the Back icon.

6. To set a schedule for an email or Microsoft Exchange ActiveSync account, tap Email or Microsoft Exchange ActiveSync in the My Accounts list (see step 2), and then tap Settings in the Common Settings section of the screen.

7. Tap the name of the specific account whose schedule you want to view or change.

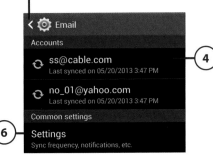

8. In the Sync Settings section of the account screen, tap Sync Schedule.

9. Tap Set Sync Schedule.

10. Select a sync interval. The interval will be used to sync all data elements selected in step 5.

The Never Interval

Select Never for accounts that you never want to update or to sync with other devices, as well as for those accounts that you intend to sync manually.

11. Review the other scheduling settings on the Sync schedule screen and then press the Back key or tap the Back icon until your email account list reappears. Repeat steps 7–10 for each additional account whose sync schedule you want to view or modify. (See Chapter 8 for additional information about and options for scheduling email checks.)

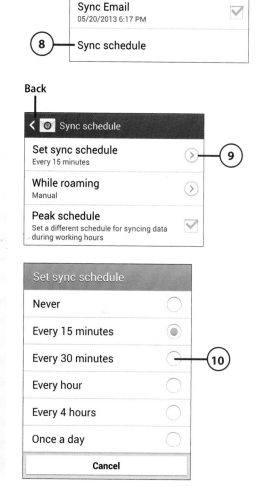

Performing Manual Syncs

You can perform manual syncs whenever you want—on an entire account or selected data elements within an account—regardless of whether an automatic schedule has been set.

1. On the Home screen, tap Apps, followed by Settings.

2. Select the Accounts tab, and tap the account type (such as Email) or the specific account (such as Samsung Account) that you want to sync.

3. *If multiple accounts are listed* (as may be the case if you selected Email or Microsoft Exchange ActiveSync in step 2), you can do the following:

   - To simultaneously sync all currently checked components for all listed accounts, tap Sync All.

   - To selectively sync the components of one account, tap the account name. On the Sync Settings screen, tap the Sync Now button to sync all checked components. To sync only a single component, double-tap the component. (It's necessary to double-tap to retain the component's original sync setting.)

4. *If a single account is listed and no components are displayed* (such as a Google or Samsung Account), you can do the following:

   - To simultaneously sync all currently checked components for the account, tap the Sync All button.

Selected account

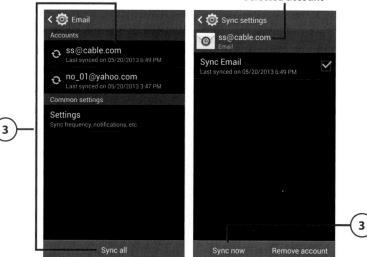

- Tap the account name. On the Sync Settings screen, tap the Sync Now button to sync all checked components. To sync only a single component, double-tap the component. (It's necessary to double-tap to retain the component's original sync setting.)

5. *If a single account is listed and components are displayed* (such as Facebook, LinkedIn, or Twitter), you can do the following:

   - To simultaneously sync all checked components for the account, tap the Sync Now button.

   - To sync only a single component, double-tap the component. (It's necessary to double-tap to retain the component's original sync setting.)

6. When you finish performing manual syncs, exit by pressing the Home key, repeatedly pressing the Back key, or repeatedly tapping the Back icon in the top-left corner of the screen.

It's Not All Good

THINK BEFORE YOU SYNC

Although syncing ensures convenient access to your data from anywhere and with any device, think carefully about the accounts you add to the phone and the types of data you elect to sync. Syncing puts your synced material (such as memos, notes, contacts, and calendar events) on Google, Samsung, and other external servers. If there's a security breach, others can potentially view your data. Thus, if you don't want certain personal or business information to be made public, you might not want to sync those items. If you're a corporate or government employee, check with your information technology (IT) department before adding non-business accounts to your phone and enabling syncing. There may be prohibitions against doing so.

>>>Go Further

ADDING ACCOUNTS

Whenever you create a new email account or launch and register an app with at least one sync component (such as email, calendar, or contacts), an account of that type is automatically added to the My Accounts list. To see if there are other accounts you can add, select the Accounts tab in Settings and tap Add Account (see the figure for step 2 in the previous task).

The Add Account screen presents a list of all eligible accounts and account types. Those followed by a green dot currently have at least one registered account on the phone. To add an account, tap an entry and follow the instructions to create or sign in to an account. (Note that you can have multiples of some account types, such as Email and Microsoft Exchange ActiveSync. Only a single instance of other accounts, such as Facebook and LinkedIn, is supported.)

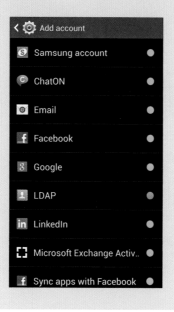

Personal message ——

Time ——

Date ——

Help text ——

Shortcuts ——

In this chapter, you discover simple methods for securing your phone from prying eyes and unauthorized use. Topics include the following:

→ Securing the lock screen
→ Setting options for the current locking method
→ Unlocking the phone
→ Other security measures for you to consider

Securing the Phone

Do you occasionally leave your phone unattended? If you don't like the idea that someone might use your phone and see everything you've stored on it, you can secure it using lock screen and security settings.

Securing the Lock Screen

Whenever you turn on the phone or restore it from a darkened state, you normally see the *lock screen*. Its purpose is twofold. First, when the phone is idle, the lock screen appears, providing a bit of privacy from casual observers. Second, you can secure the phone by requiring that a pattern, PIN, password, or face unlock be supplied to clear the lock screen—rather than simply swiping it away.

As with the Home screen wallpaper, you can customize the lock screen wallpaper by choosing a different image to display. See Chapter 3 for instructions.

Changing the Screen Locking Method

Use the following general steps whenever you want to review or change the locking method or its settings. Details for setting specific screen locking methods are presented later in this chapter.

1. On the Home screen, tap Apps, followed by Settings.

2. Select the My Device tab, and then tap Lock Screen.

Current Screen Locking Method

You can always view the current lock setting in the Screen Security section. It's displayed in the Screen Lock item.

3. Do either of the following:

- To change the screen locking method (requiring or removing a PIN, password, pattern, or face unlock), tap Screen Lock.

- To change options for the current screen locking method, tap the settings in the lower part of this screen. See "Setting Lock Screen Options" for instructions.

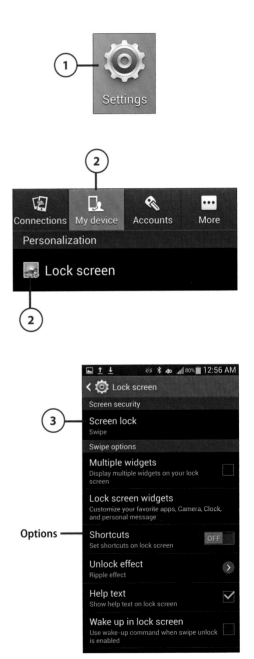

Setting a Lock Pattern

A *pattern* consists of four or more connected dots that you trace on a 3×3 grid.

1. As explained in the beginning of this section, open Settings and navigate to the Lock Screen.

2. Tap Screen Lock.

3. If a secure locking method is in use, you'll be asked to perform the unlock procedure. Otherwise, go to Step 4.

4. Tap Pattern.

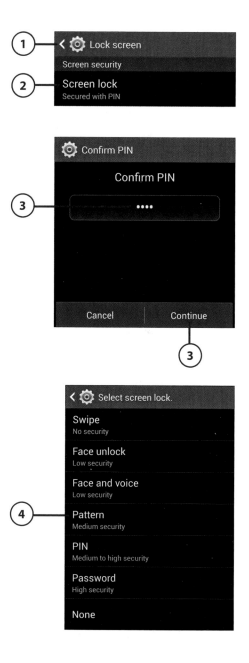

5. In a continuous motion, trace an unlock pattern that connects at least four dots. Tap Continue.

6. To confirm that you know the pattern, trace it again and tap Confirm.

7. Enter a backup PIN containing at least four digits (to use if you forget the pattern). Tap Continue.

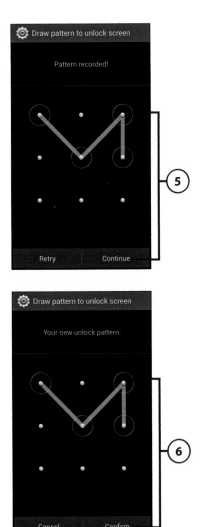

8. To confirm that you know the PIN, reenter it and tap OK.

9. The Lock Screen reappears, displaying your new security method. Review the options in the Secured with Pattern section of the screen (as explained later in this section). See "Setting Lock Screen Options" for instructions.

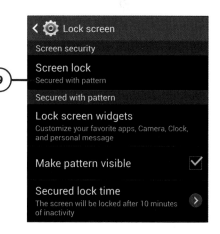

Setting a Lock PIN

A *PIN* is a number consisting of four or more digits that you enter on the onscreen keyboard to unlock the phone.

1. As explained in the beginning of this section, open Settings and navigate to the Lock Screen.

2. Tap Screen Lock.

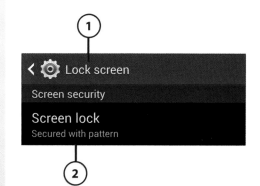

Current Lock Method

If a secure screen lock (PIN, password, or pattern) is currently in use, you'll be asked to perform the unlock procedure before continuing.

3. Tap PIN.

4. Use the keyboard to enter a PIN of four or more digits. Tap Continue.

Oops!

If you make a mistake while entering your PIN, you can tap the Delete key to backspace over the incorrect character(s).

5. To confirm that you know the PIN, enter it again and tap OK.

6. The Lock Screen reappears, displaying your new security method. Review the options in the Secured with PIN section of the screen (as explained later in this section). See "Setting Lock Screen Options" for instructions.

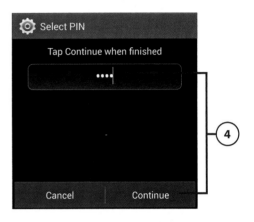

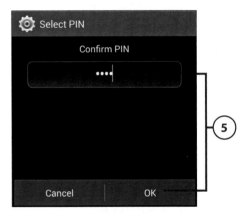

Setting a Lock Password

A *password* is a combination of uppercase and lowercase letters, numbers, and special characters that you enter on the onscreen keyboard to unlock the phone.

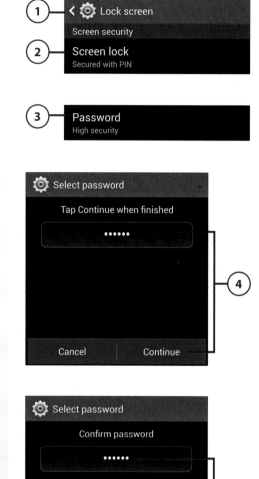

1. As explained in the beginning of this section, open Settings and navigate to the Lock Screen.

2. Tap Screen Lock.

Current Lock Method
If a secure screen lock (PIN, password, or pattern) is currently in use, you'll be asked to perform the unlock procedure before continuing.

3. Tap Password.

4. Use the keyboard to enter a password containing at least four characters. Tap Continue.

Letter Case Counts
If your password contains letters, be aware that letter case counts. *Knot*, *knot*, and *KNOT* are considered different passwords.

5. Confirm the password by entering it again and tap OK.

6. The Lock Screen reappears, displaying your new security method. Review the options in the Secured with Password section of the screen (as explained later in this section). See "Setting Lock Screen Options" for instructions.

Enabling Face Unlock

Face Unlock uses the front-facing camera and facial recognition to determine whether you or someone else is attempting to unlock the phone.

1. As explained in the beginning of this section, open Settings and navigate to the Lock Screen.

2. Tap Screen Lock.

Current Lock Method

If a secure screen lock (PIN, password, or pattern) is currently in use, you'll be asked to perform the unlock procedure before continuing.

3. Tap Face Unlock.

4. Read the three informational screens (Face Unlock, About Face Unlock, and Set Up Face Unlock). Tap Next, Set It Up, and Continue, respectively.

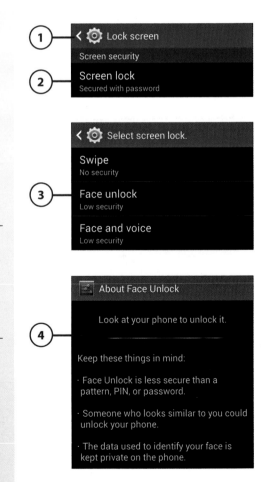

Face and Voice

If desired, you can choose Face and Voice to augment the facial recognition by adding voice recognition. Each time the phone is locked and it recognizes your face, you'll be prompted to say the unlock phrase.

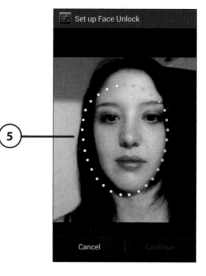

5. Hold the camera level with your face. When your face is successfully captured, the oval of dots turns green.

6. The Face Captured screen appears. Tap Continue.

7. Tap Pattern or PIN to create an alternative unlock method that will be used in instances when your face isn't recognized. (See "Setting a Lock Pattern" or "Setting a Lock PIN" earlier in this section for instructions.) Tap OK to dismiss the final screen.

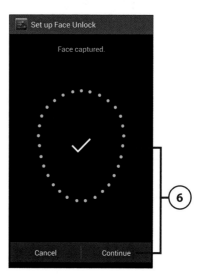

8. The Lock Screen reappears, displaying your new security method. Review the options in the Face Unlock Options section of the screen (as explained later in this section). See "Setting Lock Screen Options" for instructions.

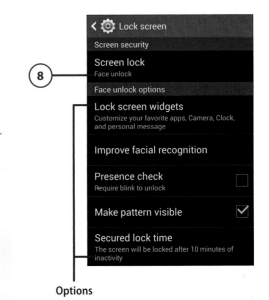

Options

Improve Facial Recognition

You can improve recognition by taking additional photos while varying the lighting, facial expression, and camera angle. See the explanation for the Improve Facial Recognition option in "Setting Lock Screen Options," later in this chapter.

Setting a Non-Secure Unlock Method

If security isn't an issue for you, you can select Swipe to simply *hide* the screen or None to dispense with the lock screen altogether.

1. As explained in the beginning of this section, open Settings and navigate to the Lock Screen.

2. Tap Screen Lock.

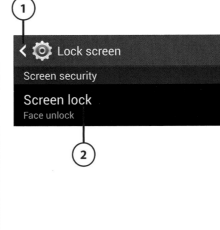

Current Lock Method

If a secure screen lock (PIN, password, or pattern) is currently in use, you'll be asked to perform the unlock procedure before continuing.

3. Tap to select one of these screen lock methods:

- *Swipe.* This is the default screen locking method. When restoring from a dark display, the lock screen wallpaper appears. Dismiss it by swiping in any direction.

- *None.* Select None to make the screen turn black following a screen timeout. When restored, the most recent screen immediately displays.

Setting Lock Screen Options

With the exception of None, each screen locking method has options that you can set. To view or change these options, open Settings, select the My Device tab, and tap Lock Screen.

In alphabetical order, these are the options and the locking method(s) to which each option applies:

- *Help Text (Swipe).* When enabled, text appears on the lock screen that explains how to unlock it.

- *Improve Facial Recognition (Face Unlock).* Snap additional photos of yourself with different expressions, lighting, and so on to improve the phone's ability to recognize you.

Current locking method

Options

Help text

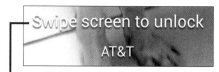

- *Lock Screen Widgets (Face Unlock, Password, Pattern, PIN, Swipe)*. You can optionally display any combination of the current time, date, and a custom text string on the lock screen. Tap Clock to display only the clock and date or tap Personal Message to display a text string.

  To edit, replace, or delete the Personal Message, tap Edit Personal Information, edit the message text, and set the text color, highlighting, and font by tapping icons. You can set the color of text or highlighting by tapping a color swatch or by dragging in the color picker. (The font size adjusts automatically to accommodate the Personal Message text string.) If desired, you can remove the date and/or time by clearing their check boxes. When you finish, tap Save.

- *Make Pattern Visible (Face Unlock, Pattern)*. When enabled, the traced pattern displays. When disabled, the traced pattern is hidden to prevent others from seeing it.

- *Multiple Widgets (Swipe)*. When this option is checked, you can enable the Favorite Apps or Camera setting (found within the Lock Screen Widgets option). If you unlock the phone by swiping from right to left near the top of the screen, a palette of your favorite apps appears or the Camera app launches.

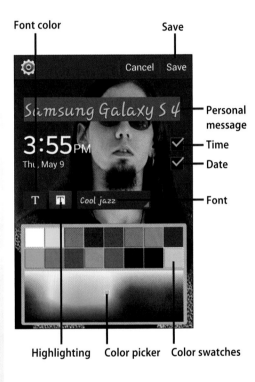

Font color   Save

Personal message

Time

Date

Font

Highlighting   Color picker   Color swatches

Editing the Favorite Apps Palette

To add an app to the palette, tap an Add App icon, and then select the app from the list of all installed apps. To remove an app from the palette, tap the Edit icon, and then tap the app that you want to remove.

- *Presence Check (Face Unlock).* To ensure that someone isn't attempting to unlock your phone by using a photo of your face, a request to Blink Now is added to the recognition process.

- *Secured Lock Time (Face Unlock, Password, Pattern, PIN).* This setting is what makes it practical to apply a secure locking method. In prior versions of Android, you were requested to perform an unlock *every time the lock screen appeared*. The Secured Lock Time is the length of inactivity (in seconds or minutes) before you're asked to perform your unlocking procedure. If less time has passed, you can clear the lock screen with a simple swipe.

- *Shortcuts (Swipe).* Shortcuts to your five favorite apps can be displayed across the bottom of the screen. Drag the slider to the On position to enable this feature. To replace a shortcut, tap its icon. To delete a shortcut, press and drag it onto the trash can. To change the order of the shortcuts, press and drag the shortcut to a new position.

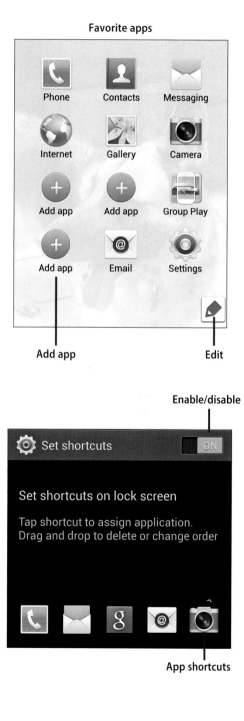

Favorite apps

Add app   Edit

Enable/disable

App shortcuts

When this option is enabled, you can launch an app from the lock screen by swiping its shortcut upward.

- *Unlock Effect (Swipe)*. Specify the visual effect that occurs whenever your finger approaches or touches the lock screen.

- *Wake Up in Lock Screen and Set Wake-Up Command (Swipe)*. When Wake Up in Lock Screen is checked, you can speak a wake-up phrase (such as *unlock* or *clear*) to clear the lock screen. To set the phrase, tap Set Wake-Up Command; tap an unassigned Wake-Up Function (1, 2, 3, or 4); tap Unlock; and record the phrase by repeating it four times.

Wake-up commands

< 🎤 Set wake-up command

Unlock

Check for missed calls

Check for missed messages

Open Camera

Check Schedule

Play Music

Record Voice

Driving mode on/off

Do More Than Clear the Lock Screen

In addition to assigning Unlock as one of the Wake-Up Functions, you can use the remaining three to perform other functions from the lock screen, such as playing music, opening the camera, or checking for missed messages.

SHOWING/HIDING PASSWORDS AND PINS

If you're concerned that people might peek as you enter passwords or PINs, you can disable Make Passwords Visible to obscure the characters as you type. Conversely, when enabled, this setting briefly shows each character that you type and then quickly replaces it with a bullet.

1. On the Home screen, tap Apps and then Settings, select the More tab, and tap Security.

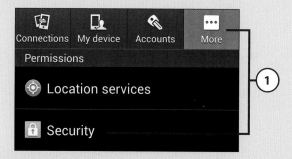

2. In the Passwords section of the Security screen, remove or add the Make Passwords Visible check mark.

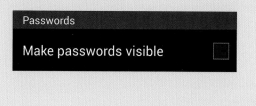

Unlocking the Lock Screen

The manner of clearing the lock screen depends on whether you've set a secure or unsecure locking method. When the lock screen is cleared, it reveals the Home screen or whatever you were doing when the screen darkened—working in Email, for example.

- *Swipe.* Using your finger, swipe the lock screen in any direction.

- *Pattern.* Trace your unlock pattern, connecting dots in the correct sequence. Don't lift your finger from the screen until you complete the pattern.

- *PIN.* Using the keyboard, enter your PIN and tap OK. If you make a mistake while entering the PIN, tap the Delete key to backspace over the incorrect character(s).

- *Password.* Using the keyboard, enter your password and tap Done. As previously noted, if the password contains letters, make sure that you use the correct letter case for each one. If you make a mistake while entering the password, tap the Delete key to backspace over the incorrect character(s).

Lock screen (Swipe)

Lock screen (Pattern)

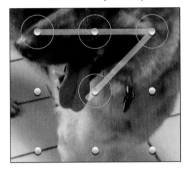

PIN   Delete

Lock screen (PIN)

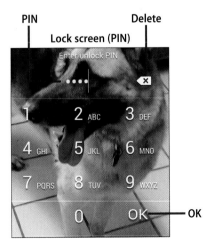

OK

- *Face Unlock.* Hold the phone at eye level, parallel to your face. If Face Unlock determines that it's you, the screen unlocks. Otherwise, it requests the backup PIN or pattern that you designated.

Password

Lock screen (Password)

Delete

Done

>>>Go Further

IF AT FIRST YOU DON'T SUCCEED…

You're allowed five tries to correctly enter your unlock pattern, PIN, or password. If you fail, an alert appears, explaining that the phone will remain locked for the next 30 seconds. Tap the OK button. A countdown timer in the center of the screen shows the seconds remaining until you can try again.

You have incorrectly drawn your unlock pattern 5 times.

Try again in 30 seconds.

OK

>>>Go Further

HEIGHTENED SECURITY

Securing the lock screen is as far as most users go to protect their phone and its data. However, just like your computer, your smartphone is susceptible to a variety of other threats. If you're concerned about security (or are *required* to have a secure phone by your company), here are some additional steps you can take:

- Review the Security section of Settings. (Open Settings, select the More tab, and tap Security.) Options enable you to encrypt the device and external memory card, lock the SIM card with a PIN, and verify apps to prevent installing known malware.

- Consider installing an antivirus app, such as Antivirus Security (AVG Mobile Technologies) or Norton Security Antivirus (NortonMobile). Both are available from the Google Play Store and are designed to protect the phone from viruses, malware, and theft.

- Corporate users can install/enable Samsung KNOX, a business security solution for the Galaxy S 4.

- When you download a new app from the Play Store, a list of permissions appears. (*Permissions* are activities that the app is requesting your permission to perform whenever it's active.) If you don't want to grant these permissions, don't download the app.

App permissions

Angry Birds Friends needs access to:

Storage
Modify or delete the contents of your USB storage

Phone calls
Read phone status and identity

Network communication
Full network access

Your location
Approximate location (network-based)

See all   ⌄

ACCEPT

Hotspot activated icon

Enabled

Hotspot network name

Connected device name

Connection instructions

In this chapter, you find out how to use your phone to provide Internet access for other devices and to control external devices. Topics include the following:

→ Creating a Wi-Fi hotspot with the phone
→ Using a USB cable to tether your phone to a Windows PC
→ Controlling a television set with the WatchON app
→ Using the optional Samsung MHL 2.0 HDTV Adapter to mirror the phone's screen on an HDTV

Powering Other Devices

If your laptop or desktop computer currently lacks Internet access— when traveling or during a provider outage, for example—you can use your phone as the equivalent of a USB (*tethering*) or wireless (*mobile or portable hotspot*) modem. Because the S 4 has infrared capabilities, you can configure the included WatchON app to control your TV with the phone. And if you buy the optional MHL 2.0 HDTV Adapter, anything on the phone can be displayed on your HDTV.

Creating a Mobile HotSpot for Wi-Fi Devices

Using the phone's Tethering and Mobile HotSpot settings in combination with your 3G or 4G data connection, your phone can become a *hotspot* through which up to eight Wi-Fi devices can simultaneously connect to the Internet. (Some carriers call this a *mobile* hotspot and others call it a *portable* hotspot.)

A Plan Add-On

Creating a mobile hotspot and tethering may not be included in your data plan. They frequently cost extra and must be ordered from your carrier as needed. Before trying these features, check with your carrier for details on the cost and the procedure for enabling/disabling this add-on service.

1. On the Home screen, tap Apps, followed by Settings.

2. Select the Connections tab and tap More Networks.

3. Tap Tethering and Portable HotSpot.

4. Drag the Mobile Hotspot slider to the On position.

Or Simply Launch the App

Some carriers provide an app that—when launched—takes you directly to the Tethering and Mobile HotSpot settings. It's not special software; it's just a shortcut that takes you directly to this step.

5. If Wi-Fi is currently enabled for the phone, an Attention dialog box appears. Tap OK to turn Wi-Fi off. (The hot spot runs only over a cellular connection, not Wi-Fi.)

6. Tap Mobile Hotspot to see the Mobile Hotspot screen that shows the current connection settings, connected devices, and password.

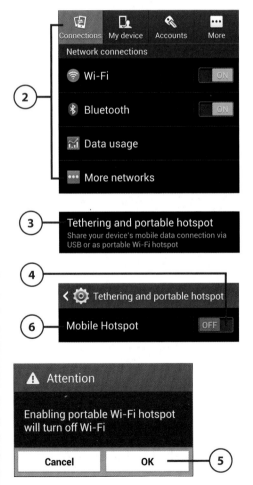

7. You can optionally edit the default settings—changing the connection name, selecting a security protocol, and setting a different password—by tapping Configure. Otherwise, go to step 9.

8. Make any desired changes to the settings and tap Save.

9. Connect up to eight Wi-Fi-enabled devices (laptops, tablets, iPods, and so on) to the hotspot network by selecting the hotspot network's name on each device and entering the password when prompted. (The figure shows this process for a Windows PC.)

Connected Devices

While the hotspot is active, the Mobile Hotspot screen displays a list of all connected devices.

10. When you finish, deactivate the hotspot by dragging the Mobile HotSpot slider to the Off position. Mobile HotSpot quits, all devices are disconnected, and Wi-Fi is automatically re-enabled (assuming a Wi-Fi network is available).

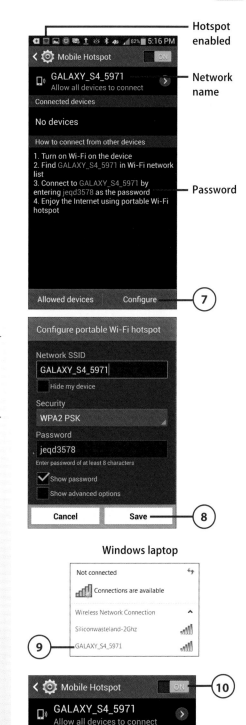

Hotspot enabled

Network name

Password

Windows laptop

It's Not All Good

TEST YOUR CONNECTION SPEED

As with other cellular connections, the faster the network and the stronger your signal strength, the more usable a hotspot connection will be. If enabling a hotspot will incur an added fee, you might want to use your phone's current connection to run a speed test at http://speedtest.net. You should also consider where you'll be using the hotspot and what networks will be available to you. Check your carrier's coverage map for information. If the data connection is less than 3G, a mobile hotspot will likely produce disappointing results.

Tethering the Phone and a PC

Another way to provide Internet access to a computer is to connect the phone and computer with the phone's USB cable (referred to as *tethering*). Unlike a mobile hotspot, tethering is restricted to only one computer at a time and is currently available only for Windows and Linux-based computers.

Bluetooth Tethering

In addition to USB tethering, some carriers may support wireless tethering using Bluetooth.

1. *Windows users only:* Visit the Support section of Samsung's site (http://www.samsung.com/us/support/) to download and install the USB driver for your carrier's Galaxy S 4. Note that installing the device driver is a one-time process.

Support Overview	Manuals	Downloads	FAQs & How-Tos	Community Q&A

| | Operating System: All | | Language: All |

Description ∧	OS	Release Date	Language	Size (MB)	Download File
⊙ Device(Install),USB Driver (Software) (ver.v1.5.14.0)	Win XP/Vista/Win 7/Win 8	Nov 12, 2012	ENGLISH	23.06	EXE

Finding Your Model Number

You can find your phone's carrier-specific model number by opening Settings, selecting the More tab, and tapping About Device.

Model number ——— SAMSUNG-SGH-I337

2. Connect the phone's USB cable to the phone and to one of the PC's available USB ports.

An Extra Step

In Windows, you may see a notice that the necessary drivers are being installed. When installation finishes, an AutoPlay dialog box appears, asking what you want to do with the new connected device; that is, the phone. Click Open Device to View Files.

Open device ———

3. On the Home screen, tap Apps, followed by Settings.

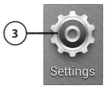

4. Select the Connections tab and tap More Networks.

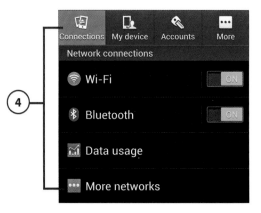

5. Tap Tethering and Portable Hotspot.

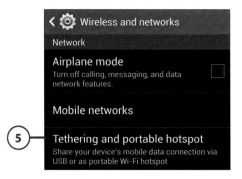

6. Enable tethering by tapping USB Tethering.

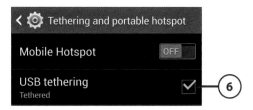

7. After the computer recognizes the phone, you can use the PC's browser and other Internet applications.

8. When you're done using the phone as a USB modem, remove the check mark from USB tethering (see step 6), eject the phone hardware in the same way that you do with other connected USB devices, and disconnect the USB cable.

Disconnection Details

You should never simply unplug a USB data device. Click the Safely Remove Hardware icon at the far right of the Windows task bar, choose the Eject *phone model* command from the pop-up menu that appears, and—when you're told that it's safe to do so—disconnect the USB cable. (If the Safely Remove Hardware icon *isn't* displayed, wait until you're certain that no data is being transferred between the phone and PC, and then disconnect the USB cable.)

Safely Remove —————— Hardware icon

Mirroring the Phone on an HDTV

With Samsung's optional MHL 2.0 HDTV Adapter, you can use your flat-screen TV to display whatever is shown on the phone.

1. Plug an HDMI cable into the adapter.

2. Connect the other end of the HDMI cable to your flat-screen television.

3. Using your television's Input menu, select the HDMI input to which the adapter is connected.

4. Plug the adapter's cable into your phone's USB port.

5. On the phone, run any application that you want to display on the TV.

MHL 2.0 HDTV ADAPTER TIPS

Note the following when using the adapter:

- *Playing music.* Depending on the quality of your television's speakers, stored and streamed songs may sound excellent.

- *Viewing videos and games.* Video quality can vary greatly, depending on its source and the application. For example, streamed video using an app, such as HBO Go, is generally encoded for playback on the phone's diminutive screen rather than on a large, flat-screen TV. Expect the quality to be only passable. Games, on the other hand, may look wonderful. Experimentation should teach you what displays well and what doesn't.

- *Viewing photos.* Multimegapixel photos may look fine when displayed on a TV. When viewing pictures, you can rotate the phone to switch from portrait to landscape display.

- *Viewing slide shows.* Slide shows don't have to be silent or dull. When playing a Gallery photo folder as a slide show, you can select a song to accompany the show and a transition effect to use when switching to each new slide.

- *Using the adapter with other phones.* When using the adapter with an MHL 2.0 compatible device such as the Galaxy S 4, the necessary power is supplied by the phone. However, if you use the adapter with the Samsung Galaxy S III or Note II, you must use the phone's USB cable/wall charger to power the adapter.

CONTROLLING YOUR TV WITH WATCHON

In combination with the Galaxy S 4's built-in infrared hardware, you can use the new WatchON app as an intelligent remote control for one or more television sets. WatchON supports most brands and set models (as long as they respond to remote control), as well as the major cable and satellite providers. WatchON can also control a set-top box/DVR, if you have one.

After configuring WatchON for your hardware and television provider, and optionally specifying your viewing preferences, there are a host of features you can use:

- Use the remote to turn the set on and off, adjust or mute the volume, change channels, change the input source, and display the TV's internal menu. You can access a basic version of the remote in the Notification panel with which you can issue common commands to the TV or DVR, as well as launch or switch to the WatchON app.

- Open the Channel Guide to see a list of the shows that are on. It can be scrolled by hour or day and used to select a show to watch. (The channel list can optionally be edited to display only the channels to which you subscribe.) If you see an upcoming show that you want to watch, you can set a reminder for it that will appear in the Notification Bar at the designated time.

- Swipe the screen to the right to select a subset of channels to display, such as Favorites, Movies, Sports, or Just for You (show recommendations, based on your viewing preferences).

- Tap the Video tab to see a list of streaming movies and TV shows that you can rent.

- Use the remote to instruct your DVR to record the current show or play a previously recorded show.

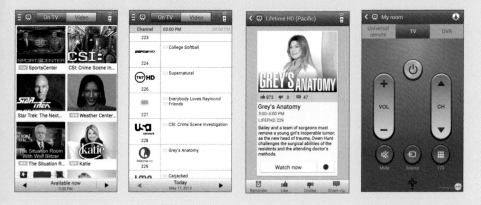

Refresh

Remaining charge

Time since last restart

In this chapter, you discover how to use your phone more efficiently by managing your plan, available storage, and memory; adding a memory card; updating system software; and performing basic troubleshooting. Topics include the following:

19

→ Using Task Manager to manage memory
→ Conserving the battery manually and by enabling Power Saving Mode
→ Making the most of your talk and data plans
→ Viewing and expanding current storage
→ Installing or replacing your SIM card
→ Performing system updates
→ Troubleshooting and resetting the phone

Optimizing and Troubleshooting

There's more to understanding your Galaxy S 4 than making phone calls and mastering a handful of favorite apps. This chapter delves into material that you don't need to commit to memory or even read immediately—but when you need it, you'll be happy to have it.

Managing Memory

You've noticed that most apps don't have a Quit or Exit command. That's because the Android operating system is designed to handle memory management behind the scenes. If free memory is running low, for example, unnecessary processes automatically shut down. However, if you occasionally feel the need to take a hands-on approach to quitting apps and freeing memory, you can use the Task Manager.

1. Press and hold the Home key. A vertically scrolling list of apps that you've recently run or are currently running appears.

2. To launch Task Manager, tap its icon.

Other Options

In addition to launching the Task Manager, you can do any of the following on this screen:

- Tap an app thumbnail to immediately switch to or launch the app.

- Drag an app thumbnail off the left or right edge of the screen to remove it from the list. If the thumbnail is that of a running app, the app quits.

- To clear the list and simultaneously quit any apps within the list that are running, click the Clear All icon. (The list is also cleared whenever you restart or power off the phone.)

- Click the Google Search icon to perform a search.

3. Select the Active Applications tab to view the currently running applications. To close a listed app, tap its End button. To simultaneously close all running applications, tap End All.

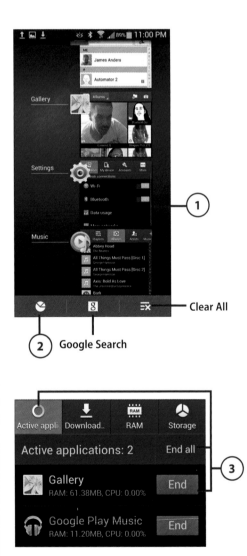

Clear All

Google Search

4. Tap OK in the End or End All confirmation dialog box.

5. *Optional*: If exiting running applications doesn't solve your memory issue, select the RAM tab, and then tap Clear Memory to clear all inactive and background processes. Note the change in the memory bar.

Clear Memory Consequences

As is the case with using the Force Stop command (described in "Viewing Battery Usage by Features and Apps" later in this chapter), Clear Memory can have consequences other than simply freeing memory that unnecessary processes are using. As the RAM screen explains, "Completed and ongoing application functions will be removed from RAM." This causes running apps to abruptly quit and background processes to halt.

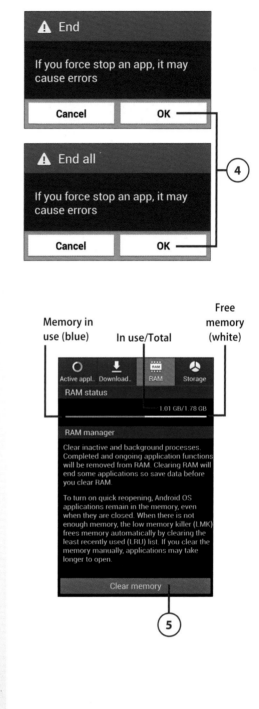

Memory in use (blue) In use/Total Free memory (white)

Conserving the Battery

Depending on how frequently you use the phone and what you typically do with it, there are several approaches to conserving the battery. First, you can automatically conserve the remaining charge by enabling Power Saving Mode. Second, if you prefer to take the *manual* approach, you can disable features that aren't currently needed or change certain default settings so that less power is used. Finally, to monitor how various apps and the operating system use the battery, you can run the Battery utility.

Show the Battery Percentage

Although the battery indicator in the status bar gives a rough indication of the remaining charge, you can alter it to show the percentage remaining. Open Settings, select the My Device tab, tap Display, and enable Display Battery Percentage.

Configuring and Enabling Power Saving Mode

When Power Saving Mode is enabled and a low battery level is detected, selected features are automatically changed or disabled to extend the remaining charge.

1. On the Home screen, tap Apps, followed by Settings.

2. Select the My Device tab. Scroll as necessary and tap Power Saving Mode.

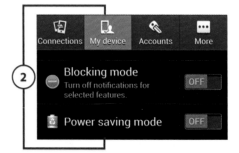

3. Ensure that the Power Saving Mode switch is in the On position.

4. Enable or disable power-saving options by tapping check boxes. To view a brief explanation of what each option does, tap Learn About Power Saving Mode.

Using the Notification Panel

If you don't need to change the Power Saving Mode settings, you can quickly enable or disable Power Saving Mode by opening the Notification panel, scrolling the icons to the right, and tapping the Power Saving icon. To quickly make changes to the settings, you can press and hold the icon to go directly to the Power Saving Mode screen in Settings.

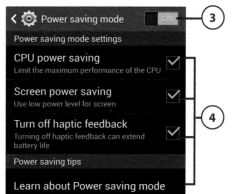

Enable/disable Power Saving Mode

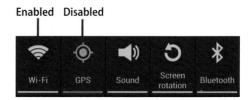

Tips for Manually Conserving the Remaining Charge

If the battery is generally draining too quickly or you want to extend usage time when the battery is almost depleted, you can manually change certain settings as needed or set new defaults.

- If you aren't currently using some services, such as GPS or Bluetooth, disable them in the Notification panel by tapping their icons. Turn them back on only when you need them.

Enabled   Disabled

- The phone's screen draws considerable power. Consider reducing the Screen Timeout value or the Brightness setting (Settings, My Device tab, Display). Whenever you're done using the phone for a bit, tap the Power button to instantly darken the display—rather than waiting for the Screen Timeout.

Display Settings

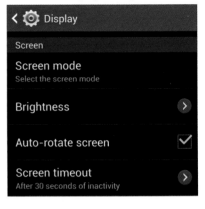

- Consider checking less frequently for new email. For unimportant email accounts, you could set the frequency to Once a Day or Never, for example. You can still perform manual checks as often as you want. To change the retrieval frequency, launch Email, press the Menu key, tap Settings, and tap the account that you want to manage. Tap Sync Schedule, tap Set Sync Schedule, and then select a new frequency.

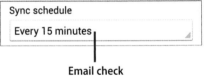

Email check frequency

- Avoid battery-intensive activities. Playing videos and games prevents the display from timing out. Streaming videos or music transfers large amounts of data to the phone, requiring that the connection be constantly running.

- In standby mode, the phone consumes little battery power. Although it may be sacrilege to suggest this, you can take things a step further by powering off the phone when you won't need it for an extended period. For instance, if you *never* answer the phone after you go to bed, consider turning it off nightly—or leave it on while you charge it during this period.

Plug It In

Before the battery dies, you can continue a conversation and other activities by quickly plugging the phone into a wall outlet or USB port. The phone charges as you continue to work. When your call or app activity concludes, power off the phone and allow the battery to charge normally.

It's Not All Good

WHY IS THIS APP USING GPS?

It's amazing and rather sad that so many apps now have a GPS component (given that it contributes to battery drain and data usage, and it frequently seems an unnecessary feature). For example, although a game might use GPS information to pair you with or show nearby players, is the feature essential? Will the app function without it? My attitude is that, unless enabling GPS benefits me, I'd rather not play "Where in the World Is Steve Schwartz?"

You have several options with GPS-enabled apps. First, turn off GPS and see whether the app still functions or whether GPS is forced back on. Second, if the app has a Settings command, you may be able to disable its GPS component or substitute a manually entered location. Third, enable GPS while using the app and quickly disable it when you finish. Fourth, decide whether the app is *really* important to you. If not, uninstall it and search for a similar app that doesn't require GPS. Fifth, reconcile yourself to recharging more frequently. If an app is critical to your business or life, it's probably worth the battery drain.

Viewing Battery Usage by Features and Apps

If you want to get a handle on which features and applications are draining your battery the most, you can find the answer in Settings.

1. On the Home screen, tap Apps, followed by Settings.

2. Select the More tab, and then tap Battery.

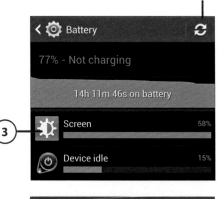

3. The scrolling summary that appears lists the features and applications that have been consuming the battery since the last time you charged the phone and shows the percentage of consumption attributable to each.

Refreshing the Data

While viewing the Battery screen, you can force a refresh to display up-to-date consumption figures.

4. *Optional:* Tap an entry to view additional information. Depending on the item, you may be able to alter its settings to reduce battery consumption or execute a force stop for it (in the case of an application).

Refresh

Display Settings

It's Not All Good

ABOUT FORCE STOP

Android is responsible for handling memory management, halting applications and processes as needed. In general, you should avoid using the Force Stop button for items that present it. (In Task Manager, tapping End is the same as performing a Force Stop.) Don't assume that Force Stop is the equivalent of a computer program's Quit or Exit command. Similar to the capability to force quit a misbehaving Mac or PC application, Force Stop's main purpose is to give you a way to semi-gracefully shut down an app or feature that isn't responding.

When used as a means to temporarily halt battery consumption or free memory, the consequences may not always be what you intend. You may lose information; the phone, app, or feature may be left in an unstable state; or you might have difficulty restarting the application or feature.

Managing Talk Time and Data Usage

If you're on a limited talk, messaging, or data plan, the key to avoiding overage charges is relatively simple: *Know and monitor your plan.*

Checking Current Usage

Each carrier generally offers several ways for you to check the current month's usage. For example, if AT&T is your carrier, usage data can be viewed in the myAT&T app.

Carriers typically provide a phone number that you can call to check your minutes and other usage. If you use Sprint, for example, dial ***4** from your cell phone. If you're a T-Mobile customer, you can dial **#MIN#** to check minutes, **#MSG#** for text messages, or **#WEB#** for Internet and data usage.

You can also check the carrier's website. At a minimum, you should see your usage for the current billing cycle. In addition, there might be an option to automatically receive a notification if you come close to exceeding a plan limit. *Forewarned is forearmed.* (It has taken my entire life to come up with a decent reason for using that phrase.) For example, when you're precariously close to hitting your monthly data limit, you can take steps to ensure that additional data-intensive activities (such as streaming videos or music) occur only over Wi-Fi.

Managing Data Usage

If your data plan has a monthly limit, you can enable the Data Usage setting on the phone to automatically warn you when you come close to exceeding your data limit—ignoring data transmitted over Wi-Fi, which doesn't count toward usage. You can also manually disable *mobile data* (using the cell network to transmit data) if you're close to exceeding your plan limit.

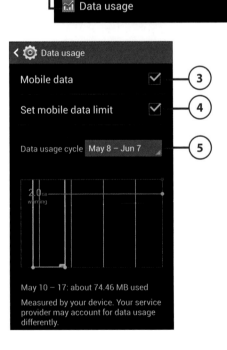

1. On the Home screen, tap Apps, followed by Settings.

2. Select the Connections tab, and then tap Data Usage.

3. The Data Usage screen appears. The state of the Mobile Data check box determines whether the cell network can be used to transfer data to and from the phone (checked) or whether you're restricting it to Wi-Fi data transfers (unchecked). If you're close to or have exceeded your monthly limit, disable it to prevent additional overage charges.

4. Tap the Set Mobile Data Limit check box to instruct the phone to warn when you're approaching your monthly limit. Read the explanatory material in the Limit Data Usage dialog box and tap OK. When the data limit (red

line) is reached, mobile data is automatically disabled; you must do additional data transfers over Wi-Fi. Continue with the remaining steps.

5. Ensure that the Data Usage Cycle matches your monthly billing cycle and represents the current cycle. If the billing period is incorrect, tap it, tap Change Cycle, specify the date when the usage cycle resets, and tap Set. If the cycle is incorrect, tap it to select a different 30-day period.

6. Set the red slider to match your plan's data limit (in gigabytes), set the orange slider to reflect the usage amount at which you want to be warned, and set the white bars to the period that you want to monitor.

7. Press the Menu key to enable or disable these additional Data Usage options:

- Enable Data Roaming to allow your phone to use other networks for data access when roaming.

- Enable Restrict Background Data to prevent background data access of apps and services, restricting them to working only when a Wi-Fi connection is available.

- Enable Auto Sync Data if you want your accounts to sync automatically—regardless of whether only a cellular connection is available.

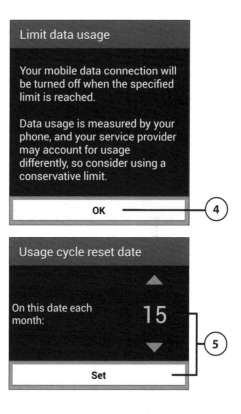

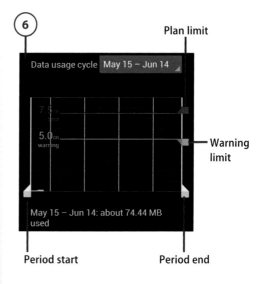

- Enable Show Wi-Fi Usage to add a separate Wi-Fi tab to the Data Usage screen, showing the last 30 days of Wi-Fi data usage and the apps that contributed to the usage. You aren't billed for Wi-Fi data usage, so it can be useful to see how much of your usage was free (Wi-Fi) versus paid (cellular).

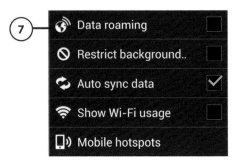

- Tap Mobile Hotspots to view enabled Wi-Fi hotspots within range of your phone.

What's Cheaper?

If you have unlimited or inexpensive text messaging, it may be advantageous to send texts rather than make short calls. Conversely, if you're billed 25¢ per message, it may be cheaper to call. Note that your carrier may allow you to *block* incoming text messages (see the carrier's website for details). Received text messages—including unwanted ones—may be billed to your account at the same rate as messages that you send.

Can This Call Be Made Later?

The distinction between free and paid calls is typically determined by the time of day at the location where you make the call. If your free minutes begin at 7:00 p.m. each weeknight, for example, try to reserve lengthy, chatty calls for evenings and weekends.

If you're traveling and are in a different time zone, your daytime and evening calling periods generally change to match the current time zone. Before heading out, check your plan to be sure. Similarly, if you're leaving the country, ask how out-of-country minutes are billed. Thinking that he was covered or that the rate would be reasonable, a friend didn't bother to check before leaving and returned to discover that his handful of international calls resulted in a bill of several hundred dollars.

Viewing and Expanding Storage

Although the 16GB version of the Galaxy S 4 has almost 10GB of internal memory available for storage, you can exhaust it with a combination of apps, photos, videos, music, and other data. You can expand the available storage by inserting a *microSD* (Secure Digital) or *microSDHC* (Secure Digital High Capacity) card into the phone's internal slot, adding as much as an additional 64GB.

Viewing Used and Available Space

Consult the Storage section of Task Manager to view the total, used, and available storage on your phone.

1. Launch the Task Manager by pressing and holding the Home key, and then tapping the Task Manager icon at the bottom of the screen.

2. Select the Storage tab.

3. Interpret the displayed information as follows:

   - *System Storage* is the phone's built-in storage.

   - An *SD Card* entry is shown if you've inserted a microSD or microSDHC card into the phone's internal slot.

   - The blue section of each bar represents the used space; the white section is the unused/ available space. Above each bar are two figures. The first represents used space; the second is the total space.

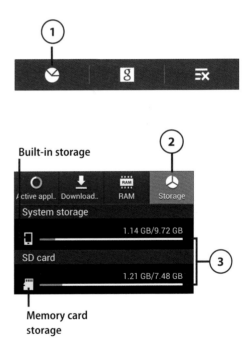

Storage Shrinkage

When viewing the Storage section of Task Manager, you may think that the total space listed is less than the stated specs. Don't be alarmed; the figures are correct. Although the Galaxy S 4 includes at least 16GB of internal storage, part of it is used as system memory. And when formatted for use, an 8GB microSDHC card has only 7.48GB of usable space, for example.

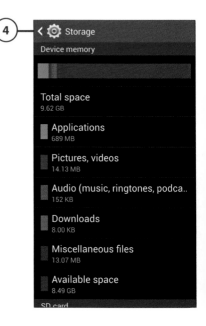

4. *Optional:* To view a breakdown of the storage space being used by different types of data, open Settings, select the More tab, and tap Storage.

Adding a Memory Card

The Galaxy S 4 can accommodate up to a 64GB memory card in its internal slot. When picking a card, take note of its *class* in the item description. The lower the class number (2, 4, 6, 8, or 10), the slower the card. Under current class specifications, the class indicates the card's minimum sustained write speed in megabytes per second. Thus, a Class 2 card should be capable of writing data to the card at 2 Mps (megabytes per second) or faster. (If a card's description or packaging doesn't mention a class, assume that it's Class 2 or slower. That frequently explains why such cards are so inexpensive.) Currently, you can purchase Class 10 cards for less than $1 per megabyte. Unless you already have an older, slower card, there's little monetary incentive to go slower than Class 10.

Next, determine the amount of storage you need. An 8GB or 16GB card suffices for most people. If you intend to pack it with videos and music or regularly shoot hundreds of photos or lengthy movies, go for the highest-capacity card you can afford—64GB is the max.

All Cards Aren't Equal

Even within a class, cards aren't identical. First, some Class 10 cards can sustain a minimum 10MB/second *read* speed, as well as write speed. Second, the minimum speed on some of these cards is occasionally much faster than 10MB/second. Third, based on user reviews and ratings on sites such as Amazon.com and NewEgg.com, some cards appear to be knockoffs that are slower than their stated class, fail quickly, or don't work at all.

When choosing a card from an online source, read the user comments, note the ratings, and check the seller's return policy. Amazon.com, for example, sells a card called AmazonBasics that's highly rated by purchasers and is inexpensive, too.

Although it isn't necessary, make a note of whether your chosen card includes a microSD to SD adapter. If it does, you can slip your tiny card into the postage stamp-sized adapter and use it in devices that require an SD card rather than a microSD card. (In the same vein, be sure that your chosen card is a *microSD* or *microSDHC*, not an SD or SDHC. Only a micro card will fit in the phone's slot.)

Inserting a Memory Card

Whether the card is new or being moved from another phone or device, the first step is to insert it into your phone.

1. Shut down the phone by holding down the Power button, tapping Power Off in the Device Options dialog box, and then tapping OK in the confirmation dialog box.

2. Remove the cover from the back of the phone by slipping your fingernail into the slot on the side (above the Power button) and prying off the back.

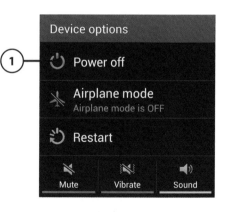

3. Grasp the memory card by its edges and turn the card so that its gold contact strips face down. The labeled side of the card should face up.

4. Carefully push the card into the slot until it clicks into place, and then replace the phone's back cover. Ensure that the cover is sealed around all edges.

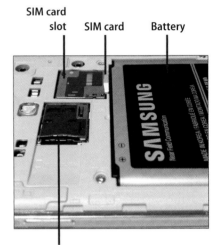

SIM card slot   SIM card   Battery

Memory card slot

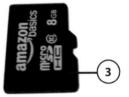

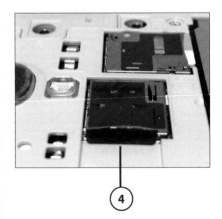

Formatting a Memory Card

If the memory card contains unwanted data from another phone or device or isn't recognized by the phone as formatted, you can *format* the card (erasing any current data and preparing it for use in the phone).

1. On the Home screen, tap Apps, followed by Settings.

2. Select the More tab, and tap Storage.

3. Scroll down to the SD Card section, and tap Format SD Card.

4. Tap the Format SD Card button.

5. Tap the Delete All button.

6. The memory card is unmounted, formatted, and remounted to enable the phone to see and use it.

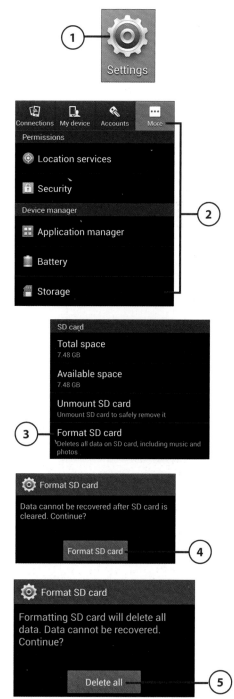

Removing a Memory Card

The following steps explain how to safely remove a memory card from the phone to replace it with a different card or to move the card to another device. You begin by *unmounting* the card so that it can be safely removed.

1. On the Home screen, tap Apps, followed by Settings.

2. Select the More tab, and tap Storage.

3. Scroll down to the SD Card section, and tap Unmount SD Card. Tap OK in the confirmation dialog box.

4. Shut down the phone by holding down the Power button, tapping Power Off in the Device Options dialog box, and then tapping OK in the confirmation dialog box.

5. Remove the cover from the back of the phone by slipping your fingernail into the slot on the side (above the Power button) and prying off the back. For photos relevant to this and the remaining steps, see "Inserting a Memory Card," earlier in this section.

6. To free the SD card, press it *into* the slot. The card will spring free. Carefully slide the card out of the slot. (When handling the card, be sure to grasp it only by its edges.)

7. Replace the battery cover.

Using a Memory Card as a USB Drive

By following the instructions in "Transferring Files over USB" in Chapter 15, you can mount your phone as an external drive on your Mac or PC (like a flash drive), enabling you to freely copy files in either direction. You can view and access the files on your phone by going to the Home screen and tapping Apps, My Files. When you open the All Files folder, you can see separate icons for the phone's built-in memory (Device Storage) and your installed memory card (SD Memory Card). If you tap these icons to view the files within, you'll note that all files stored in built-in memory have the path prefix `/storage/emulated/0/`. Files on an installed memory card have the path prefix `/storage/extSdCard`.

Built-in memory

Installed memory card

Installing or Replacing the SIM Card

To be recognized by your carrier's network, every Galaxy S 4 must have a carrier-specific Subscriber Identify Module (SIM) card. If the SIM card wasn't preinstalled when you purchased the phone, follow the procedure and photos in "Inserting a Memory Card" to open the case and insert the SIM card into its slot. Ensure that the notched edge goes into the slot first and that the card's gold contacts face down.

To replace an existing SIM card with a new one, start by removing the battery. (Although you can remove and replace the SIM card with the battery in place, it's much easier if you take it out.) To remove the current SIM card, gently press it into its slot until it pops out. Remove the card. Slide the new SIM card into the slot—notch first, gold contacts down—until it clicks into place. Finish by replacing the battery and the phone's back cover.

Checking for System Updates

It's a good idea to periodically check for system updates. Although you may automatically receive notices of firmware updates, for example, you can still perform manual checks whenever you like, as explained in the following task. The notification method and process of updating to a newer version of the Android operating system and firmware are carrier-dependent. When notified of an available update, refer to your carrier's website for additional instructions.

Check the Battery First
Before performing any kind of system update—especially firmware and Android—be sure you have sufficient charge to complete the process. Interrupting updates can have dire consequences for the phone.

1. On the Home screen, tap Apps, followed by Settings.

2. Select the More tab.

3. Depending on your carrier, do one of the following:

   - *AT&T.* Tap About Device, Software Update, Check for Updates, OK.

   - *T-Mobile, U.S. Cellular.* Tap About Device, Software Update, OK.

   - *Sprint.* Tap System Update, followed by Update *item type* to check for a particular type of update, such as Update Samsung Software or Update Firmware.

   - *Verizon.* Tap About Phone. Check the Build Number and Baseband Version for the software that's currently installed on your phone.

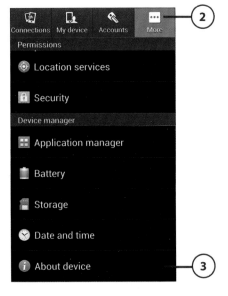

What Version of Android Do I Have?

The About Device or About Phone screen shows the version of the Android operating system that's currently installed.

Troubleshooting

This section provides suggestions for correcting simple and complex problems that can arise with the phone.

General Troubleshooting

When trying to correct an app-related or OS-related problem, you should generally work from the least to the most extreme solution.

- Try appropriate button presses. Try pressing the Home or Back key to leave the current screen, or press the Power button.

- Use the Task Manager to close unnecessary apps. (Press and hold the Home key, and then tap the Task Manager icon at the bottom of the screen.)

AT&T

< About device

Software update

Status
Show status of battery, network, and other information

Legal information

Device name
AT&T 1

Model number
SAMSUNG-SGH-I337

Android — Android version
version   4.2.2

Task Manager icon

- For app-related issues, check the app's settings (if it provides them) by pressing the Menu key and tapping Settings. You can also try uninstalling and reinstalling the app to see if the problem is corrected. If the issue continues, check Google Play for an update, visit the developer's website for troubleshooting information, or consider uninstalling the offending app.

- For battery-drain issues, turn off services that you aren't currently using, such as GPS, Bluetooth, and Wi-Fi. Open the Notification panel and tap icons to enable or disable services.

Active services (green)

- Restart or shut down the phone by pressing and holding the Power button, tapping Restart or Power Off, and then tapping OK in the confirmation dialog box.

Power Off

- To determine if a downloaded app or update is causing the problem, restart the phone in Safe Mode (as described in the section "Testing in Safe Mode").

- For a complete lock-up or similar issue, remove and replace the battery (as described in the section "Fixing a Lockup").

Restart

- Perform a Factory Data Reset (as described in the section "Performing a Factory Data Reset"), but only if the phone is so messed up that no other solution remains. Call your carrier's customer service/technical support before performing this procedure or, if one of its stores is nearby, take the phone in to be checked out.

Testing in Safe Mode

When the phone is in *Safe Mode*, only the standard, built-in apps are active; apps that you've downloaded are disabled. If the problem isn't present in Safe Mode, the likely culprit is an app that you've recently installed or updated. To enable Safe Mode, start by turning the phone off. Then turn the phone back on and—when the Samsung logo appears during the start-up sequence—press and hold the Volume down key until the lock screen appears. (You can exit Safe Mode at any time by restarting the phone normally.)

Safe Mode enabled

While in Safe Mode, test to see if the problem persists. If it does, refer to the section "Performing a Factory Data Reset." On the other hand, if the problem isn't present in Safe Mode, you'll have to determine which new app is the troublemaker. Uninstall the most recently installed app (see "Uninstalling Apps" in Chapter 10), restart the phone normally, and test again. One by one, continue uninstalling the newest apps until the problem goes away. Others that you've uninstalled during this testing can generally be reinstalled.

Fixing a "Lockup"

Yes, some apps have bugs, so what you *expect* to happen sometimes doesn't match what *actually* happens. When the worst occurs—the phone locks up so solidly that it ignores all taps, swipes, button presses, and attempts to power down, restart, or recharge—there's still something you can try. Open the back cover, remove the battery, wait 2 minutes, and reinsert the battery. Note that this is a solution of last resort. If you perform it while the phone is writing to memory, you can lose data.

Performing a Factory Data Reset

Using the Factory Data Reset procedure, you can restore your phone to its initial factory-default apps and settings. If you're planning to trade it in, sell it, or give it to a family member, performing a factory data reset also removes the applications you've installed and erases your personal data, such as contacts, photos, and music files. If this data is important to you, be sure to back it up to a memory card prior to performing the reset.

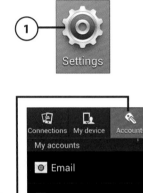

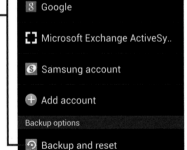

1. On the Home screen, tap Apps, followed by Settings.

2. Select the Accounts tab, and tap Back Up and Reset.

3. In the Personal Data section, tap Factory Data Reset.

4. On the Factory Data Reset screen, review the explanatory text.

5. *Optional:* Tap the Format SD Card check box if you also want to erase an installed memory card.

6. Tap the Reset Device button.

7. Tap the Delete All button to perform the factory reset. (Or if you've changed your mind, press the Back key.)

Index

muting
  calls, 126
  ringtone, 121
My Files
  choosing email
    attachments, 241
  emailing songs from,
    422-423
  locating downloads,
    235, 416
  selecting videos to
    play, 384
  transferring files, 425, 495
  viewing files, 286

N

naming phone, 425
navigating
  Apps view, 284
  Home screen pages, 42
  web pages, 206
  within apps, 289
Navigation. *See* Google
  Navigation; GPS (Global
  Positioning System)
Near Field Communication
  (NFC), 426-428
networks. *See* connection
  methods; Wi-Fi
Never sync interval, 441
new message notifications,
  263-264
NFC (Near Field
  Communication), 426-428
night detection for
  photos, 355
Night shooting mode, 358
noise reduction
  enabling, 134
  for phone calls, 125
Nokia phones, transferring
  data from, 15
non-alphabetic characters,
  entering, 53

non-secure lock methods
  for lock screen, setting,
  456-457
notes
  Google Voice Search, 96
  writing on photos, 368
Notification bar, 40-41
Notification panel, 48-49
  accessing during phone
    calls, 126
  Back key usage, 47
  Input Method,
    switching, 58
  Music controls, 331
  Power Saving Mode, 481
notifications
  in Amazon Appstore, 306
  managing, 48-49
  reminders, 187-189
  ringtone settings, 83-84
  text message settings,
    273
number dialed, changing, 101
numbers, entering, 53

O

opening. *See* launching
operating systems
  Android 4.2.2, 9
  checking version, 497
Optical Reader, 97
options. *See also* settings
  call logs, 107
  Contacts app display
    options, 168-169
  Google Navigation,
    320-321
  in-call options, 124-127
  Messaging app,
    configuring, 270-275
  running apps list, 478
  in Samsung Kies, 406
  for synchronization,
    439-441
  for text messages,
    268-269

order of playback (Music app)
  for songs, 330
  in playlists, changing, 337
organizing bookmarks,
  211-212
orientation, viewing web
  pages, 202
outgoing email messages,
  copying, 228
Outlook 2011 (Mac)
  synchronization, 436-437
Outlook contacts (Windows),
  exporting, 165

P

pages, Home screen, 42
pairing phone
  and Bluetooth
    headsets, 21
  and computer, 413-415
Palm Motion settings,
  enabling, 78-80
Pandora Internet Radio
  app, 344
Panorama shooting
  mode, 358
parental controls in Amazon
  Appstore, 305
passwords
  creating, 25-26
  for lock screen, setting,
    453-454
  retrieving, 277
  Show Password, 35
  unlocking lock
    screen, 462
  viewing/hiding when
    typing, 461
pasting
  Clipboard material, 61
  text, 60
pattern for lock screen
  setting, 449-451
  unlocking lock
    screen, 462

Your purchase of **My Samsung Galaxy S**® **4** includes access to a free online edition for 45 days through the **Safari Books Online** subscription service. Nearly every Que book is available online through **Safari Books Online**, along with thousands of books and videos from publishers such as Addison-Wesley Professional, Cisco Press, Exam Cram, IBM Press, O'Reilly Media, Prentice Hall, Sams, and VMware Press.

Safari Books Online is a digital library providing searchable, on-demand access to thousands of technology, digital media, and professional development books and videos from leading publishers. With one monthly or yearly subscription price, you get unlimited access to learning tools and information on topics including mobile app and software development, tips and tricks on using your favorite gadgets, networking, project management, graphic design, and much more.

Activate your FREE Online Edition at
informit.com/safarifree

STEP 1:   Enter the coupon code: ADABNXA.

STEP 2:   New Safari users, complete the brief registration form.
Safari subscribers, just log in.

If you have difficulty registering on Safari or accessing the online edition,
please e-mail customer-service@safaribooksonline.com